RAGHAVAN IYER

SMASHED
MASHED
BOILED
AND BAKED

AND FRIED, TOO!

WORKMAN PUBLISHING • NEW YORK

Library of Congress Cataloguing-in-Publishing Data is available.

ISBN 978-0-7611-8547-5

Cover and book design: Lisa Hollander
Cover and interior photography: Matthew Benson
Author photo: Bonnie Powell
Food styling: Nora Singley
Prop styling: Sara Abalan

Workman books are available at special discount when purchased in bulk for premiums and sales promotions as well as for fund-raising or educational use. Special editions or book excerpts can also be created to specification. For details, contact the Special Sales Director at the address below or send an email to specialmarkets@workman.com.

Workman Publishing Co., Inc.
225 Varick Street
New York, NY 10014-4381
workman.com
WORKMAN is a registered trademark of
Workman Publishing Co., Inc.

Printed in China
First printing October 2016

10 9 8 7 6 5 4 3 2 1

This book is dedicated to the one in my life who stood by me over the years and tirelessly supported my decision to come to the United States to make a life in the culinary world—Dr. Lalitha Iyer, my sister. Without you, I would never have come this far!

ACKNOWLEDGMENTS

To get a potato varietal to the marketplace often takes ten years or more of creation, cultivation, and testing for its survival in disparate climates. Writing a cookbook can be similar in so many ways. My passion for potatoes spans over fifty-five years, but the idea to put it in writing was relatively quicker than that. An evening dinner at a Turkish restaurant with my dear friend, who happens to be my editor, was enough to get the dialogue started over a side of potatoes. Within weeks I was on my way to start creating and writing *Smashed, Mashed, Boiled, and Baked—and Fried, Too!* And for that I thank the amazing editor Suzanne Rafer and my agent, Jane Dystel, for making it happen.

Researching the material was a monumental task for which I have Phyllis Louise Harris's diligence to thank. Sita Krishnaswamy, a close Canadian friend, led me to Agnes Murphy, the research scientist who provided crucial info on the life of a tuber. Her friends became mine as I spent a long weekend getting to know all about french fries from the owners of McCain Foods—Allison McCain, his wife, Clare, and their son, Brian.

A plethora of recipe sharers and testers came through to nurture the project. Tukkur Vanvark, Nancy Hayer, Sandra Gutierrez, Mary Evans, Esperanza Constellano, Nancy Coune, Mary Jane Miller, Scott Edwin Givot, Suraj Pradhan, Yukari Sakamoto, Perrine Medora and her son, Zubin, Priscilla Feral (who shared Miyoko Nishimoto Schinner's recipe), Meredith Deeds, Mette Nielsen, Sandra Mandel, Guanghe Luo, Natasha MacAller, Florence Lin, David and Martha Dovart, Shirley Corriher, and Rohan Singh. A huge debt of gratitude to my dear friend Jim Dodge, who was an incredible wealth of information and recipes—there is a reason why he is a world-renowned and revered pastry chef! And the book signings he organizes at various Bon Appétit Management Company accounts nationwide are so very supportive and for that, I give my heartfelt thanks.

Thanks, too, to the folks in my Canola oil world—Dorothy Long Sandercock, Leah Mann, Ellen Pruden, Simone Demers Collins, and Shaunda Durance-Tod. And to my boys' night group: Dr. Jeff Mandel, R J Singh and Tara Jebens-Singh, Raymond and Terra Vaughn, Jiten and Jennifer Gori, Ben and Zaidee Martin—even though they all take credit for my work, pretending it's the result of their collective minds (whatever gets them through the day!). Gratitude to Robert Schueller from Melissa's for sending me remarkable potato varietals to test and Don Odiorne and his team from the Idaho Potato Commission for their valuable support.

Many thanks to the astounding team put together by Workman Publishing (I still miss you, Peter Workman) that pulled off a mind-blowing book: Suzanne Fass and her attention to detail while copyediting and maintaining my voice; Lisa Hollander, who breathed life into the pages with her colorful and evocative layout; Anne Kerman, who assembled a great team to photograph the book, including photographer Matthew Benson, food stylist Nora Singley, and prop stylist Sara Abalan; Sarah Brady, who assisted Suzanne with the editing; production editor Kate Karol; typesetting manager Barbara Peragine; and production manager Doug Wolff. Thanks to Katie Workman for her support, friendship, and great sense of humor; Selina Meere and Jessica Wiener, who lead the band of drum beaters promoting and marketing the book, along with the incredibly brilliant Rebecca Carlisle and Jenny Lee.

Finally, loving thanks to my family, who was there for me with their quiet support as I plowed through the manuscript: Terry Erickson, my partner of thirty-four years, and our son, Robert Iyer-Erickson, and my siblings and all their families in India (you all know who you are—there are so many!).

So, I invite you to enjoy the amazing flavors in these recipes that mean the world to me. Savor them every which way: smashed, mashed, boiled, baked, and fried, too!

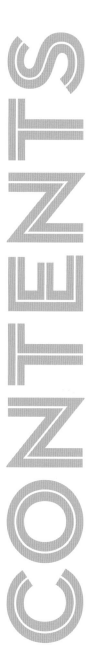

A DEEP-ROOTED OBSESSION

I am not petrified to openly admit my addiction. It may be the first step toward recovery but, honestly, I have no intention of recovering. There are billions like me who fall into this category. We are all victims of the easy-to-love vegetable known simply as the potato. Once its dirt-smothered skin is scrubbed and cleaned, it's amenable to being smashed, mashed, whipped, stir-fried, roasted, baked, poached, fried, and even braised.

I feel fortunate to have been born in India post-sixteenth century, after the Spanish and Portuguese traders and settlers introduced the country to potatoes (along with tomatoes and chiles). My love affair with this tuber began the moment I was weaned off milk into the world of spices and solids. My mother smashed a variety similar to the American russet and peppered it with crushed blackened red chiles, roasted lentils, and black mustard seeds. A generous drizzle of clarified butter, a sprinkle of coarse sea salt, and a handful of finely chopped fresh cilantro stirred into the smash and the whole concoction made its way into my eager mouth.

And when it came to my evening snack (that she so graciously made all throughout my childhood days), invariably my answer was "chips," the British Raj influence manifesting itself through their word for french fries. My mother had an unusual way of making them. As she fried the cut potatoes, she salted the oil (even though that was a disaster for the oil's life expectancy—a fact I was unaware of at that time), making the saltiness more intense. I was hooked.

I think it's pretty obvious that I'm not the only one who is a potato-holic. Potatoes are the fourth-largest crop in the world, next to wheat, rice, and maize. This member of the nightshade family (which includes eggplant, peppers, and tomatoes) was rooted in the Andean civilization that cultivated it around 10,000 BCE. But it wasn't until the Inca civilization (around 1500 CE) that the potato's true agricultural impact was unleashed. The Incas' intricate and sophisticated agricultural planning and tools, along with the ability of the potato to survive severe shifts in climate within short time periods, made for a winning partnership. Now

THE POTATO WHISPERER

I met Agnes Murphy, a senior research scientist with Canada's Potato Research Centre in Fredericton, New Brunswick, while investigating the tuber's past, present, and future. With an impressive one hundred-year history, the Potato Centre, also known as the "spud stud farm," is the go-to organization in the international science community; it is also linked to the International Potato Center in Lima, Peru, and other similar research centers across Europe.

Agnes's aspiration is to bring to fruition varieties that are uniform, have an appealing look, taste great, and are capable of being grown in a wide range of conditions. A modern-day matchmaker who is passionate about the science of breeding, she also possesses that rare quality of balancing the ethical concerns of the current consumer with the need to create a breed that feeds the world economically. Almost half of the current crop of potatoes are grown for processing in the french fry and chip industries, and new varieties, most desired in the consumer household, are constantly being tested and cultivated.

A Star Is Born

Agnes walked me through the process of how a potato variety gets born, a birds-and-bees lesson along the reproductive tater trail. It all starts with a desirable male and female that have all the attributes needed to create progeny that can feed the world. A controlled cross is carried out on an emasculated potato flower—that is, blossoms in varied hues of pink, white, and purple, from which the stamens have been removed. Pollen is then amassed from the potential father and applied to the stigma of the mother-to-be. The controlled cross is labeled with the parental info on the flower cluster, and these pollinated flowers produce seed berries that are cocooned in plastic wrap until they are ready to be harvested. The true potato seeds are then harvested from these berry-like fruits that resemble small green tomatoes (they are, after all, part of the family of nightshade vegetables). They are dried, counted, packaged, and labeled for planting, usually in the spring.

The seeds are sown in trays in a controlled environment to produce seedlings. The seedlings are then grown in a greenhouse and one tuber from each plant is harvested, producing a plant with a specific set of genetic qualities (unlike humans, deep-set eyes are not desirable). Its tubers are harvested after three months and stored until planted outdoors as the first field generation. If successful—after multiple years of replanting to ensure a hearty and productive cultivar—these become the new kid on the tater block.

potatoes are an essential ingredient in billions of kitchens in more than one hundred countries around the globe.

SO MANY POTATOES, SO LITTLE TIME

Gone are the days, pretty much, when most of us didn't know potatoes by their proper names—except maybe the russet. In the supermarket, they were offered by generalization: baking potatoes, boiling potatoes, sweet potatoes, and yams. Boy, is that changing. But the purpose of this book is not to list the names and properties of the more than five thousand varieties of potatoes in the world. Instead I've selected potatoes you're likely to find now—or soon—in your local market. I threw in a few that haven't really arrived in the United States yet (a couple I sampled in Canada), but in all likelihood will.

Most of us buy potatoes based on how we'll be cooking them, as opposed to a specific cultivar. So here's a handful that's readily available in most supermarkets or farmers' markets, divided into two groups based on their starch content: floury and waxy.

Floury (Starchy) Potatoes

High in starch, low in moisture and sugar content, floury potatoes are the ones you want if you're baking, roasting, deep-frying, or mashing. There are a few telltale signs that give you a clue to the potato's starch content. When you slice a potato, sometimes a potato slice sticks to the knife, and other times it cuts easily and falls off the blade. The ones that stick to the knife are much starchier, while the waxier ones slide off effortlessly. A more home-science way of determining starchiness is by dunking the uncut potato in a brine of salt and water (1 part salt to 10 parts water). If it sinks, it has a starchy persona; if it floats, it's waxy.

ULTIMATE FRENCH FRIES | Page 175

RUSSET: Around 1870, Luther Burbank, an American botanist and horticulturist, introduced the granddaddy of floury types, russet potatoes, and more specifically the cultivar called Burbank. This is a late-summer-into-fall crop with a brown, almost coarse, tough skin and white, dense flesh. It is by far the most cultivated of all potato crops in the United States. Russets are harvested as late as November and store well even if not used until June of the following year. This versatile tuber is great for baking, french frying, and mashing (as they are fluffy when boiled, dried, and riced).

YUKON GOLD: This hybrid, formulated in Canada, is by far the best-marketed potato in North America (named after the Yukon River in Canada and with a nod to the gold rush of the West). Gold-skinned and -fleshed, this medium-starch potato is a great multipurpose tuber that has fried, baked, and boiled its way into millions of kitchens. These potatoes are also much higher in vitamin C and potassium compared with other baking cultivars.

PURPLE CREAMER: Genetically rooted in Peru, these beautifully tinted tubers are simply known in the United States as purple potatoes. Medium in size, they have dark purple skin and deep purple flesh, which, when sliced and soaked in cold water, lightens up to a beautiful soft shade of purple (if it were a paint, it would have a froufrou name, perhaps Petulant

Patagonia). Purple creamers are more readily available now in supermarkets than they once were. With medium starch and a subtle hint of chalkiness (in my opinion), they are a visually stunning presence in any recipe in which they appear. Great for roasting, baking, and in stews, purple creamers are high in antioxidants (anthocyanin to be exact) as well.

YELLOW FINN: No relation to tuna, these pear-shaped potatoes have a speckled light yellow skin and gold-hued flesh. Yellow Finn is a versatile cultivar, similar to Yukon Gold, but far sweeter in taste. Higher in starch, too, they work better fried, baked (love this potato in the recipe for Hasselback Potatoes with Cardamom Butter on page 192), or in casseroles. They originated in Europe but lately have gained popularity in North America.

KENNEBEC: Versatile and perfect for making chips, this thin-skinned potato is oval in shape with a flesh color ranging from white to a very pale yellow. It is similar to the Yukon Gold in terms of culinary use, adapting well to mashing and baking as well as boiling because of its medium starch and moisture content. As the name suggests, it is a hybrid that originated in Maine and is named after the Kennebec River.

ONAWAY: Named after a Michigan town, this is an oval-shaped, rough-skinned, hearty potato that is quite desirable among cultivators

POTATO NUTRITION

Potatoes are technically tubers and not, as you may think, root vegetables. They are enlarged stems, higher in starch and complex carbohydrates than root vegetables, which are simply enlarged roots. Potatoes excel in providing essential energy from complex carbohydrates—necessary for the body to perform optimally. They are also a great source of vegetable proteins, with a ratio of protein to carbohydrates higher than in most cereals and other roots and tuber crops. An average potato contains high amounts of vitamin C and potassium, in addition to vitamin B_6 and magnesium; and some darker-skinned potatoes contain a higher level of antioxidants than others. And yes, a plain potato has no fat, sodium, or cholesterol and is vegan and gluten-free!

because of its high resistance to disease and extreme temperature. Quite prolific, multiple crops a year are common. The first time I tasted an Onaway was at an organic potato farmer's stall in Canada. It has white flesh and a high nutrient level, and is a great baking potato. It's an ideal mate for pot roasts and even stews.

SHEPODY: A 1980 cultivar that was primarily created in New Brunswick, Canada, to be the best french fry potato, this tuber was exclusively owned by McCain Foods (page 178) for a number of years. Once the ownership expired, it became available for world use. It is long in size (just right for a french fry), has smooth skin and white flesh, and is moisture-balanced and high in starch content. Because the growing season is short, multiple crops are possible in a year.

MARIS PIPER: One of Ireland's own, Maris Piper is considered the largest cultivated potato in the United Kingdom. Harvested late in the summer, these potatoes are oval-shaped with a light yellow skin and high starch content. They remain the best choice for french fries in the UK. Although I found them at a farmers' market in Canada, they are not commonly available in North America. They are comparable to the russet and Kennebec.

KING EDWARD: Oval with shallow eyes (shallow eyes are far more desirable in the potato world than deep-set ones), light brown speckled skin that is slightly thick, and a light pinkish flesh, King Edwards are great for baking. According to the English cook and TV star Delia Smith, they are perfect for making gnocchi. A few farmers are now growing them in the United States as well although it is not a mainstay cultivar in North America. There are now pink-skinned Edwards with a white flesh, very floury and high in starch, being cultivated all over the UK.

MOJITO POTATO-POMEGRANATE SALAD
Page 87

Waxy Potatoes

Unlike their floury counterparts, waxy potatoes do not fall apart when they are boiled, making them ideal to use in salads, stews, and roasts, where they are required to hold their shape. A high moisture and low starch content keep them cohesive. Perfect if you have potato salad on your mind.

CAROLA: A golden, thin-skinned small potato with a deep yellow flesh, these are great for that perfect potato salad. A German variety with genetic roots in Peru, Carolas are popular with home gardeners for their easy growing characteristics. There's no need to peel these potatoes before use, as the skin is thin enough to be enjoyed as much as the flesh.

RUSSIAN BANANA: One of the best-known fingerling potatoes, these yellow-skinned, yellow-flesh varieties are shaped like mini bananas. Ideal for boiling or roasting, they should be used unpeeled, as their skin is very thin. Nutty and buttery in taste, native to the Andean culture, Russian bananas were introduced in the 1700s to Europe's Baltic regions. Later, Russian sailors introduced them to North America via Alaska.

AMAROSA: This fingerling with deep red skin and flesh, when sliced, has a marbled meat-like look (sort of like salami, to my eyes). The cultivar hails from the tri-state areas of Washington, Oregon, and Idaho (the Burbank russet capital of the United States). Almost nutty in texture and buttery, I love to include it in recipes that would benefit from some color. Many farmers are now selling packages of these fingerlings mixed with Russian bananas and Peruvian purples. Remember, you eat with all your senses.

PERUVIAN PURPLE: Part of the new marketing and packaging of varietals in supermarkets these days, these purple-colored and -fleshed fingerlings are boilers and roasters (sounds like chicken talk!). They are native to Peru, Bolivia, and Ecuador, are known to have a high resistance to disease, and are able to grow in tough conditions. Fingerlings like these are harvested early and tend to have thinner skins so peeling is not recommended.

NORDONNA: This cultivar was created in North Dakota in 1982. It has a red skin with creamy white flesh, is medium-size, and is ideal in recipes requiring boiling, roasting, pan-frying, and even baking. Nordonnas have a long storage life and are not susceptible to bruised skin or flesh. I'm sure you've experienced cutting into a potato and discovering hollow flesh. Well, that's called a hollow heart, and this cultivar is known to produce tubers that are not genetically predisposed to that condition as often as other varieties are.

Jewel
Sweets

Stokes
Purple

Yukon
Golds

Peruvian
Purple
Fingerlings

Russets

New Reds

Purple
Regulars

White
Jersey
Sweets

Russian
Banana
Fingerlings

La Ratte
Yellow Fingerlings

Japanese
Sweets

New Reds
& Whites

Red
Fingerlings

Ruby
Crescent
Fingerlings

Papa Cachos

Okinawa
Sweets

Ruby
Crescents

Adirondack
Blues & Reds

Sweet Potato
Fingerlings

ORGANIC, CONVENTIONAL, OR GMO?

Pesticides and fertilizers are nothing new in the world of agriculture. In fact, one of the first fertilizers came from Peru and was associated with the potato. Called Peruvian guano, it was a by-product of their coastal seabirds—the pelican, cormorant, and booby. In the 1850s, it became the most sought-after fertilizer (for its ability to produce more nitrogen, an essential chemical in generating chlorophyll), with Peru controlling its distribution. Because the potato revolutionized the agricultural industry among the major players worldwide, pesticides and other harmful chemicals were formulated to keep diseases and bugs at bay. No one wanted a repeat of the blight that had annihilated the potato crop in Ireland or of the infestation of the Colorado potato beetle (which had taken arsenic and copper to get rid of). These pesticides were eventually replaced by the chemicals used in the modern pesticide industry. Conventionally grown potatoes have a tendency to absorb and retain some of the chemicals and no amount of washing and scrubbing ensures complete elimination. Spreading the pesticides is harmful to the farmers applying them as well as to the environment. Truth be told, even organic potatoes are sprayed with naturally occurring chemicals like sulfur and copper.

Which brings us to the ever-controversial introduction of genetically modified organisms (GMOs), wherein the genetic code of a plant is manipulated with increased precision to make it far more resilient. Resiliency results in a dramatic decrease in the use of harmful pesticides and chemicals to ward off disease and decay. Farmers have been doing this for centuries with natural plant-breeding crossovers, hoping to come up with the same answers we seek even now in the twenty-first century. Whichever side of the debate you rest on, these are all legitimate concerns as we look at the future of food, and of the fourth-largest crop in the world.

So while we grapple with a solution to these complex issues, I, for one, continue to purchase organic potatoes as much as I can, paying attention to the Environmental Working Group's (ewg.org) Shopper's Guide to Pesticides in Produce.

PINK FIR APPLE: Another waxy fingerling potato, this has a pinkish red skin, flesh that is almost creamy yellow in color, and a flavor that is very nutty. In 1850, France (where it's called *corne de gatte*) exported it to the United Kingdom under the name pink fir apple, where these knobby-looking tubers became a popular variety. Almost ginger-like in appearance, they are great in roasts, salads, plainly boiled and tossed with fresh herbs, and even steamed.

New Potatoes

I feel this category of potatoes, with its range of skin tones, needs to be on its own podium. Sure, they are small, but please don't mistake just any baby potatoes (or B-size potatoes) as new potatoes. The difference in new potatoes and other kinds has to do with harvest times. New ones are plucked fresh from the ground when the leaves and stems are still verdant. Normally tubers are uprooted after the vine dies and when the leaves are dried up. Regular potatoes are temperature-cured and then stored for months before they make their way into supermarkets. New ones are never stored and usually land in the bins and farmers' markets within hours of being harvested. As Elizabeth Schneider so eloquently states in her amazing work *Vegetables from Amaranth to Zucchini: The Essential Reference*, "Perhaps new potatoes might be better served by the name fresh-harvest or first-crop potatoes." I couldn't agree more. New ones have such tender skin that I highly recommend that, after a good scrub and rinse, you leave them unpeeled. They are very expeditious in their cooking times and are great pan-fried in butter with the simplest of spices and fresh herbs.

SWEET POTATOES

In 1492, Christopher Columbus tasted sweet potatoes, called *batatas*, in the Caribbean islands. He took them back to Spain, where they came to be thought of as having aphrodisiac powers. No relation to the potato, sweet potatoes are part of the morning glory family (and to make this more complicated, orange-fleshed sweet potatoes are referred to as yams even though yams have nothing to do with sweet potatoes and belong to an entirely different botanical family). Unlike those of potatoes and yams, the leaves of the sweet potato plant are lusciously edible (page 74).

Nutritionally comparable to the potato in terms of most nutrients, sweet potatoes— especially the darker varieties—deliver more antioxidants, minerals, and vitamin A than potatoes, and, because of their higher sugar content, they leave your sweet tooth satisfied.

Most of the sweet potatoes in North America are cultivated in North Carolina, Mississippi, Louisiana, and California. Here are a handful of sweet potato cultivars that are common in most of our supermarkets:

SWEET POTATOES WITH
CHICKEN AND LEMONGRASS | Page 112

and even to shades of pink. It has a dry, mealy flesh that is exceptionally sweet and creamy and retains its form when cooked, especially baked. I love its texture (almost like poached pears) in the Sweet Potato Pithivier (page 237).

JAPANESE (KOTOBUKI, SATSUMA-IMO, AND YAMAIMO): Often, supermarkets label all these varieties as Japanese or just Asian sweet potatoes. White-fleshed and ranging in skin color from reddish brown to almost pink with white flesh, these are all luscious even when they are simply baked. Try them steamed, sprinkled with a hint of freshly ground cardamom and a drizzle of butter. Street vendors in India throw them directly on burning embers and roast them. They peel and cut them, tossing the pieces with black salt and cayenne. They are not overly sweet, and they are perfect in some of the dessert recipes in this book.

PURCHASING AND STORING POTATOES

Ideally, buy the specific or comparable variety of potatoes needed for a particular recipe or two. Oftentimes natural food stores will sell them loose, so you are not stuck with a 5- or 10-pound bag (not that there is anything wrong with that) of a particular cultivar. Choose tubers that are firm to the touch, with no sprouts or greening just under their skin. Green coloration is chlorophyll and also is evidence of elevated

ORANGE-FLESHED JEWEL AND GARNET: These North American cultivars are by far the most popular in supermarkets all across the United States. Deep orange in their hues, I find them very pumpkin-like in their flavor and mouthfeel. Because of their creaminess when mashed, I love them in the Sweet Potato Rolls with a Creamy Cointreau Glaze (page 228).

JERSEY WHITE AND JERSEY YELLOW: Often when I want a true sweet potato, I reach for a tan-skinned Jersey, a cultivar that ranges in flesh color from light yellow to creamy white

levels of glycoalkaloid, a chemical compound that is deemed toxic among the nightshade family. It is a potato's internal mechanism to guard against certain diseases. High levels are indicative of improper and long storage times, especially when they are exposed to sunlight. It is best to keep potatoes in a dark spot in a well-ventilated pantry or even your cool basement or garage. If you have the opportunity to buy potatoes toward the tail end of a growing season at a farmers' market, buy them in a heartbeat, as some vendors may sell them to you with plenty of dirt still clinging to them—which is ideal for storage. Buy them and store them as is in that cool dark spot. Scrub and wash what you intend to use for a meal. This way you will be ensured a constant supply of fresh-dug potatoes even during the winter months. In simple words, keep potatoes in the dark.

When your potatoes start to sprout, it is an indication that they have been around too long. Sprouts signify new growth from the potato's eyes. Once the sprout takes over (the eye and the sprout planted underground will yield a new plant), it will absorb all the nutrients from the parent, drying out the tuber in the process, which is great for the new progeny, but not great for an eater. I have been known in times of need to peel away any small sprouts, if the potato is still firm and does not appear wrinkled and soft. But that's certainly not optimal!

In terms of storage, the other big no-no, is stashing potatoes in the refrigerator. In that environment, the potato's starch gets converted to sugar. The only time you want that sugar is if you're making oven fries—the raised sugar level ensures a surface browning that is usually not possible when you're making french fries the low-fat way.

POTATO FLOUR AND POTATO STARCH

Both potato flour and potato starch—not the same thing, by any means—are widely available in large supermarkets and natural food stores. Potato flour goes back to the Inca civilization around the thirteenth century (although archeological sites date it back 2,200 years) when potatoes were eaten freshly dug and raw, or, after storage, roasted or used in stews. Potato flour is made from peeled, dried potatoes and, because of its ability to help increase moisture content, is an excellent addition to breads and other baked goods.

Potato starch is fashioned from the dried starch component of peeled potatoes and like cornstarch is used as a thickener. Unlike the flour, potato starch has no potato flavor.

MUNCHIES MORSELS TIDBITS & FINGER FOODS

When I go to restaurants, especially with a group of friends, I get accused of going overboard with appetizers. Practically every item on the starters list grabs my attention, and soon small plates of delectables appear at the table. I am perfectly content stopping after that course.

Of course, if I see potatoes anywhere, well, that does me in. So to imagine an array of potato offerings that spans the globe as a precursor to a meal, it's all I can do to contain myself. Cheesy tots, a perfect balance of crispy exterior and creamy interior, bursting with the perfume of fresh tarragon, excite my palate. *Llapingachos*, those classic Ecuadorian potato cakes with a winsome combination of salty Cotija cheese and creamy peanut sauce are so irresistible, I could consume them in one sitting. My weakness for fried foods commands me to include a plate of crispy fried potato skins with a zesty crème fraîche—a great accompaniment to a gin martini, extra-dry, straight-up, twist, no olives! The French know a thing or two about *gougères*, addictive puffs that are airy and rich with egg. Filled with citrusy mashed potatoes and asparagus, they make for a great Sunday brunch, and you know every guest will want that recipe.

I could go on and on about each of the recipes in this chapter, but see for yourself. Starters may introduce the meal or be the meal—your very own global tapas.

SMASHED
BOILED
BAKED
MASHED
FRIED
SHREDDED
ROASTED
RICED

— A TALE OF TWO CITIES —

MUSTARD- OR GARLIC-SPIKED
CRISPY
POTATO CAKES

Maybe I'm partial to India, but I marvel at the country's fascination with the potato, even though it is a relatively new crop. (It was brought in by Spanish and Portuguese merchants in the sixteenth century.) It's the most affordable vegetable for even the poorest of the poor and no Indian meal feels complete without it.

From two disparate regions with remarkably different cooking and spicing styles—Mumbai on the west coast and Madras (now called Chennai) on the southeast coast—come two variations of crispy cakes: one spiked with roasted mustard seeds and lime, the other fragrant with garlic. Both are enrobed in a chickpea flour batter and fried to a gorgeous brown. They cannot be any more different in terms of flavors, but are equally addictive. **MAKES 24 CAKES (12 OF EACH VERSION)**

2 pounds medium-size red-skin potatoes

FOR THE MUMBAI VERSION

6 slices fresh ginger (each about the size and thickness of a quarter; no need to peel first), coarsely chopped

4 large cloves garlic

2 or 3 fresh green serrano chiles, stems discarded

1 cup firmly packed fresh cilantro leaves and tender stems

1 teaspoon coarse sea or kosher salt

½ teaspoon ground turmeric

FOR THE MADRAS VERSION

¼ cup finely chopped fresh cilantro leaves and tender stems

¼ cup finely chopped fresh curry leaves (optional; see Tater Tip)

2 or 3 fresh green serrano chiles (see Tater Tips, page 18), stems discarded, finely chopped (do not remove the seeds)

2 tablespoons canola oil

1 teaspoon black or yellow mustard seeds

1 teaspoon coarse sea or kosher salt

½ teaspoon ground turmeric

¼ cup freshly squeezed lime juice

FOR THE BATTER

1 cup chickpea flour, sifted

¼ cup white rice flour, sifted

1 teaspoon coarse sea or kosher salt

½ teaspoon ground turmeric

Canola oil, for deep-frying

1. Peel the potatoes and place them in a medium-size saucepan. Cover them with cold water and bring to a boil over medium-high heat. Lower the heat to medium-low, cover the pot, and simmer until the potatoes are tender when pierced with a fork or knife, 20 to 25 minutes. Scoop out 1 cup of the potato water and set it aside. Drain the potatoes. Divide them equally between 2 medium-size bowls. Mash each portion with a potato masher.

2. Lay out 2 large pieces of wax paper or parchment paper on the counter.

3. To make the Mumbai version, pile the ginger, garlic, chiles, and cilantro into a food processor. Pulse the medley into an herbaceous mince (do not puree). Scrape this into one of the bowls of potatoes. Sprinkle in the salt and turmeric and give it all a good mix. Divide the mixture into 12 equal portions, setting each portion onto one of the pieces of wax paper. Shape each into a ball, then flatten each into a disk about ½ inch thick and return it to the wax paper.

To make the Madras version, add the cilantro, curry leaves (if using), and chiles to the second bowl of potatoes. Heat the oil in a small skillet over medium-high heat. Once the oil appears to shimmer, sprinkle in the mustard seeds. Cover the pan right away as the seeds will start to pop, not unlike popcorn. Once the seeds finish popping, 10 to 15 seconds, remove the pan from the heat. Uncover it and sprinkle in the salt and the turmeric, which will bathe the oil with its sunny disposition. Scrape this all into the potatoes and pour in the lime juice. Stir well to incorporate all these ingredients into the

TATER TIP

▲ Fresh curry leaves, a member of the citrus family, are common in the produce aisle of any Indian grocery. I have also seen them on occasion at health-food stores and Southeast Asian markets (since folks with roots in Malaysia use them). They strip off the sprig very easily and are often used in stews and stir-fries, especially among India's coastal cuisines. We normally don't eat them if they are left whole in a recipe, but if they are chopped or pureed, they can be consumed. Since there is no substitute to replicate their flavor, leave them out if you can't find them. If you buy a bunch and fear you won't use them often, dry them out under a sunny window or freeze them fresh in a zip-top bag.

TATER TIPS

▲ I often give a range of chiles to use in a recipe. The tolerance for heat varies among diners. Use the minimum or even less for a very mellow presence. The maximum delivers a pleasant punch while still maintaining a balance. Of course, use more if you are a hothead like me.

▲ I cannot emphasize too strongly the importance of a thermometer if you wish to fry perfectly. It's all about temperature control. But if you have no thermometer, an alternate way to see if oil is at the right temperature is to gently flick a drop of water over it. If it skitters across the surface, the oil is ready. Or safer yet, stick a wooden skewer or wooden spoon into the oil. When bubbles form around the bottom of the skewer, the oil is ready.

potatoes. Divide, shape, and flatten this mixture as you did the Mumbai version, using the other piece of wax paper as the holding area.

4. To make the batter, combine the chickpea and rice flours in a medium-size bowl and sprinkle in the salt and turmeric. Pour in half of the reserved potato water and whisk it in, making sure there are no lumps. Continue drizzling and whisking as much potato water as you need to make a batter that is slightly thicker than pancake batter.

5. Pour oil to a depth of 2 to 3 inches into a wok, Dutch oven, or medium-size saucepan. Heat the oil over medium heat until a candy or deep-frying thermometer inserted into the oil (without touching the pan bottom) registers 350°F. Line a cookie sheet with several layers of paper towels, for draining the cakes of excess oil. If you want to serve all the cakes at one time, set a wire rack over another cookie sheet,

place it in the center of the oven, and preheat the oven to 175°F.

6. Once the oil is ready, carefully scoop out ¼ cup of the hot oil and gently whisk it into the batter. The hot fat makes the cakes crispier when fried.

7. Pick up a cake with your hand (a little messy but it works well) and gently drop it into the batter. Use your hand or a fork to carefully flip it over, then lift it out. (Make sure the cake gets completely coated.) Slide it into the hot oil. Coat and add another 5 cakes to the oil. Deep-fry the cakes, flipping them over with a slotted spoon, until they are reddish brown and crispy, 5 to 8 minutes. Transfer them with the spoon to the paper towels to drain. Repeat with the remaining cakes and batter. Serve each batch fresh from frying (can't imagine why not!); or, after draining, set them on the wire rack in the oven preheated to 175°F to keep warm.

CHEESY
TARRAGON TOTS

The year 1860 witnessed a plethora of deep-fried potatoes on the streets of France and in US restaurants. Home cooks could not afford to make them because of the large amounts of oil and special equipment required. These cheesy tater tots need neither. Yes, enough oil for deep-frying, but nothing that breaks the bank, and all that is essential in terms of equipment is a thermometer.

Among all the potato dishes I have eaten over the years, I have never turned down an opportunity to eat a Tater Tot or two (I lie—it's more like half a pound or more). The saltier and crispier they are, the more I eat. Most commercial tots are sold frozen and ready-to-cook, and coming up with a home version was a bit of a challenge. Your work is easy since I have tested multiple options to bring you the best. Tot-lovers, you will not be disappointed. SERVES 4

1 pound russet or Yukon Gold
   potatoes

Canola oil, for deep-frying

1 small yellow or white onion,
   coarsely chopped

4 ounces fresh cheese curds
   (see Tater Tips)

2 tablespoons finely chopped fresh
   tarragon leaves

1 tablespoon potato starch

½ teaspoon coarse sea or
   kosher salt

1. Fill a medium-size bowl with cold water. Peel the potatoes and give them a good rinse under cold running water. Cut them into 2-inch pieces. Submerge them in the bowl of water to rinse off surface starch and to prevent them from turning gray.

2. As the potatoes soak, pour oil to a depth of 2 to 3 inches into a wok, Dutch oven, or medium-size

TATER TIPS

▲ Here the cheese curds, similar to feta but firmer and with no moisture, work their magic to maintain a meaty and firm texture. If you can't get cheese curds, use white cheddar.

▲ These tots are freezable once they have been shaped. Line them up in a single layer on a cookie sheet and place the sheet in the freezer. Once they have frozen, transfer them to a zip-top bag. They will keep for up to 3 months. No need to thaw them before you fry them. Just allow for an extra minute or two to get done on the inside as well.

▲ Tater Tots, an American invention by the frozen potato giant Ore-Ida, were conceived in 1953 to address the issue of wasted potato slices and designed to be marketed to children. Production is now estimated at 70 million pounds a year in the United States alone.

SMASHED
FRIED
MASHED
CHOPPED
BAKED
BOILED
SHREDDED
RICED

saucepan. Heat the oil over medium heat until a candy or deep-frying thermometer inserted into the oil (without touching the pan bottom) registers 325°F. Lay out a clean cotton kitchen towel or several layers of paper towels on the counter, for drying the potatoes. Set a wire rack on a cookie sheet, for draining the partially cooked potatoes of excess oil.

3. Drain the potatoes in a colander and rinse them a bit under cold running water. Give the colander a good shake or two to rid the potatoes of excess water. Transfer the potatoes to the kitchen towel and dry them well.

4. Divide the potatoes into 2 equal portions. Drop a portion gently into the oil. You will notice the temperature dip down by 30°F or so. Allow the potatoes to poach at that temperature just until they appear pale brown and are a bit soft, about 5 minutes. Lift them out immediately with a slotted spoon and transfer them to the rack to drain. Let the oil return to 325°F and repeat with the remaining potatoes.

5. Once they've all had a chance to drip excess oil, transfer the potatoes to a clean, dry, medium-size bowl. Allow them to cool for 10 minutes. For a quicker chill, place them in the freezer for about 5 minutes.

6. Transfer the potatoes to a food processor and pulse them until finely chopped. Scrape them back into the same bowl. Add the onion and cheese curds to the food processor and pulse them to a texture similar to that of the potatoes. Add them to the potatoes. Add the tarragon, potato starch, and salt and give it all a good mix.

7. Lay out a large sheet of wax paper or parchment paper on the counter. Take a heaping teaspoon of the bumpy potato "dough" and shape it into a mini football about 1 inch in length, compressing it as you form the shape. Set it on the wax paper. Repeat until all the dough is used up.

8. Reheat the oil over medium heat until a candy or deep-frying thermometer registers 375°F. Line a cookie sheet with several layers of paper towels, for draining the finished tots.

9. Once the oil is ready, gently slide in a handful of the tots; do not crowd the pan. Fry, flipping them occasionally with a slotted spoon, until they are caramel brown and crisp all over, 3 to 5 minutes. Remove them with the spoon and place them on the paper towels to drain. Repeat until all the tots are fried. You may need to adjust the heat to maintain the oil's temperature at 375°F. And I don't need to say this, but eat them while they are hot and crispy.

"The potato has proved one of the greatest blessings bestowed on mankind by the creator."

—*Noah Webster, American lexicographer*

BOILED
MASHED
FRIED
SMASHED
BAKED
SHREDDED
ROASTED
RICED

"I have these big piano-playing hands. I feel like I should be picking potatoes."

—*Sandra Bullock, actress*

CRASH & BURN POTATOES
WITH CINNAMON MALT VINEGAR

This style of cooking potatoes, made popular by Australian food writer Jill Dupleix, showcases a crispy crunchy exterior and a creamy middle. But after they are crisped, my version bastes them with a potent chile-vinegar sauce, making this really hot. A crash and burn kind of recipe. **SERVES 4**

1½ pounds new red potatoes

¼ cup malt vinegar (see Tater Tips, facing page)

3 to 5 dried red chiles (such as cayenne or chile de árbol), stems discarded

1 teaspoon cumin seeds

1 teaspoon coarse sea or kosher salt

½ teaspoon black peppercorns

1 small yellow onion, coarsely chopped

4 medium-size cloves garlic

2 slices fresh ginger (each about the size and thickness of a quarter; no need to peel first)

1 stick (3 inches) cinnamon, broken into smaller pieces

Canola oil, for brushing

Sour cream or crème fraîche, for serving (optional)

1. Scrub the potatoes well, give them a good rinse under cold running water, place them in a medium-size saucepan, and cover with cold water. Bring to a boil over medium-high heat and cook, uncovered, until the potatoes are just tender but still firm, 20 to 25 minutes. Take care not to overcook the potatoes. Drain them in a colander and rinse under cold running water to cool them down. Give the colander a few good shakes to rid the potatoes of excess water.

2. As the potatoes cook, combine the vinegar, chiles, cumin seeds, salt, peppercorns, onion, garlic, ginger, and cinnamon in a blender jar. Puree until a highly pungent, reddish-brown paste forms, scraping the inside of the jar as needed. Add just enough water to make it brushable. Pour into a small bowl.

3. Position a rack in the center of the oven and preheat it to 375°F. Line a cookie sheet with parchment paper or lightly grease it with oil.

4. Smash the potatoes one by one on a cutting board with a potato masher. Place each potato on the cookie sheet. Be sure to keep them separate. Liberally brush each of the smashed potatoes with oil on both sides.

5. Bake the potatoes until crispy brown, 25 to 30 minutes. Flip them over after about 12 minutes and rotate the cookie sheet front to back.

6. Once the potatoes are crisp, liberally brush each of them on both sides with the chile-vinegar sauce. Try to use all of it. Return the pan of potatoes to the oven and continue to bake them until they have a nice dried coat, 5 to 8 minutes. Serve hot, with sour cream or crème fraîche for dipping if you want to modulate the heat from the chiles.

TATER TIPS

▲ Go with cider vinegar as an alternative to malt, if gluten is an issue.

▲ These potatoes can be fiery hot for some in terms of chile heat. I personally find it quite well balanced, but I suggest serving cooling sour cream or crème fraîche as a great accompaniment.

CRISPY POTATO SKINS
WITH CRÈME FRAÎCHE

Potatoes arrived in North America in the late 1600s but did not become a field crop until the next century when Scottish immigrants brought potatoes to New England from Ireland. This happened in the town of Derry, New Hampshire (then known as Londonderry), in 1719. Over the years, much has been garnered in terms of potato nutritional knowledge. A skin-on potato around 5 ounces in weight contributes 45 percent of the daily value for vitamin C, 2 grams of fiber, a healthy dose of vitamin B$_6$, magnesium, and more potassium than a banana, with no fat or cholesterol. But contrary to popular belief, the skin itself is not nutritious. What *is* nutritious is the thin layer immediately under the skin, mere millimeters thick. These crispy potato skins include that nutritious layer, making them a guilt-free indulgence. Crème fraîche is, of course, ridiculously sinful! SERVES 4

3 pounds russet potatoes

Canola oil, for deep-frying

¼ cup chickpea flour

1 teaspoon coarse sea or kosher salt

1 teaspoon cayenne pepper

Zest of 1 medium-size lime
(see Tater Tip)

½ cup crème fraîche or sour cream
(see Tater Tips, page 26)

¼ cup finely chopped fresh chives

½ teaspoon coarsely cracked black peppercorns

1. Fill a medium-size bowl halfway with cold water. Scrub

TATER TIP

▲ To zest a lime or lemon, wash it well. (I prefer washing mine with a bit of dish soap to remove any surface dirt or pesticide, then rinsing it under running water.) Dry it well. Using a Microplane or the small holes of a box grater, finely shred just the colored part of the skin. Make sure not to include the white pith underneath, as it makes the zest bitter.

TATER TIPS

▲ Sour cream is a good alternative to crème fraîche, but I prefer the latter's richness and satiny mouthfeel.

▲ Save the peeled potatoes in a zip-top bag filled with cold water for up to 2 days in the refrigerator. I think they are perfect to whip up a batch of Ultimate Mashed Potatoes (page 169).

the potatoes well under running water. Peel the potatoes with a paring knife, cutting about ¼ inch deep into the flesh. Try to get long strips of skin, as they are easier to fry and look prettier. Submerge them in the bowl of water to prevent them from discoloring. Save the peeled potatoes for another recipe (see Tater Tips).

2. As the potato skins soak, pour oil to a depth of 2 to 3 inches into a wok, Dutch oven, or medium-size saucepan. Heat the oil over medium heat until a candy or deep-frying thermometer inserted into the oil (without touching the pan bottom) registers 350°F (see Tater Tips, page 18).

3. Set a wire rack over a cookie sheet, for draining the fried skins of excess oil.

4. Drain the potato skins in a colander and rinse them a bit under cold running water. Give the colander a good shake or two to rid the skins of excess water. Transfer the skins back to the same bowl and sprinkle with the chickpea flour and ½ teaspoon

of the salt. Toss the skins to coat them with the flour. There should be enough moisture in the skins to get the flour to cling to them. If they feel dry, wet your hand and use it to toss the skins.

5. Remove about a quarter of the skins and gently disperse them in the hot oil. Use a slotted spoon to separate them as they sizzle and turn reddish brown, 4 to 6 minutes. You will need to adjust the heat under the pan to make sure the oil stays at 350°F. Scoop the cooked skins out of the oil with the spoon and transfer them to the rack to drain. Repeat with the remaining skins.

6. As the potatoes fry, combine the remaining ½ teaspoon salt, the cayenne, and the lime zest in a medium-size bowl. Whisk the crème fraîche, chives, and peppercorns in a small bowl.

7. Once all the potato skins are fried and drained, add them to the seasonings and toss to coat them. Serve the zesty skins with the creamy sauce right away.

LLAPINGACHOS

ECUADORIAN FILLED POTATO CAKES
WITH PEANUT SAUCE

This Ecuadorian classic is an adaptation of a family recipe that came to me via Jaime Sierra, a sous chef who trained under me at a restaurant I consulted at briefly years back. It showcases potatoes in their simple form. This recipe is nothing short of a showstopper. Even though the name is difficult to pronounce, these potato cakes are easy in their execution. They house salty Cotija cheese and smoky paprika—definitely a lively filling. And a mellow peanut sauce, dairy-rich and pungent with onion, is perfect to cloak each bite of this well-balanced starter to any meal. MAKES 12 CAKES

FOR THE SHELLS

1½ pounds russet potatoes

3 tablespoons potato starch

1 teaspoon coarse sea or kosher salt

FOR THE FILLING

2 ounces Cotija cheese, crumbled (see Tater Tips, page 160)

2 tablespoons finely chopped fresh cilantro leaves and tender stems

2 tablespoons thinly sliced scallions (green tops and white bulbs)

½ teaspoon smoked paprika

FOR THE SAUCE

1 cup whole milk

1 small yellow onion, cut into ½-inch pieces

¼ cup chunky or smooth natural peanut butter

¼ teaspoon coarse sea or kosher salt

Canola oil, for pan-frying

FOR THE TOPPING

1 large ripe Hass avocado, cut into ¼-inch cubes (see Tater Tip)

1. To make the shells, peel the potatoes and give them a good rinse under cold running water. Cut them into large chunks. Place them in a medium-size saucepan and cover them with cold water. Bring to a boil over medium-high heat. Partially cover the pan, lower the heat to medium-low, and

TATER TIP

▲ A Latin American fruit, the avocado (an adaptation of the Aztec word *ahuacaquahuitl*, or "testicle tree") is a powerhouse of nutrients, easily accessible in every nook and corner of the world. The Hass avocado is bright green when unripe, but as it ripens it acquires a dark greenish-black skin, soft to the touch. Get one that is firm but yields to a gentle press. Cut straight into the fruit until you feel the pit in its center, then follow the curve of the pit to split the avocado in two. Twist the two halves in opposite directions to yield a clean separation with the pit embedded in one half. I usually hold the half with the pit securely in one hand and gently whack the pit with a chef's knife. Then I twist the avocado half and lift the pit from its bed. To remove the pit from the knife, I whack the handle against the edge of the garbage can and the pit falls right in. I score the fruit into the desired cut (slices or cubes) with a paring knife, and scoop them out with a spoon.

simmer briskly until the chunks are tender when pierced with a fork or knife, 12 to 15 minutes.

2. Lay out a large sheet of wax paper or parchment paper on the counter. Drain the potatoes in a colander and return them to the pan. Set it over medium-low heat and stir the potatoes once or twice to dry them out, about 1 minute. Working in batches if necessary, transfer the chunks to a ricer and press them directly into a medium-size bowl. Sprinkle on the potato starch and salt and stir them in while the potatoes are still warm, until the dough is satin smooth. Once the dough is cool enough to handle, divide it into 12 equal portions and set them on the wax paper.

3. To make the filling, lay out a smaller sheet of wax paper or parchment paper on the counter. Combine the cheese, cilantro, scallions, and paprika in a small bowl. Divide this into 12 equal portions as well and set them on the small sheet of wax paper.

4. One at a time, shape each portion of dough into a disk about 3 inches in diameter. Place a portion of the filling in the center and fold over the dough to cover it. Reshape each half-moon into a cake roughly 2½ inches in diameter and ½ inch thick. Return each to the wax paper while you finish flattening, filling, and shaping the remaining cakes.

5. To make the sauce, bring the milk and onion to a boil, uncovered, in a small saucepan over medium heat. Lower the heat to medium-low and simmer the milk, uncovered, stirring occasionally, to allow it to absorb some of the onion flavor, about 5 minutes. Fish out and discard the onion pieces (a slotted spoon works well). Whisk in the peanut butter and salt and continue to simmer the sauce, stirring occasionally, until it thickens, about 2 minutes. Cover the pan, remove from the heat, and keep the sauce warm while you pan-fry the cakes.

6. Set a wire rack over a cookie sheet and place it in the center of the oven. Preheat the oven to 200°F.

7. Heat 2 tablespoons of oil in a medium-size nonstick or cast-iron skillet over medium heat. Once the oil appears to shimmer, place 6 of the cakes in the pan. Fry them until reddish brown and crispy on the underside, 3 to 5 minutes. Flip them over and fry on the other side, 3 to 5 minutes more. Transfer the cakes to the rack in the oven to keep warm as you finish pan-frying the remaining cakes. Add more oil to the pan as necessary.

8. Serve the cakes warm, drizzled with the peanut sauce and topped with avocado. Pass around any extra peanut sauce for those wanting a bit more of that nutty goodness.

"A diet that consists predominantly
of rice leads to the use of opium,
just as a diet that consists
predominantly of potatoes leads
to the use of liquor."

—*Friedrich Nietzsche, German philosopher and poet*

NUTTY POTATO PHYLLO TRIANGLES

I have always been a fan of Thai food. Strong flavors, crunchy peanuts, and the perfumed allure of freshly chopped basil are enough to make me swoon (yes, I am dramatic). Throw all that into the mix with shreds of Yukon Gold potatoes, and you have pushed me over the edge. These savory phyllo-wrapped triangles are a great snack even at room temperature, and if I consume a half dozen or more at once, I can safely skip dinner. A better alternative to the peanut roll candy bars! **MAKES 16 TRIANGLES**

1 pound Yukon Gold potatoes

1 large carrot or 2 medium-size carrots

3 tablespoons canola oil, plus extra for brushing

½ cup unsalted dry-roasted peanuts, ground to coarse crumbs (see Tater Tip, page 32)

¼ cup firmly packed fresh basil leaves, finely chopped

¼ cup firmly packed fresh cilantro leaves and tender stems, finely chopped

2 scallions, beards trimmed, green tops and white bulbs thinly sliced

2 fresh green serrano chiles, stems discarded, finely chopped (do not remove the seeds)

1 teaspoon coarse sea or kosher salt

½ teaspoon coarsely cracked black peppercorns

Cooking spray, for greasing the pan

1 package frozen phyllo sheets (18-by-14-inch sheets), thawed (see Tater Tip, page 34)

Thai-Style Peanut Sauce (page 50), for serving (optional)

SHREDDED
SMASHED
FRIED
MASHED
BOILED
BAKED
ROASTED
RICED

"There's a science to ordering potatoes. Are they skinny shoestring or big, fat steak fries? You just have to let your taste buds guide you when deciding what to eat."

—*Gayle King, American entertainer*

TATER TIP

1. Lay out a clean cotton kitchen towel or several layers of paper towels on the counter, for drying the vegetables. Fill a medium-size bowl halfway with cold water. Peel the potatoes. Shred them through the large holes of a box grater, the fine teeth of a mandoline, or the shredding disk of a food processor. Immediately transfer the shreds to the bowl, making sure there is enough water to keep them submerged; add more water if needed. Soak the shreds for 30 minutes to get rid of excess starch. The water also prevents the potatoes from oxidizing and turning gray.

2. Peel the carrots and trim the ends. Shred the carrots and add them to the potatoes. Drain the shredded vegetables in a colander and rinse them well under cold running water. Give the colander a good shake or two to rid the vegetables of excess water. Spread out the shreds on the towel and pat them dry.

3. Preheat a large skillet or wok over medium-high heat. Once the pan is hot (holding your palm close to its base will make you pull back within 2 seconds), drizzle in 1 tablespoon of the oil, which will instantly heat and appear to shimmer. Add a third of the shreds to the hot oil. Stir-fry briskly to allow the shreds to warm through but barely cook, about 2 minutes. They should still have a slight crunch. Transfer them to a large plate or a cookie sheet to cool. Repeat twice more with the remaining oil and shredded vegetables, adding them, once cooked, to the first batch of cooling shreds. Place the plate in the freezer to quickly chill them, about 5 minutes.

4. As the shreds chill, lay out a large sheet of wax paper or parchment paper on the counter. Once the shreds are chilled, transfer them to a medium-size bowl and add the peanuts, basil, cilantro, scallions, chiles, salt, and peppercorns. Give it all a good mix. Go ahead and sneak a taste. If you need a bit more salt, by all means sprinkle some on. Divide the mix into 16 equal portions and place them on the wax paper.

5. Position a rack in the center of the oven and preheat the oven to 375°F. Line a cookie sheet with parchment paper or lightly grease it with cooking spray.

6. Unroll the phyllo on the clean countertop and cover the stack of sheets with a damp, clean cotton kitchen towel. Carefully peel off

TRIANGLES STEP-BY-STEP

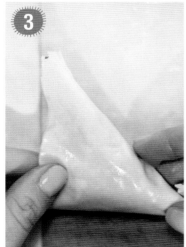

1. Spoon a portion of the filling onto the bottom of a strip of phyllo.

2. Fold the lower right-hand corner up and over the filling.

3. Fold the triangle up onto the phyllo.

4. Fold the triangle from left to right. Continue, repeating Step 3 and Step 4, between folding the triangle from one side to the other until you come to the end of the phyllo strip. Brush the end of the strip with oil and tuck it under, if necessary.

TATER TIP

▲ Unbaked phyllo triangles can be stored in the refrigerator, wrapped in plastic, for up to 2 days. They freeze well for up to 2 months (freeze them on the cookie sheet, then transfer them to a zip-top bag) but do not thaw them out before baking them or the thin casing will become very soggy and unwieldy. Preheat the oven to the recommended temperature and place the frozen triangles on a parchment paper-lined cookie sheet to bake. They may need the longer baking time to heat the filling completely. Any remaining sheets of phyllo? I roll them back into a log, wrap them in 2 layers of plastic wrap, and refreeze them for up to 2 months.

a sheet of phyllo and place it on a cutting board with the broader end facing you. Re-cover the remaining phyllo with the towel to keep it from drying out. Brush the phyllo on the board with some oil. Repeat stacking and brushing three times more so you end up with a stack of 4 sheets. Cut the stack from top to bottom into 4 equal strips. Cover those strips with another damp towel.

7. Working quickly with 1 strip-stack at a time, spoon a portion of the filling onto the center of the narrow end closest to you. Here is where your flag-folding skills come in handy: Form a triangle by folding the lower right-hand corner up and over the filling to the opposite side. Repeat folding that triangle up and over to the opposite side, maintaining

the triangle until you get to the end of the strip. You should have a neat-looking triangle. If you have an uneven lip at the end, brush that lip with oil and tuck it under. Place the triangle on the prepared cookie sheet and brush it with a little oil. Repeat with the remaining 3 strips. Repeat making the 4-sheet stack, cutting strips, dolloping filling, and folding triangles 3 times more, to yield 16 phyllo triangles.

8. Arrange the triangles in a single layer on the cookie sheet so there is a little space between them. Bake until they are sunny brown and crispy, 25 to 30 minutes.

9. Serve warm as is, or with a bowl of Thai-Style Peanut Sauce (page 50), slightly warmed.

POTATO EMPANADAS

J ust about every country in the world has some sort of dough turned into a shell to house delectable morsels of meats, vegetables, cheeses, and what-have-you's. These Latin-influenced pies, made with masa harina (a type of corn flour), conceal waxy purple potatoes and salty Cotija cheese, and the results are very addictive. My friend and colleague Sandra Gutierrez calls them handheld pies in her book *Empanadas*, and my version of these grab-and-go packages is a convenient bundle for a snack or a meal-on-the-run. MAKES 12 EMPANADAS

FOR THE DOUGH

2 cups masa harina (see Tater Tips)

1 teaspoon coarse sea or kosher salt

About 1½ cups hot tap water

FOR THE FILLING

8 ounces purple potatoes

¼ cup finely chopped fresh oregano leaves

¼ cup finely chopped fresh cilantro leaves and tender stems

1 fresh green serrano chile, stem discarded, finely chopped (do not remove the seeds)

½ teaspoon coarse sea or kosher salt

4 ounces Cotija cheese, crumbled (about 1 cup; see Tater Tips)

Canola oil, for pan-frying

Creamy Jalapeño Sauce (page 133), for serving

1. Lay out 2 large sheets of wax paper or parchment paper on the counter.

2. To make the dough, combine the masa harina and salt in a medium-size bowl. Use your hand to give it a good mix. Pour in 1 cup of the water and start mixing

TATER TIPS

▲ Look for bags of masa harina in the Latin American aisle of your supermarket. Regular cornmeal is not a substitute for this flour, as it is grainier and does not hold together as well to make a soft and cohesive dough. Masa dough is easy to work with once you understand it has a tendency to dry out very quickly. Keep the rest covered under damp paper towels as you press your individual dough rounds to make the shells. Keep a bowl of hot water around so you can wet your hand and work that moisture into the dough. As you shape the round, if it cracks around the edges, that's a telltale sign that the dough is dry. Reconstitute it by kneading in more moisture with a wet hand.

▲ If Cotija cheese is unavailable, use feta as an alternative.

"Zen does not confuse spirituality with thinking about God while one is peeling potatoes. Zen spirituality is just to peel the potatoes."

—*Alan Watts, English philosopher*

it in (yes, with your hand). It should start to come together to form a slightly gritty, textured dough. Add an additional ¼ cup of water at a time, making sure it gets well incorporated. The dough should feel soft but like coarse Play-Doh, a bit grainy to the touch.

3. Break up the dough into 12 equal portions. Roll each into a ball and place them on one of the sheets of wax paper. Keep the balls covered securely with wet paper towels. The moisture from the paper towels will keep the dough moist.

4. To make the filling, scrub the potatoes well under cold running water. Shred them into a large bowl using the fine teeth of a mandoline or the large holes of a box grater. Or use the shredding disk of a food processor. (I like to leave the skin on since it looks pretty.) Add the oregano, cilantro, chile, salt, and cheese, and thoroughly combine. Divide the filling into 12 equal portions and set them aside on the other sheet of wax paper.

5. Cut two 12-inch-square pieces of parchment or wax paper. Place a dough round on one sheet, cover it with the second sheet, and flatten it either with a rolling pin or by pushing down on it with a pie plate. You want a circle roughly 6 inches in diameter. If you have a tortilla press, by all means, use it. Place a portion of the filling on one half of the dough round, making sure you leave about

½ inch of the edge exposed. Fold the other half over the filling, sealing the edges shut by pressing them with a fork or fluting them (see Canadian Lamb-Potato Tourtière, page 109, for fluting instructions). I use a fork. Return the filled empanada to the large piece of wax paper and re-cover it with damp paper towels. Repeat with the remaining dough rounds and filling.

6. Line a cookie sheet with several layers of paper towels and set a wire rack on top, for draining the empanadas of excess oil.

7. Heat a large nonstick or cast-iron skillet over medium heat. Pour enough oil into the pan to form a layer about ¼ inch deep. Once the oil appears to shimmer, gently place 4 empanadas into the hot oil. Allow the underside to turn crispy and sunny gold, 3 to 4 minutes. Flip them over and cook on the other side for an additional 3 to 4 minutes. If you feel the dough at the fold is being ignored as the empanada cooks, stand the empanada on that base to let it brown as well. Transfer the empanadas to the rack to drain.

8. Repeat with the remaining empanadas, adding more oil as needed.

9. Serve the empanadas warm, with Creamy Jalapeño Sauce (page 133) for dipping.

SMASHED
MASHED
BAKED
SHREDDED
BOILED
ROASTED
FRIED
RICED

European

POTATO LATKES
WITH CLOVE-SCENTED APPLESAUCE

These perfectly cooked, sun-yellow, crispy-on-the-surface-and-tender-inside latkes shed light on another star (besides potatoes, of course): turmeric, a tad bit astringent but tasty sibling of the ginger family. Native to India, this is an anti-inflammatory, cancer-fighting spice and a key ingredient in the dyes that yellow the fabrics that drape Hindu priests. I love that it bathes the potatoes in its golden hue—a perfect backdrop to the clove-scented applesauce. MAKES 8 LATKES

1 pound russet or Yukon Gold potatoes

1 small onion, finely chopped

3 tablespoons finely chopped fresh cilantro leaves and tender stems

1 teaspoon coarse sea or kosher salt

½ teaspoon ground turmeric

2 fresh green serrano chiles, stems discarded, finely chopped (do not remove the seeds)

Canola oil, for pan-frying

Clove-Scented Applesauce, for serving (recipe follows)

1. Fill a medium-size bowl with cold water.

2. Peel the potatoes. Shred them through the large holes of a box grater, the fine teeth of a mandoline, or the shredding disk of a food processor. Submerge the shreds in the water for 15 to 30 minutes to allow the surface starch to settle to the bottom and to prevent them from discoloring due to oxidation.

3. When you're ready to continue, use a slotted spoon to scoop the potatoes out of the water into a colander to drain a bit. Carefully pour out the soaking water, making sure you save the potato starch that has sunk to the bottom (see Tater Tip). Dump the shreds back into the bowl and add the onion, cilantro, salt, turmeric, and chiles. Thoroughly mix all the ingredients.

4. Line a cookie sheet with several layers of paper towels, for draining the latkes of excess oil. Heat a large nonstick skillet or a griddle over medium heat. Drizzle in a tablespoon of oil. Once the oil appears to shimmer, drop in a heaping ¼ cup of the potato batter (it will be a bit wet because of the liquid starch). Flatten it out with a spatula into a pancake roughly ¼ to ½ inch thick and about 3 inches in diameter. Shape as many latkes as you can fit in the skillet without overcrowding. Cook them until the underside is golden brown and crispy, 3 to 5 minutes. Flip them over and continue cooking until the flipped side is golden brown and crispy, 3 to 5 minutes. Remove them from the skillet and drain them on the paper towels. Repeat with the remaining batter.

5. Serve them warm, with the spiced applesauce on the side.

TATER TIP

▲ If, like me, you sometimes drain the potatoes and forget to scoop out that starchy slurry, don't beat yourself with a potato shred. Sprinkle 2 tablespoons of store-purchased potato starch into the mix. Works great!

TATER TIP

▲ Ghee is easy to make. Indians take clarification of unsalted butter a step farther than the French (see Tater Tips, page 139) and eliminate all the milk solids, ending up with a clear, light amber–colored fluid. The flavor from this process is far nuttier and richer than French clarified butter, in my not-so-humble opinion. Removing all the milk solids makes ghee shelf stable. Ghee is also conveniently available in the international aisle of your supermarket.

CLOVE-SCENTED
APPLESAUCE

I often make a double batch of this rich, pleasantly sweet-tart applesauce because, as well as being a perfect accompaniment, it's a perfect afternoon pick-me-up. It appeases my appetite and doesn't load me down with an insane amount of sugar. MAKES 1 CUP

1 large tart-sweet apple (such as Honeycrisp or Braeburn), peeled, cored, and cut into 1-inch pieces

2 tablespoons firmly packed dark brown sugar

2 tablespoons ghee (see Tater Tip) or unsalted butter

3 slices fresh ginger (each about the size and thickness of a quarter; no need to peel first)

½ teaspoon ground cloves

Juice from 1 small to medium-size lime (about 2 tablespoons)

Place the apple, brown sugar, ghee, ginger, cloves, lime juice, and ¼ cup water in a small saucepan and bring to a boil over medium-high heat. Lower the heat to medium, cover the pan, and simmer briskly, stirring occasionally, until the apples soften and most of the water is absorbed, 12 to 15 minutes. If you have an immersion blender (also called a stick blender), puree the medley in the pot to a smooth and saucy consistency. If not, transfer the pan's contents to a blender jar. Puree, scraping the inside of the jar as needed, until smooth. Scrape the sauce into a serving bowl and set it aside as you make the latkes.

Or refrigerate, covered, until ready to serve. The applesauce will keep for up to 2 weeks. Warm it up in the microwave before serving.

POTATO-STUFFED GOUGÈRES

Nothing says "French food" better than airily light gougères with an eggy, cheesy interior and a pleasant crisp exterior. These baked wonders are a cross between popovers and biscuits. This is one of those recipes I retested half a dozen times. My initial batter included freshly squeezed lime juice—and each time the gougères fell flat, as opposed to puffing up to create a hollow interior. Apparently, the acid caused a reaction with the flour and prevented the eggs from doing their puffy magic in that hot oven. Once I removed the lime juice from the equation, voilà—the recipe worked great.

These great starters are filled with herbaceous and citrusy (yes, I get that from the zest in the filling) mashed potatoes, asparagus, and an indulgent dollop of crème fraîche. MAKES ABOUT 30 GOUGÈRES

FOR THE GOUGÈRES

6 tablespoons (¾ stick) unsalted butter, cut into 6 slices

1 teaspoon coriander seeds, ground (see Tater Tips)

1 teaspoon coarse sea or kosher salt

1 teaspoon coarsely cracked black peppercorns

1 cup unbleached all-purpose flour

3 or 4 large eggs

1 cup shredded Gruyère cheese

1 tablespoon finely chopped fresh rosemary leaves

FOR THE POTATO STUFFING

8 ounces Yukon Gold potatoes

2 tablespoons unsalted butter

8 ounces fresh asparagus, ends trimmed off, finely chopped

½ cup crème fraîche

2 tablespoons finely chopped fresh chives

1 teaspoon Dijon mustard

½ teaspoon coarse sea or kosher salt

Zest of 1 large lemon (see Tater Tip, page 25)

TATER TIPS

▲ If you wish, you can double the dough recipe and make an extra batch of gougères to freeze. Then the next time you have an urge, you can whip up a fresh batch of stuffing and spoon it into the reheated gougères. (To reheat gougères, place them on a cookie sheet and bake them in an oven preheated to 300°F until they re-crisp on the surface and are warm inside, 5 to 8 minutes.)

▲ Small amounts of coriander seeds are not easy to grind in a spice grinder (like a coffee grinder). I have better luck grinding them with a mortar and pestle. Or you could grind a couple of tablespoons of seeds in a spice grinder and reserve the rest for another recipe.

A French encyclopedia once defined potato as a "weapon against famine."

1. To make the gougères, position a rack in the center of the oven and preheat the oven to 425°F. Line 2 cookie sheets with parchment paper.

2. Pour 1 cup of water into a small saucepan and add the butter, coriander, salt, and peppercorns. Bring to a boil over medium heat. Once the butter melts, dump in all the flour and stir it in vigorously, making sure you have no lumps. Keep stirring the flour paste over the heat until it starts to separate from the sides of the pan a bit and looks slightly opaque, 3 to 5 minutes.

3. Transfer the paste to the bowl of a stand mixer and attach the paddle. Beat on medium speed to allow some of the steam to escape and to cool it down, about 30 seconds. Turn off the mixer. Add 1 egg and turn the mixer back on at medium speed to blend it in, about 15 seconds. Repeat with 2 more eggs. You want a dough that holds soft peaks. If your dough is not there, an extra egg should do the trick.

4. Remove the bowl from the mixer and fold in the cheese and rosemary. Using 2 teaspoons (the tableware kind—one to scoop, the other to slide it out), spoon a walnut- to golf ball-size mound of the dough onto the prepared cookie sheets, leaving about an inch of space between the gougères to allow them to rise and spread. Bake until the gougères puff up, are evenly brown, and when gently tapped with a finger sound slightly hollow and feel firm, 25 to 30 minutes. Remove them from the oven and set them on a wire rack to cool.

5. As the gougères bake, make the stuffing. Peel the potatoes and rinse them under cold running water. Cut them into quarters, place them in a small saucepan, and cover them with cold water. Bring to a boil over medium-high heat. Lower the heat to medium-low, cover the pan, and boil the potatoes until they are fall-apart tender, 15 to 20 minutes.

6. As the potatoes boil, melt the butter in a medium-size skillet over medium heat. Once the butter foam subsides, add the asparagus and stir-fry until tender but still very firm, 3 to 5 minutes. Remove the pan from the heat and stir in the crème fraîche, chives, mustard, salt, and lemon zest.

7. Once the potatoes are tender, drain them into a colander. Give the colander a few good shakes to get rid of any excess water. If you wish, you can return the potatoes to the saucepan and heat them over medium heat to dry out any surface water, 1 to 2 minutes. Working in batches if necessary, transfer the potatoes to a ricer and push them through, directly into the creamy asparagus. Fold to blend, and set aside.

8. Once the gougères are cool enough to handle, cut about a 1-inch slice off the tops; set aside the tops. Scoop out and discard the slightly wet dough with a spoon to create a hollow space. Fill each with the stuffing, mounding it if you like; use up all the stuffing.

9. Place the top back on each, hat-like, and serve. These are best at room temperature.

VARIATION: For a brunch version, fold ¼ cup finely chopped smoked salmon into the stuffing.

FRIED
STEAMED
SMASHED
MASHED
BAKED
BOILED
SHREDDED
RICED

TATER TIPS

▲ If you have access to fresh water chestnuts, there is nothing better! They are crisp, juicy, sweet, and as addictive as candy. It takes patience to peel them, but it is so well worth the effort. Use a paring knife and ample rinsings with water to get rid of the chocolate-brown skin and mud that clings to it. But, unfortunately, fresh is not an option for many, so the canned ones, drained, are what we make do with.

▲ When purchasing these round potsticker wrappers (also labeled as "gyoza wrappers" on some packages), make sure you see the individual disks as you fan them out a bit through the packaging (if it's loose enough). If all you see is a hockey puck-like mass with no separation, set them down and choose another package. You want to be able to separate them easily.

Asian

WATER CHESTNUT POTATO POTSTICKERS

With China leading the world in growing potatoes (a surprise fact, perhaps!), it is no wonder they house four national potato research institutes and, in Beijing, the International Potato Center. It is evident that to the Chinese, the humble tuber is really anything but! And I cannot think of anything more iconic than China's world of dumplings to showcase potatoes in all their glory. There's nothing more comforting than these little pouches of scallion-ginger potatoes pan-fried and steamed to fashion a crispy exterior and a tender, juicy interior. Yes, if you have a bit of time, by all means make your own wrappers; if not, the store-purchased ones will be perfectly palatable. **MAKES ABOUT 24 POTSTICKERS**

8 ounces Yukon Gold potatoes

6 tablespoons canola oil

1 tablespoon finely chopped fresh ginger (no need to peel first)

¼ cup finely chopped water chestnuts (see Tater Tips)

¼ cup thinly sliced scallions (green tops and white bulbs)

2 tablespoons finely chopped fresh cilantro leaves and tender stems

2 tablespoons soy sauce

1 teaspoon coarsely cracked black peppercorns

½ teaspoon toasted sesame oil

1 teaspoon cornstarch

1 package store-purchased potsticker wrappers (see Tater Tips)

Scallion-Pepper Dipping Sauce (page 51), for serving

1. Fill a medium-size bowl halfway with cold water. Peel the potatoes and drop them into the bowl of water to keep them from discoloring. One at a time, slice the potatoes lengthwise into ¼-inch-thick planks (a chef's knife or mandoline works well). Stack a few planks at a time and cut them into ¼-inch-wide strips. Run your knife perpendicular to the strips to make ¼-inch dice, then finely chop the dice. Scrape them off the cutting board, back into the bowl. Repeat with the remaining potatoes.

2. Lay out a clean cotton kitchen towel or several layers of paper towels on the counter. Drain the potatoes in a large fine-mesh sieve and rinse them with cold running water. Spread them out on the towels to dry.

3. Heat 2 tablespoons of the canola oil in a wok or large skillet over medium-high heat. Once the oil appears to shimmer, add the potatoes and ginger. Stir-fry to allow the pieces to cook briefly but still remain firm, about 2 minutes. Remove the pan from the heat and stir in the water chestnuts, scallions, cilantro, soy sauce, peppercorns, and sesame oil. Set the skillet aside.

4. Whisk together the cornstarch and ¼ cup of warm water in a small bowl to make a thin milk-colored slurry. Lay out a large sheet of wax paper or parchment paper on the counter.

5. Place an individual potsticker wrapper in the palm of your hand; keep the package covered with a damp towel so as not to dry out the rest of them. Place a scant tablespoon of the potato filling in the center of the wrapper you're holding. Dip a finger in the cornstarch slurry and apply a coating about ¼ inch wide all around the wrapper's edge. Lift one side over the filling to the opposite side and press the edges together to seal. If you wish, you can crimp the edges while sealing the potsticker. Set the potsticker aside on the wax paper. Repeat until all the filling is used up. Save any unused wrappers in a zip-top bag in the refrigerator for up to 2 weeks or in the freezer for up to 3 months.

6. Heat 2 tablespoons of the canola oil in a large nonstick skillet over medium-high heat. Once the oil appears to shimmer, place about 12 potstickers in the pan in a single layer. Allow the bottoms to brown, about 2 minutes. Flip them over and repeat with the other side for an additional 2 minutes. Pour ½ cup of water over the dumplings. The heat from the pan will heat the water instantly and create a cloud of steam. Quickly cover the pan and give the skillet a good shake to loosen up the potstickers and allow the water to coat the bottom. Continue to steam them, 1 to 2 minutes. Remove the cover and allow the water to evaporate, an additional 2 to 3 minutes. Transfer the potstickers to a plate and cover them loosely with aluminum foil to keep them warm. Add the remaining 2 tablespoons of oil to the skillet and repeat with the remaining potstickers.

7. Serve the potstickers warm, with individual bowls of the scallion-pepper sauce for dipping.

SMASHED
MASHED
BAKED
BOILED
SHREDDED
FRIED
ROASTED
RICED

Asian

RICE PAPER-WRAPPED
POTATO ROLLS

TATER TIPS

▲ Rice paper is available in the Asian aisle of well-stocked supermarkets. The Asian grocery in your town may stock many varieties of rice paper. Brown rice, red rice, and white rice are all fair game for these almost plastic-like thin rounds. I will often get a few different kinds and offer a kaleidoscope of colors, making for a pretty platter. These are shelf stable so they will keep forever (well, almost!) in your pantry.

▲ An alternative, less messy way to fold the rice paper? Once the paper is wet, place it on a dry cutting board and fold it in half. Place the filling across the middle and fold the rice paper into a tight wrap, left to right (or the other way).

These tightly packed rice paper skins are the hit of the party, should they even make it there. I have been known to have all good intentions to take them along, but then I eat half of them at home and don't have enough left over to share.

The potatoes, when shredded lengthwise, have a noodle-like quality, especially when they are barely cooked, providing that essential toothsomeness. Peanuts inject a protein-rich crunch and fresh herbs and greens liven the roll. Even though shrimp are a part of the package, by all means, leave them out if you are vegetarian, are allergic, or keep kosher. MAKES 24 ROLLS

1 pound purple potatoes

½ pound Yukon Gold or russet potatoes

1 medium-size head red leaf lettuce, about 8 ounces

1 large red bell pepper

6 to 8 scallions (1 bunch), green tops and beards trimmed

1 pound (24 count) peeled cooked shrimp (optional)

¼ cup canola oil

½ cup dry-roasted salted peanuts, coarsely ground (see Tater Tip, page 32)

1 tablespoon rice vinegar

1 teaspoon coarse sea or kosher salt

4 fresh green serrano chiles, stems discarded, finely chopped (do not remove the seeds)

2 cups loosely packed fresh mint leaves

2 cups loosely packed fresh cilantro leaves and tender stems

Boiling water, as needed

2 packages (12 ounces each) rice paper wraps

Thai-Style Peanut Sauce (recipe follows), for serving

Scallion-Pepper Dipping Sauce (recipe follows), for serving

> "What I say is that, if a man really likes potatoes, he must be a pretty decent sort of fellow."
>
> —*A. A. Milne, English author of the Winnie-the-Pooh books*

1. Fill a medium-size bowl halfway with cold water. Peel all the potatoes. Using the medium teeth of a mandoline, the julienne disk of a food processor, or a julienne peeler (see Tater Tips, page 72), shred the potatoes. Immediately submerge them in the bowl of water. Allow the shreds to soak for 30 minutes or so, to remove excess starch.

2. While the potatoes soak, separate the lettuce leaves. Rinse them well and spin them dry in a salad spinner. Keep them wrapped in damp paper towels so they don't wilt.

3. Slice the red pepper in half lengthwise and discard the stem, ribs, and seeds. Cut the pepper into thin strips (matchstick-like) and pile them onto a large plate.

4. Slice each scallion (white bulb and green top) crosswise into three equal portions. Cut each portion lengthwise into thin shreds. Place them in a pile on the plate next to the red pepper. If using the shrimp, split them in half lengthwise (down the back). Place them next to the vegetables.

5. Lay out a clean cotton kitchen towel or several layers of paper towels on the counter, for drying the potato shreds. Drain the potato shreds into a colander and rinse them under cold running water to wash off the excess starch. Give the colander a good shake or two to rid the potatoes of excess water.

Spread out the shreds on the towel and pat them dry.

6. Set out a large plate, for the cooked potatoes. Preheat a wok or large skillet over medium-high heat. Drizzle 2 tablespoons of the oil into the wok, which will instantly get hot and appear to shimmer. Drop half of the potato shreds into the pan. Stir-fry the shreds by constantly tossing them around, until they appear a bit translucent but still are firm and toothsome-tender (al dente), 1 to 2 minutes. Transfer them to the plate. Repeat with the remaining oil and potato shreds, adding them to the cooked pile.

7. Add the peanuts, vinegar, salt, and chiles to the potatoes and mix them well. Spread them out a bit to allow them to cool quickly.

8. Place a cutting board near one end of the counter. Set a pie plate on one side of the board and a platter on the other (to receive the completed rolls). Line up the fillings above the board, in order: shrimp, lettuce leaves, potatoes, red pepper strips, scallions, mint, and cilantro. Have plenty of paper towels or dry kitchen towels on hand.

9. Fill the pie plate with the boiling water. Take a single rice paper wrapper and briefly dip it in the water. Don't keep it submerged; a quick and even dunking will ensure proper wetness. (I usually grab the edge of the wrapper with both hands to dunk and rotate it, getting the entire wrapper wet.) Place the wet wrapper on the dry cutting board. Place 2 shrimp halves flat side down alongside the lower fourth of the wrapper, closest to you. Arrange a lettuce leaf over them and top it with a liberal tablespoon of the potato filling, followed by a red pepper strip or two, some scallion shreds, and a few leaves each of mint and cilantro. Fold the lower part of the wrapper up and over the filling. Fold in the ends, burrito style. Now roll the wrap tightly into a log, making sure everything is contained in this snug cocoon. Set it on the plate. Dry the cutting board and repeat with the remaining papers and filling. Replace the water in the pie plate with a fresh batch if it gets cold.

10. Cut each roll diagonally into two halves and serve with the two dipping sauces.

THAI-STYLE PEANUT SAUCE

With flavors that showcase the balanced nuances of Thai cooking with assertive spices and herbs, this sauce is a great accompaniment to many of the potato dishes in this book, especially potato rolls (page 47) and the Nutty Potato Phyllo Triangles (page 31). Addictive enough to sip with a spoon, it is also great to drape on a simply grilled fish, planks of pan-fried tofu, or tempeh. But don't stop there. Try it on freshly cooked pasta as well. MAKES 1 GENEROUS CUP

4 fresh or dried red Thai chiles

Boiling water (optional)

1 tablespoon coriander seeds

1 teaspoon cumin seeds

1 cup unsweetened coconut milk

¼ cup firmly packed fresh cilantro leaves and tender stems

2 tablespoons finely chopped fresh lemongrass (see Tater Tips, facing page)

4 slices fresh ginger (each about the size and thickness of a quarter; no need to peel first)

2 large lime leaves (see Tater Tips, facing page) or 1 tablespoon lime rind

1 tablespoon chunky or smooth natural peanut butter

1 teaspoon fish sauce or 1 tablespoon soy sauce

¼ teaspoon coarse sea or kosher salt

1. If using dried chiles, place them in a small bowl and cover them with boiling water, to reconstitute them.

2. Heat a small skillet over medium-high heat. Once the pan is hot (placing your palm close to its base will make you pull it back within 2 seconds), sprinkle in the coriander and cumin seeds. Toast the seeds, shaking the skillet very often to make sure they turn evenly reddish brown and smell aromatic, about 1 minute. Transfer the seeds to a blender jar.

3. Drain the soaking chiles and pull out the stems, or cut the stems off the fresh chiles. Add the chiles to the spices in the blender. Pour in the coconut milk, followed by the cilantro, lemongrass, ginger, lime leaves or rind, peanut butter, fish sauce, and salt. Puree these aromatic ingredients to a fluid paste, scraping down the inside of the jar as needed.

4. Transfer the sauce to a small saucepan and bring it to a gentle simmer over medium heat. Cook, uncovered, stirring occasionally, until it starts to thicken a bit, about 5 minutes. Serve warm. Any leftover sauce will keep, covered, in the refrigerator for up to 1 week and in the freezer for up to 2 months. Thaw and reheat it in a microwave or on the stovetop over low heat.

SCALLION-PEPPER DIPPING SAUCE

This is everything a dipping sauce should be: salty, hot, and redolent of the heady aroma of toasted sesame oil. It doesn't freeze well because of the scallions, but the high acidity in the sauce does contribute to extended storage. Serve it with a platter of the potato rolls or the Water Chestnut Potato Potstickers (page 44). Store it in a glass jar in the refrigerator for up to 10 days. MAKES ¾ CUP

½ cup soy sauce

1 tablespoon rice vinegar

1 teaspoon toasted sesame oil

2 teaspoons unrefined granulated sugar (such as Sugar in the Raw)

1 fresh green serrano chile, stem discarded, finely chopped (do not remove the seeds)

2 scallions, beards trimmed, green tops and white bulbs thinly sliced

Combine all the ingredients in a small glass or stainless-steel bowl and serve.

TATER TIPS

▲ Stalks of lemongrass are now a common presence in the produce section of many supermarkets, as well as farmers' markets. And of course your neighborhood Asian grocery will stock them. Unused lemongrass stores beautifully in a freezer bag for up to 6 months. To chop lemongrass, slice off the root end of the stalk and the top three fourths of the blade-like green grass. All you will use is about 3 inches of the light-colored tightly knotted stalk. Slice this in half lengthwise, then cut each half into thin strips. Stack a few of these strips at a time and cut them crosswise into teeny tiny pieces. One stalk gives you 1 generous tablespoon of finely chopped lemongrass.

▲ Lime leaves, leathery and dark green with that perfectly tapered end, are common in Asian groceries. Highly aromatic and ever so slightly sour, I use them in stir-fries and whenever I make my own Thai curry pastes. Freeze them and use them as needed; they have a long life. I have stored them for as long as 6 months. Even in a zip-top bag in the refrigerator, my stash has survived for a month.

TATER TIP

▲ Cooks often fail to look at the world of legumes for its diversity, in terms of both flavor and texture. When used in flour form (such as chickpeas) or pureed (as is the case with red lentils in this recipe), they have an egg-like quality in their ability to "coagulate" and provide lightness. A great tool for those not into eggs!

European

SAVORY POTATO AEBLESKIVERS

The Danish classic *aebleskivers* consist of mounds of batter that are a rich cross between pancakes and popovers, and often contain fruit fillings. So this rendition surprised me. Yes, it's my creation, but to fashion a savory version from lentils and potatoes—no eggs, either—well, I was pleased!

These make a great starter with any dipping sauce of your choice, or even just some sour cream with a pinch of salt and some coarsely cracked black peppercorns. MAKES ABOUT 24 AEBLESKIVERS

1 cup red lentils (also known as Egyptian lentils; see Tater Tip)

2 fresh green serrano chiles, stems discarded

4 slices fresh ginger (each about the size and thickness of a quarter; no need to peel first)

8 ounces Yukon gold potatoes

1 small yellow onion, finely chopped

¼ cup finely chopped fresh thyme leaves and tender stems

¼ cup finely chopped fresh cilantro leaves and tender stems

1 teaspoon coarse sea or kosher salt

Canola oil, for pan-frying

1. Pour the lentils into a medium-size bowl. Cover them with cold water. Agitate them with your fingertips to rinse off any surface dust. Drain off this water. Repeat once or twice more. Cover the lentils with warm water and allow them to soak for about 1 hour.

2. Drain the lentils in a colander. Pour ½ cup of warm water into a blender jar followed by the lentils, chiles, and ginger. Puree to a smooth light-pink batter speckled with green and brown from the chiles and ginger, scraping the inside of the jar as needed. Scrape this into the bowl you soaked the lentils in.

3. Scrub the potatoes under running water. Shred them through the large holes of a box grater, the fine teeth of a mandoline, or the shredding disk of a food processor. As soon as you finish shredding them, add them to the lentil batter along with

the onion, thyme, cilantro, and salt. Vigorously beat the batter in a circular motion with a wooden spoon to incorporate some air (which makes the batter lighter), about 2 minutes.

4. Line a large plate with several layers of paper towels, for draining the cooked aebleskivers of excess oil.

5. Preheat an aebleskiver pan (see Tater Tips) over medium heat. Once the pan is hot, pour 1 teaspoon of oil into each of its indentations. Using 2 teaspoons (the tableware kind—one to scoop, the other to slide it out), spoon a heaping teaspoon of batter into each hole. As the batter cooks and turns reddish brown on the underside, 2 to 4 minutes, use a skewer to loosen it and flip it over. Brown the flipped side as well, 2 to 4 minutes. Tease out the spherical aebleskivers onto the paper towels to drain.

6. Repeat with the remaining batter. Serve warm.

TATER TIPS

▲ Any kitchen store (online or retail) will be able to fill your aebleskiver pan order. Usually available in cast iron, this pan normally has seven indentations. Modern ones now come preseasoned, so working with them cannot be any easier. You can also make aebleskivers in a mini muffin pan. Oil each muffin cup, place the pan in a preheated 400°F oven for 3 minutes to get hot, add a heaping tablespoon of batter, and bake until browned on the underside and ready to be flipped, 2 to 4 minutes. Brown the flipped side for 2 to 4 minutes, remove, and drain the aebleskivers. Enjoy.

▲ Aebleskivers are ideally consumed right away, as their crispness dissipates as they sit. But you can rewarm them in a 250°F oven on a wire rack over a cookie sheet for about 10 minutes.

STEAMED POTATO-CHIVE BUNS

Chinese steamed buns, called *bao*, are a cinch to make. This easy food processor dough—adapted from grande dame of Chinese cooking Florence Lin's excellent *Complete Book of Chinese Noodles, Dumplings, and Breads*—makes it an anytime-you-want-it recipe. My sesame-chive potato filling, addictive on its own, is a perfect complement to the buns, while the hot pepper sauce brings you tears . . . of joy. Dramatic, perhaps, but have yourself an extra bun. You won't regret it since the caloric count is very low. **MAKES 8 BUNS**

FOR THE FILLING

½ pound russet potatoes

1 tablespoon canola oil

1 tablespoon finely chopped fresh ginger (no need to peel first)

2 tablespoons finely chopped fresh chives

1 teaspoon toasted sesame oil

½ teaspoon coarse sea or kosher salt

½ teaspoon coarsely ground black peppercorns

FOR THE BUNS

1 package (2¼ teaspoons) instant yeast

½ cup warm tap water

1 tablespoon unrefined granulated sugar (such as Sugar in the Raw)

1 teaspoon coarse sea or kosher salt

2 tablespoons canola oil

2 cups unbleached all-purpose flour

Hunan Pepper Sauce (page 206), for serving

TATER TIP

▲ The light density of the unsteamed bun (due to the yeast dough) works to its advantage in freezing and then steaming. To freeze, let them rest for 30 minutes, then transfer them—paper and all—to a cookie sheet covered with plastic wrap. Place the cookie sheet in the freezer. When the buns are frozen, transfer them with the parchment paper to a zip-top freezer bag for up to 2 months. You don't have to thaw the buns before steaming them. An extra few minutes in the steamer ensures a hot interior.

1. To make the filling, fill a medium-size bowl halfway with cold water. Peel the potatoes and drop them into the bowl. One at a time, slice the potatoes lengthwise into ¼-inch-thick planks (a chef's knife or mandoline works well). Stack a few planks at a time and cut them into ¼-inch-wide strips. Run your knife perpendicular to the strips to make ¼-inch dice, then finely chop the dice. Scrape them off the cutting board, back into the bowl. Repeat with the remaining potatoes.

2. Lay out a clean cotton kitchen towel or several layers of paper towels on the counter. Drain the potatoes in a large fine-mesh sieve and rinse them with cold running water. Give the sieve a good shake or two to rid the potatoes of excess water. Spread them out on the towel and pat them dry.

3. Heat the oil in a wok or a large skillet over medium-high heat. Once the oil appears to shimmer, add the potatoes and ginger. Stir-fry to allow the pieces to cook briefly but still remain firm, 1 to 2 minutes. Remove the pan from the heat and stir in the chives, sesame oil, salt, and peppercorns. Divide the filling into 8 equal portions, placing them on a large plate. Set it aside as you make the dough.

4. To make the dough, stir the yeast into the warm water to dissolve it. Allow the yeast to activate, 2 to 4 minutes. Stir in the sugar, salt, and oil.

5. Place the flour into a food processor. Dribble the yeasty liquid through the feeding chute as you pulse the machine to fashion a soft dough. If it's very sticky, add a little more flour. You don't want it too dry, either, because then it won't form a ball. Soft and pliable is what you are going for.

Lightly dust the clean countertop with flour from a shaker (see Tater Tips, page 131). Transfer the dough to the counter and knead it for a minute or two to smooth it out a bit more. Cut the dough into 8 equal portions. Shape each portion into a ball. Cover them with plastic wrap to prevent them from drying.

6. Prepare a steamer, wok, or Dutch oven with a basket for steaming, making sure there's enough water to facilitate that (usually a depth of 2 to 3 inches is enough). Cut eight 3-inch squares of parchment paper or wax paper.

7. Grab a dough ball and roll it out on the lightly floured counter to a circle about 5 inches in diameter. Spoon 1 portion of the filling onto one half of the circle. Lift the other half over it and seal the edges by crimping or pressing them together, to form a sealed half-moon. Lightly score the top once or twice with a knife. Place it on a parchment square in the steamer basket. Repeat with the remaining rounds and filling. Cover the buns loosely with plastic wrap and allow them to rest for 30 minutes. Unless you have a large enough steamer basket or have one of those wooden steamer baskets that are stacked on top of each other, you may have to steam them in batches, without overcrowding. Keep the ones that do not fit into the steamer covered under plastic wrap.

8. Steam the buns until the dough appears opaque and dry, about 15 minutes. Serve them hot with the pepper sauce.

SPINACH-STUFFED POTATO CAKES

I have sampled many a stuffed potato cake in my life, but only this one harbors all my favorite ingredients within a crispy breaded potato shell studded with scallions. In an unusual way to create instant dough, bread slices are dampened, then blended with riced potatoes to create that bond needed to fashion dumpling-style wrappers. If you would rather not use bread, mix 2 tablespoons potato starch into the riced potatoes while they are still warm. **MAKES 8 CAKES**

FOR THE SHELLS

1 pound russet potatoes

6 scallions, beards trimmed, green tops and white bulbs thinly sliced

1 teaspoon coarse sea or kosher salt

6 slices firm good-quality white bread, regular or vegan

1 tablespoon canola oil

FOR THE FILLING

12 ounces fresh baby spinach leaves, thoroughly rinsed and dried (see Tater Tips)

½ cup finely chopped fresh cilantro leaves and tender stems

2 fresh green serrano chiles, stems discarded, finely chopped

½ teaspoon coarse sea or kosher salt

FOR PAN-FRYING AND SERVING

About 6 tablespoons canola oil

Golden Raisin-Ginger Sauce (recipe follows)

TATER TIPS

▲ After all the water gets wrung out, the spinach weighs 8 ounces. So if you are planning on using frozen chopped spinach (thawed, of course, and squeezed dry), you will know how much to use.

▲ A great do-ahead, these hold well for up to 2 days in the fridge, covered with plastic wrap to prevent drying. Pan-fry them just before you plan to serve them. If you wish to freeze the cakes, I feel you should first pan-fry them. And when you're ready to eat them, allow them to thaw a bit at room temperature and warm them on a cookie sheet in the oven at 300°F until the shells re-crisp and the interior is hot, 10 to 15 minutes.

1. To make the shells, peel the potatoes and cut them into quarters. Rinse them and place them in a medium-size saucepan. Add enough water to cover the pieces. Bring to a boil over medium-high heat. Cover the pan, lower the heat to medium-low, and boil gently until the potatoes are tender, about 20 minutes.

2. Working in batches if necessary, fish the potatoes out with a slotted spoon and place them in a ricer. Continue to keep the water warm for the spinach. Rice the potatoes into a medium-size bowl. (If you don't have a ricer, use a potato masher and fluff them with a fork when completely mashed.) Stir in the scallions and salt.

3. Hold the bread slices (including crusts) under running water to drench them, then squeeze out as much water as possible. You should end up with a wad of moist but firm bread. Use your hands to work the bread, a third of the wad at a time, into the potatoes, squeezing the mixture together to blend it, then kneading it to create a slightly sticky dough. You may not need to use all the softened bread to get the right consistency. Rub the tablespoon of oil over the dough, cover the bowl with plastic wrap or with a damp paper towel, and allow the dough to rest for 15 to 20 minutes.

4. Meanwhile, make the filling: Bring the potato water back to a boil. Pile in the spinach leaves, pushing them under as necessary. As soon as they all wilt, about 1 minute, drain them in a colander. Cool them under cold running water until you can handle them. Squeeze the spinach to get rid of all the excess liquid.

5. Finely chop the squeezed spinach and place it in a medium-size bowl. Mix in the cilantro, chiles, and salt. Lay out 2 sheets of wax paper or parchment paper on the counter. Divide the filling into 8 equal portions and set them on one of the wax paper sheets.

6. To assemble the shells, divide the dough into 8 equal portions and set them on the other sheet of wax paper. Shape each portion into a ball. Working with one ball at a time, flatten it between the palms of your hands and shape it with your fingers into a wrapper roughly 3 inches in diameter and ¼ inch thick. Place 1 portion of the filling in the center of the wrapper. Gather the edges and bring them together in the center, pinching the seam to seal it tightly, forming a mound that looks like a Hershey's Kiss. Gently flatten the top, making sure the filling stays completely covered. Press and shape it into a cake roughly 3 inches in diameter and 1 inch thick. Return it to the wax paper and repeat with the remaining dough balls and filling.

7. Line a large plate or cookie sheet with several layers of paper towels, for draining the cakes.

8. Heat about 3 tablespoons of canola oil in a large nonstick or well-seasoned cast-iron skillet over medium heat. Arrange 4 cakes in a single layer in the skillet (do not crowd them), and cook until they are golden brown and crisp on the underside, about 5 minutes. Flip them over to cook the other side until golden brown and crisp, about 5 minutes. Transfer the cooked cakes to the paper towels, and repeat with the remaining cakes, adding more oil as needed.

9. Serve the cakes hot, with the sauce.

GOLDEN RAISIN-GINGER SAUCE

A luscious and thick-bodied sauce, sweet with a pleasant kick from chiles, this is great as a dip for almost anything, from kettle-cooked potato chips to the incredible Spinach-Stuffed Potato Cakes (page 57). I often liven up leftover chicken by tearing up the cooked meat into bite-size morsels (discarding skin and bones) to mix into this sauce, slightly warmed—great for lunch or dinner, served with warm and supple Potato Tortillas (page 216). MAKES 1 GENEROUS CUP

2 tablespoons canola oil

1 teaspoon cumin seeds

4 slices fresh ginger (each about the size and thickness of a quarter; no need to peel first), finely chopped

½ cup golden raisins

1 large tomato, cored and coarsely chopped (no need to discard the seeds)

1 fresh green serrano chile, stem discarded, coarsely chopped (do not discard the seeds)

¼ cup firmly packed fresh cilantro leaves and tender stems

½ teaspoon coarse sea or kosher salt

1. Heat the oil in a small saucepan over medium-high heat. Once the oil appears to shimmer, sprinkle in the cumin seeds. They will instantly sizzle, smell nutty, and turn reddish brown, about 5 seconds. Add the ginger and raisins and stir-fry the medley until the ginger lightly browns and the raisins swell up and turn reddish gold, 2 to 3 minutes.

2. Stir in the tomato and chile and cook, stirring occasionally, to warm up the tomato, 2 to 3 minutes.

3. Transfer everything to a blender jar and add the cilantro and salt. Puree to a smooth sauce, scraping the inside of the jar as needed. Serve warm or at room temperature.

SMASHED
BAKED
BOILED
MASHED
SHREDDED
FRIED
ROASTED
RICED

Asian

SWEET POTATO SAMOSAS

> "Potato samosas and chutney go together like a horse and carriage, and this I tell you brother, you can't have one without the other."
>
> —*Raghavan Iyer*

Versatile in its use, pervasive in its presence, and accessible to every economic stratum, the potato always takes center stage in India. Synonymous with Indian cuisine, at home and in the rest of the world, are samosas—those triangular flaky pastry shells jam-packed with seasoned potatoes and peas. This is a dish that cooks make in home kitchens, on the streets in makeshift stalls, and in highbrow and lowbrow restaurants. My version leaves out the regular potatoes but includes sweet potatoes, and has the same assertive spices that populate the filling. Serve them as is or with any dipping sauce— a savory or sweet chutney would be heavenly. **MAKES 16 SAMOSAS**

FOR THE SHELLS

3 cups unbleached all-purpose flour

1 teaspoon coarse sea or kosher salt

8 tablespoons (1 stick) salted butter, cut into thin slices and chilled

About ½ cup ice water

FOR THE FILLING

1 pound sweet potatoes (I use a combination of white Jersey and Stoke's purple)

2 tablespoons canola oil

1 teaspoon cumin seeds

1 cup finely chopped red onion

4 slices fresh ginger (each about the size and thickness of a quarter; no need to peel first), finely chopped (about 1 tablespoon)

1 or 2 fresh green serrano chiles, stems discarded, finely chopped (do not remove the seeds)

2 teaspoons garam masala (see Tater Tip, facing page)

1 teaspoon coarse sea or kosher salt

1 cup frozen green peas, thawed and drained

¼ cup thinly sliced scallions (green tops and white bulbs)

¼ cup finely chopped fresh cilantro leaves and tender stems

Canola oil, for deep-frying

1. To make the shells, combine the flour and salt in a food processor and pulse to blend. Add the butter and pulse it into the flour until pea-size pellets form. (It's these clumps of butter that will make for a flaky shell.)

2. Drizzle in the cold water through the feeding chute a few tablespoons at a time, continuing to pulse the crumbly dough until it just starts to come together to form a soft ball. Transfer the dough to a cutting board or the clean, dry countertop. Knead it gently to form a smooth ball, then form it into a 12-inch-long log. Cut the log crosswise into 8 pieces and shape each piece into a ball. Press each ball flat to form a patty and set them on a large plate. Cover them in plastic wrap and refrigerate until ready to use.

3. To make the filling, bring a medium-size saucepan of water to a boil over medium-high heat. While waiting for the water to boil, peel the sweet potatoes, give them a good rinse under cold running water, and cut them into large chunks. Add them to the boiling water. Allow the water to return to a boil, then lower the heat to medium. Cover the pan and cook the sweet potatoes until they are very tender, 5 to 8 minutes.

4. Drain the sweet potatoes in a colander and shake off any excess water. Transfer them to a medium-size bowl. Mash them until smooth with a potato masher or fork.

5. Heat the oil in a medium-size skillet over medium-high heat. Once the oil appears to shimmer, add the cumin seeds and let them sizzle until they turn reddish brown and are aromatic, 5 to 10 seconds. Add the onion, ginger, and chiles, and stir-fry the medley until the onion is light brown around the edges and the aromas emanating from the pan are pungent, 3 to 5 minutes. Remove the pan from the heat and stir in the garam masala and salt. The heat of the pan's contents will be just right to cook the ground spice blend without burning it. Scrape this into the potatoes along with the peas, scallions, and cilantro, and thoroughly stir everything in. You will have a purple-hued mixture with specks and bumps of green. Set the filling aside.

6. Lightly dust a cutting board or clean countertop with flour from a shaker (see Tater Tips, page 131). Also lightly flour a large plate, for holding the shaped samosas. Place a small bowl of water next to the bowl of filling. Remove a firm, chilled patty from the

TATER TIP

▲ Garam masala is a warming blend of ground spices—usually cardamom, cumin, black peppercorns, cinnamon, and bay leaves—commonly used in the northern regions of India. Look for it in the spice aisle of your neighborhood supermarket.

TATER TIPS

▲ The Golden Raisin-Ginger Sauce (page 59) makes a great chutney with these samosas.

▲ Leftover fried samosas freeze well for up to 6 months. Freeze them on a cookie sheet in a single layer, then transfer them to a zip-top bag to store. Thaw them in the refrigerator and bake them in a 300°F oven until they re-crisp and are warm on the inside, 15 to 20 minutes.

refrigerator and place it on the board. Roll it out to form a disk roughly 5 to 6 inches in diameter, dusting it with flour as needed. Slice the disk in half. Lay one half across the fingers of one hand (the best position is when your four fingers are together and your thumb is pointing outward) with the straight edge of the cut dough in line with your forefinger and the curve at your pinkie. Dab a little water—about ½ inch wide—along the straight edge. Lift the corner closest to your thumb and twist it, bringing the wet edge together, and press to seal it well, fashioning a cone. Spoon a heaping tablespoon or two of the filling into the cone, pushing it down. Wet the inside of the round edge of the cone and press it together to seal it tightly shut. The step-by-steps on the facing page should clarify the process. Place the triangular samosa on the plate. Repeat with the other half of the disk and the remaining dough patties and filling.

7. Pour oil to a depth of 2 to 3 inches into a wok, Dutch oven, or medium-size deep saucepan. Heat the oil over medium heat until a candy or deep-frying thermometer inserted into the oil (without touching the pan bottom) registers 350°F (see Tater Tips, page 18).

8. Line a large plate or a cookie sheet with several layers of paper towels. Once the oil is ready, gently slide in 4 samosas; do not crowd the pan. Fry, flipping them occasionally with a slotted spoon, until they are caramel brown and crisp all over, about 5 minutes. (You may need to adjust the heat to maintain the oil's temperature at 350°F.) Remove them with the spoon and place them on the paper towels to drain. Repeat until all the samosas are fried. Then serve.

SAMOSAS STEP-BY-STEP

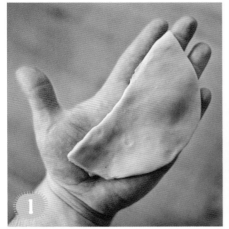

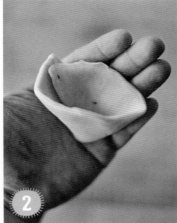

1. Roll the dough into a circle roughly 5 to 6 inches in diameter. Cut the circle in half. Dab the straight edge of the half circle with water.

2. Form the half circle into a cone. Press the straight edge onto itself to seal.

3. Spoon 1 or 2 heaping tablespoons of the filling into the cone.

4. Wet the dough at the top of the cone and press to seal.

SAVORY SOUPS & STUNNING SALADS

It works. The combination. A bowl of soup and a salad alongside. Deeply satisfying, immensely satiating, and surprisingly quick, these pairings work not only for lunch, but also for that end-of-the-day meal. Even though *locro de papas*, the Peruvian classic potato soup, is velvet-rich, I find the nuttiness of annatto seeds (the color of the setting sun) and cumin alongside buttery avocado chunks to be a pleasing contrast. A small cup of it with *dukkah*-rubbed potato slices and fresh pomegranate appeals to my senses. Or the Indonesian *soto ayam*, brothy with fresh herbs, potatoes, chicken, and eggs, makes for a complete meal, all by its lonesome but fulfilling self.

If the winter blues have you down, comforting Sweet Potato-Peanut Stew with a butter-smeared baguette and a glass of wine by the fire is just what the doctor ordered. Looking for something different to take on a picnic? How about Grandmother Ida's Russian Potato Salad with anchovies (in that creamy dressing)—chock-full of fresh dill, cucumbers, and radishes—or the boozy Mojito Potato-Pomegranate Salad that will be the surefire hit of the event? Or for your next gathering, consider offering an array of potato salads that represent flavors from all corners of the world. Tater love at its finest!

LOCRO DE PAPAS

PERUVIAN POTATO SOUP

BOILED
SMASHED
MASHED
PUREED
FRIED
SHREDDED
ROASTED
RICED

Esperanza Constellano apologized for the January weather when she picked me up from the Miami airport to take me to the Ocean Reef Club in Key Largo, where I was teaching. "It's usually not this cold," she said in her soft voice. Her South American roots, evident to me from previous encounters, led me to quiz her about her family's love affair with potatoes. We talked about a Peruvian favorite she made once a week for her husband. *Locro de papas*—the words rolled off her tongue as she described its simplicity and creaminess. This version, her steadfast, incorporates ground annatto seeds to perfume the soup with a musky aroma and splash the potatoes with a sunny disposition. I found it luscious. MAKES 8 CUPS

1½ pounds assorted fingerling potatoes (I used red and yellow)

2 tablespoons extra-virgin olive oil

1 medium-size yellow onion, cut into ½-inch pieces

4 large cloves garlic, coarsely chopped

1 small red bell pepper, stem and ribs discarded, cut into ½-inch pieces

1 teaspoon cumin seeds, ground

1 teaspoon ground annatto seeds (see Tater Tip, page 68)

1 teaspoon coarse sea or kosher salt

1 teaspoon coarsely cracked black peppercorns

½ teaspoon cayenne pepper

4 ounces cream cheese, diced

2 cups whole milk

For Serving

2 ounces queso blanco, crumbled (about ½ cup)

1 large ripe avocado, cut into ¼-inch pieces (see Tater Tip, page 27)

3 scallions, beards trimmed, green tops and white bulbs thinly sliced

¼ cup finely chopped fresh cilantro leaves and tender stems

TATER TIP

▲ Annatto seeds, also called *achiote*, are from the achiote tree and are prized for their deep yellow-orange color, mild aroma, and nutty flavor with peppery undertones. Their source, indigenous to Central and South America, is also called the "lipstick tree" as the seeds were used to infuse color into lipstick. A natural coloring of choice in many commercial food products, annatto seeds are commonly available in any store that caters to the Latin American community. Not a great alternative, but if you don't have annatto seeds, an equal combination of sweet paprika and ground turmeric will produce an annatto-like color.

1. Fill a medium-size bowl with cold water. Wash the potatoes well under cold running water. Cut them in half and submerge them in the bowl of water to prevent them from discoloring.

2. Heat the oil in a Dutch oven or large saucepan over medium-high heat. Once the oil appears to shimmer, add the onion, garlic, and bell pepper. Stir-fry the medley until the onion is light brown around the edges and the garlic and pepper have softened, 5 to 7 minutes. Remove the pan from the heat.

3. Stir in the cumin, annatto, salt, peppercorns, and cayenne. The heat of the pan's contents is just right to cook the spices without burning them, about 15 seconds.

4. Drain the potatoes in a colander and add them to the pan along with the cream cheese and milk. Return the pan to medium-high heat. As the milk comes to a boil, the cream cheese will start to melt. Lower the heat to medium-low, cover the pot, and simmer, stirring occasionally, until the potatoes are tender when pierced with a fork or knife, about 15 minutes.

5. Transfer the soup, in batches, to a blender jar and puree it until smooth, creamy, and a beautiful shade of yellow, scraping the inside of the jar as needed. You can also puree it in the pan with an immersion blender.

6. Serve the soup warm in individual bowls, topping it with the queso, avocado, scallions, and cilantro.

POTATO SOTO AYAM

Nancy Couné, along with her husband, Jody Sipe, both Minnesota natives, lived in Indonesia for four years in the early eighties. Being friends with an Indonesian ambassador exposed Nancy to many of Indonesia's classics, and the *soto ayam* was by far her favorite. It is a perfect balance of textures, temperatures, colors, tastes, and aromas. Bursting with assertive flavors, my version gives the original chicken-heavy version a nudge to the side with the inclusion of fingerling potatoes. I agree this is a lot of prep for the soup, but once you finish, this would be it for the evening meal. If you have some time over a weekend, a homemade chicken broth will make the soup even richer. **SERVES 4**

8 ounces assorted fingerling potatoes (red, yellow, and purple)

1 stalk lemongrass (see Tater Tips, page 51)

½ cup thinly sliced shallots

2 slices (each the size and thickness of a quarter) fresh galangal (see Tater Tips, page 103) or ginger

2 slices (each the size and thickness of a dime) fresh turmeric (see Tater Tip, page 71), or ¼ teaspoon ground

2 large cloves garlic

1 teaspoon coriander seeds

½ teaspoon whole black peppercorns

1 teaspoon coarse sea or kosher salt

1 tablespoon canola oil

6 cups low-sodium chicken or vegetable stock

3 medium-size to large lime leaves (see Tater Tips, page 51) or the zest of 1 medium-size lime

1 pound bone-in, skin-on chicken breasts

For Finishing and Serving

4 ounces dried vermicelli rice noodles

4 cups boiling water

1 cup shredded napa cabbage

1 cup bean sprouts, rinsed and drained

1 large carrot, peeled, ends trimmed, cut into julienne (see Tater Tip, page 72)

2 scallions, beards trimmed, green tops and white bulbs thinly sliced

¼ cup finely chopped fresh cilantro leaves and tender stems

2 fresh green serrano chiles, stems discarded, finely chopped (do not remove the seeds)

1 large lime, cut into quarters

2 hard-cooked large eggs, peeled and cut in half

1 cup store-purchased kettle-cooked potato chips

1. To make the soup, scrub the potatoes under running water. Cut them into 1-inch pieces, place them in a medium-size bowl, and cover them with cold water.

2. Slice off the root end of the lemongrass stalk and the top three fourths of the stalk. All you will use is about 3 inches of the light-colored tightly knotted stalk. Slice this in half lengthwise, then cut it into 1-inch pieces.

3. Pour ¼ cup of water into a blender jar and pile in the shallots, galangal, turmeric, garlic, coriander seeds, peppercorns, and salt. Puree the medley into a delectable paste, scraping the inside of the jar as needed.

4. Heat the oil in a Dutch oven or large saucepan over medium heat. Once the oil appears to shimmer, scrape in the paste and give it a good stir. Roast the paste in the oil, stirring occasionally, until it smells highly aromatic and a bit of it starts to stick to the bottom of the pan (called "fond"—pronounced "fohn"—in culinary lingo), 2 to 3 minutes.

5. Quickly drain the potatoes in a colander and give it a good shake or two to rid the potatoes of excess water. Add them to the paste and stir once or twice. The water still clinging a bit to the potatoes will help to release some of the stuck-on bits of paste. Pour in the stock and add the lemongrass and lime leaves. Scrape the bottom of the pan to make sure all that stuck-on goodness is now completely released and incorporated into the stock. (What you have done is deglazed the pan—not to mention made it easier to wash it later.)

6. Add the chicken and bring it all to a boil. Cover the pan, turn the heat to medium-low, and simmer the soup, stirring occasionally, until the chicken is no longer pink when cut through the middle and the potatoes are tender when pierced with a fork or knife but still firm, 15 to 20 minutes.

7. Fish out the chicken and place it on a cutting board to cool. Fish out and discard the lemongrass and lime leaves. Keep the soup on the lowest heat and cover it to stay warm as you finish getting the serving ingredients ready.

8. Place the rice noodles in a medium-size heatproof bowl and pour the boiling water over them. Give them a stir. The water will render the noodles tender, 1 to 2 minutes. Quickly drain them in a colander and rinse them under

TATER TIP

▲ Fresh turmeric looks a lot like ginger, except it is much more slender and has a yellow-orange skin. The intense color reveals itself when you snap it open. Much sweeter than its ground dried form, and mellow in its aromas and taste, the fresh rhizome is available certain times of the year in upscale supermarkets, natural food stores, and Asian groceries. Store it as you would fresh ginger, loosely bagged in plastic or a brown paper sack in the vegetable bin of your refrigerator for up to 2 weeks.

TATER TIP

▲ It's really not that difficult to julienne a carrot. An easier way is to use a julienne peeler (yes, you can get them at kitchen stores). Or do it the old-fashioned way with a chef's knife. I usually cut the carrot into three cross sections. Stand each one up on one flat end and slice it into thin (⅛-inch-thick) planks. Stack a few planks together and cut them into very thin strips, matchstick-like, to yield a julienne cut.

cold running water to prevent them from continuing to cook and turn mushy. Allow them to drain completely.

9. Discard the skin and bones from the chicken. Shred the chicken by pulling it apart with your fingers. Divide this into 4 portions and place them in individual bowls. Cut the noodles into bite-size strands with kitchen shears and divide them among the 4 bowls. Divide the cabbage, sprouts, carrot, scallions, cilantro, and chiles equally among the bowls as well.

10. Skim off and discard any fat from the chicken you may see floating on top of the soup. Ladle the soup equally among the bowls. Serve right away with a platter of the lime wedges, eggs, and potato chips.

FOR VEGETARIANS

1. Replace the chicken with tofu.

2. Use vegetable stock, instead of chicken stock.

3. The eggs are a nice addition, but if your diet doesn't include them, leaving them out won't diminish the soup in any way.

SMASHED
MASHED
BAKED
FRIED
SHREDDED
ROASTED
BOILED
RICED

Ghanaian

SWEET POTATO-PEANUT STEW

Sweet potatoes—no relation to the potato family—are eaten extensively in the northern and western countries of Africa and often include the plant's leaves and shoots. The indigenous African legume, the groundnut (more commonly known here as the peanut), is a crucial source of protein in the foods of these countries, including this Ghanaian peanut stew, which incorporates both foods. Nutritionally superior in every way when compared to the potato, sweet potatoes are rich in antioxidants; the darker the sweet potato flesh, the richer the beta-carotene. A stew that satisfies with the honeyed presence of sweet potatoes, the nutty crunch of roasted peanuts, and the pungency of ginger is grounds for being a main course offering on a wintry evening. Serve it alongside a few slices of crusty bread or try the Potato Habanero Biscuits (page 211). **SERVES 6**

1 pound sweet potatoes

½ pound sweet potato greens or collard greens (see Tater Tip, page 74)

2 tablespoons canola oil

½ cup dry-roasted unsalted peanuts, coarsely chopped (see Tater Tip)

1 medium-size red onion, finely chopped

6 slices fresh ginger (each about the size and thickness of a quarter; no need to peel first), finely chopped

4 large cloves garlic, finely chopped

1 pound boneless, skinless chicken breasts or thighs, cut into 1-inch pieces

1 teaspoon ground cumin

1 teaspoon crushed red pepper flakes

1 teaspoon coarse sea or kosher salt

1 cup canned diced tomatoes (including any juices)

¼ cup creamy or crunchy natural peanut butter

TATER TIP

▲ Dry-roasted unsalted peanuts are commonly found in the snack area or the health food section of the supermarket, often in the bulk goods aisle. If you can procure blanched raw peanuts, buy them in a heartbeat and roast them yourself in a bit of oil in a large skillet until light brown. The smells and tastes are unparalleled compared to the store-purchased variety. Often, I will still lightly roast the pre-roasted kind for a more intense peanut burst.

TATER TIP

▲ The first time I saw sweet potato greens at my farmers' market in Minneapolis, I had a million questions for the farmer. Stacks of lush, sturdy green leaves with thick stems ranging in color from green to shades of light purple-pink made for a sensual sight. What intrigued me was the line of women from Nigeria in their colorful regalia, stuffing their bags with as many bunches of the greens as they could. I have no qualms about asking people questions on food and cooking—it's the best icebreaker. "Cook them like any greens," one said. "They are very, very sweet." So I walked home with two bunches in my bag. I braised one, and she was so right. The dish was candy-sweet with a wisp of smokiness (yes, that came from the blackened red chiles I had in the mix). I was hooked. If you have access to a grocery store that caters to the African community, you will be able to find these greens with more regularity than the once-a-year guest appearance at the farmers' market.

1. Peel the sweet potatoes, give them a good rinse under cold running water, and cut them into 1-inch cubes. Drop them into a medium-size bowl and cover them with cold water to prevent oxidation.

2. Trim and discard the tough stems and ribs from the greens. Stack a few of the leaves at a time, roll them into a tight cylinder, and slice them crosswise into thin strips. Drop them into a bowl large enough to fit them with room to spare and cover them with cold water. Swish them around, then allow the sand and grit to settle to the bottom. Scoop out the greens and place them in a colander. Dump the water and rinse the bowl. Repeat this twice more or until all the sand and grit have been washed off and the greens have drained in the colander one last time.

3. Heat the oil in a Dutch oven or large saucepan over medium-high heat. Once the oil appears to shimmer, sprinkle in the peanuts and stir them around to allow the nuts to acquire that fresh-roasted aroma, about 30 seconds. Add the onion, ginger, and garlic and continue to stir-fry, uncovered, until the medley is light brown around the edges, 5 to 7 minutes.

4. Stir in the chicken, cumin, red pepper flakes, and salt. Allow the chicken to cook just a bit, uncovered, stirring occasionally, until the pieces appear a bit opaque on the outside, 3 to 5 minutes.

5. Drain the sweet potatoes and add them to the pan along with the greens, 4 cups water, and the tomatoes. Bring to a boil over medium-high heat, then lower the heat to medium, partially cover the pan, and simmer vigorously, stirring occasionally, until the potatoes are tender when pierced with a fork, and the chicken pieces are barely pink in the center when cut and their juices run clear, 15 to 20 minutes.

6. Stir the peanut butter into the stew and simmer it, uncovered, stirring occasionally, until the liquid thickens, about 5 minutes. Serve it warm.

African

DUKKAH-RUBBED POTATOES
WITH POMEGRANATE SEEDS

This is one of those recipes that falls under the "sexy" category. A sesame-flavored Egyptian spice blend, called *dukkah*, coats thin slices of buttermilk-soaked potatoes that are pan-fried crispy brown, then swathed with a yogurt-cucumber dressing. But don't judge this dish solely by its looks. While it's a great potato salad course, I often make this as an appetizer or a stand-alone lunch alongside a mini baguette. (Please don't judge me for ingesting multiple sources of carbohydrates at one meal.) In fact, potatoes are a good source of vegetable protein, with a ratio of protein to carbohydrate higher than most cereals and other root crops. **SERVES 4**

TATER TIP

▲ Sesame seeds have been unearthed in fossilized remains dating back to 20,000,000 BCE in the part of the world where India now is. Untoasted sesame seeds are the key ingredient in making tahini, a paste used in many Middle Eastern cuisines, while toasted varieties yield the darker, stronger oil drizzled on the foods of Southeast Asia. Because of their high oil content, they have a tendency to turn rancid quickly. Store sesame seeds in the refrigerator.

FOR THE DUKKAH

¼ cup raw skin-on or blanched hazelnuts

¼ cup raw shelled pumpkin seeds

1 tablespoon white sesame seeds (see Tater Tip, page 75)

2 teaspoons coriander seeds

2 teaspoons cumin seeds

2 tablespoons chickpea flour

1 teaspoon coarse sea or kosher salt

1 teaspoon coarsely cracked black peppercorns

½ teaspoon cayenne pepper

FOR THE MARINATED POTATOES

2 cups buttermilk

1½ pounds russet potatoes

Canola oil, for pan-frying

FOR THE DRESSING

1 cup nonfat plain Greek yogurt

1 teaspoon coarsely cracked black peppercorns

½ teaspoon coarse sea or kosher salt

1 small to medium-size cucumber, peeled, cut in half lengthwise, seeds discarded, and shredded

¼ cup finely chopped fresh mint leaves

1 cup fresh pomegranate seeds

1. To make the dukkah, heat a large nonstick or well-seasoned cast-iron skillet over medium heat. As the pan heats, combine the hazelnuts, pumpkin seeds, sesame seeds, coriander seeds, and cumin seeds in a small bowl. Sprinkle the medley into the pan and toast everything, stirring constantly, until the nuts and seeds smell aromatic and turn light brown, 3 to 5 minutes. Return them to the same bowl to cool.

2. Sprinkle the chickpea flour into the same skillet over medium heat and immediately start stirring it, as it will start to brown almost instantly. Once it is evenly brown—this should take only 30 seconds to 1 minute—scrape the flour into a separate small bowl. Wipe out the skillet, but there's no need to wash it yet.

3. Transfer the cooled nut medley to a blender jar, spice grinder, or clean coffee grinder and pulverize it to the consistency of finely ground black pepper. Tap this into the bowl of toasted chickpea flour and sprinkle in the salt, peppercorns, and cayenne. Give it a good stir. Often the heat from the grinder may clump up some of the nuts and sesame seeds, so break them up as you mix it.

> "There is no species of human food that can be consumed in a greater variety of modes than the potato."
>
> —*Sir John Sinclair, Scottish politician*

4. To marinate the potatoes, pour the buttermilk into a 13-by-9-inch cake pan or a similar rectangular pan. Peel the potatoes and slice them lengthwise into ⅛-inch-thick planks using a chef's knife or a mandoline. Submerge the planks in the buttermilk as you slice them, to prevent them from discoloring. Repeat with the remaining potatoes.

5. When you're ready to cook the potato planks, set a wire rack over a cookie sheet, for draining off excess oil. Pour about 2 tablespoons of oil in the skillet over medium heat. Once the oil appears to shimmer, lift a potato plank out of the buttermilk with one hand and place it, still dripping wet, on a plate. With your dry hand, sprinkle a coating of dukkah on top. Flip the plank with your wet hand. Sprinkle dukkah again with your dry hand, and place the plank into the hot oil. Add as many planks as you can without crowding the pan. Once the planks are sunny brown and slightly crispy on the underside, 2 to 3 minutes, flip them and cook the other side for an additional 2 to 3 minutes. Using tongs or a slotted spoon, lift them onto the rack to drain the excess oil. Carefully wipe any remaining oil out of the pan with paper towels. Repeat coating, pan-frying, and draining the potato planks, wiping out the pan after and heating fresh oil, until you've cooked all the potatoes.

6. To make the dressing, whisk together the yogurt, peppercorns, and salt in a medium-size bowl. Fold in the cucumber and most of the mint leaves; reserve about a tablespoon for sprinkling as garnish.

7. Transfer the potato planks to a large serving platter and spoon the yogurt dressing over them. Top them off with the pomegranate seeds and the reserved mint leaves. If you have any extra dressing, pass it at the table for those who wish to have more.

DUTCH LETTUCE

❝In Pella, Iowa, Midwest USA, you can eat Dutch lettuce at the diners in the spring. Pella is a wooden-shoe-and-tulips Dutch town, rather than a German Dutch town. However, this is essentially hot German potato salad mixed with garden lettuce. The lettuce wilts and the whole thing is ugly but utterly delish," writes Mary Jane Miller, a friend and colleague from Minnesota who is a food writer and recipe developer. Serve it for a simple lunch with a favorite sandwich, roasted chicken, or even just a few slices of toasted bread. SERVES 4

> "It's easy to halve the potato where there's love."
>
> *—Proverb*

1 pound new red potatoes

4 strips bacon

1 tablespoon unbleached all-purpose flour

½ teaspoon ground mustard

1 teaspoon celery seeds

¼ cup apple cider vinegar

1 teaspoon white granulated sugar

1½ teaspoons coarse sea or kosher salt

1 teaspoon coarsely cracked black peppercorns

4 cups firmly packed torn-up red leaf lettuce, thoroughly rinsed and dried

¼ cup finely chopped red onion

4 hard-cooked large eggs, peeled and cut into ½-inch-thick slices

1. Scrub the potatoes well under cold running water, cut them in half, and place them in a medium-size saucepan. Cover them with cold water and bring to a boil over medium-high heat. Briskly boil the potatoes, uncovered, until they are just tender but still firm, 12 to 15 minutes. Take care not to overcook the potatoes. Scoop out 1 cup of the potato water. Drain the potatoes in a colander and give the colander a few good shakes to rid the potatoes of excess water. Leave the colander in the sink with the potatoes in it as you get the other ingredients ready.

2. Heat a large skillet over medium heat. Lay the bacon strips in the pan and cook one side, then flip them over to cook the second side until crispy, 4 to 6 minutes per side. Transfer the bacon to a cutting board. Sprinkle the flour, mustard, and celery seeds into the hot grease. Stir and cook to brown the flour, 1 to 2 minutes. Pour in the reserved potato water, whisking to ensure a lump-free sauce. Simmer the liquid, uncovered, whisking occasionally, until it thickens, 3 to 5 minutes. Remove the skillet from the heat. Stir in the vinegar, sugar, salt, and peppercorns. Crumble the cooled bacon.

3. Spread the lettuce in a large bowl. Top it off with the still-warm potatoes, followed by the onion, crumbled bacon, and eggs. Pour the dressing over this and serve right away.

"I have made a lot of mistakes falling in love, and regretted most of them, but never the potatoes that went with them."

—Nora Ephron, American writer and humorist

GRANDMOTHER IDA'S RUSSIAN POTATO SALAD

BOILED
SMASHED
MASHED
BAKED
FRIED
SHREDDED
ROASTED
RICED

TATER TIPS

▲ Refrigerating the dressed salad overnight to serve the next day allows the flavors to marry. The salad keeps up to 3 days. However, it can become slightly watery. Drain off any excess liquid. Check for taste and correct with salt and pepper if needed.

▲ The use of raw eggs and/or yolks is always a cause for concern in this day and age of salmonella. You may fall on either side of the argument—should I use raw eggs from a source I am familiar with, or should I consider using pasteurized eggs? Pasteurized whole eggs are heated in the shell at a safe temperature for the requisite number of minutes to make the eggs safe for raw consumption. The emulsifying properties of the egg differ a bit but it certainly works well in any recipe that calls for raw eggs.

Scott Edwin Givot, a soulmate (a past president of the International Association of Culinary Professionals) and traveling companion, originally from Chicago, then Minneapolis, and now settled in Norway, reminisced about his grandmother Ida's potato salad. The salad reflected her history and background, and what an interesting one at that. Married at the age of seventeen, she was swept into her husband's underground world of smuggling diamonds (in Scott's father's diaper when he was a baby!), drugs, guns, and more. Grandma Ida's ancestral roots were a hodgepodge, ranging from Crimean to Catalan, Hungarian, and French. This Russian salad was special to her and to Scott, a summer tradition they shared in the kitchen as she gave him advice on all that life could throw at him. A spoonful of this gave me evidence of equilibrium in her tumultuous life—a true fine balance of taste, color, temperature, and texture.

"Even as a kid, I never minded the idea of the salty little fish

"The value of the potato in calamity and wartime has been proved repeatedly."
—*Anonymous*

[anchovies] being used in the dressing. It's what gave the salad that undeniable umami flavor," Scott mused, a love for the years-that-were in his voice. "She always served it next to her sweet 'n' sour 'Swedish' meatballs, which had a mellifluous tomato sauce punctuated with whole allspice. I loved both dishes and still make them to this day." SERVES 4

FOR THE SALAD

1½ pounds new red potatoes

6 medium-size to large red radishes, scrubbed, trimmed, and thinly sliced

4 ribs celery, leaves discarded, thinly sliced

1 large English cucumber, peeled, cut in half lengthwise, seeds discarded, and thinly sliced

4 scallions, beards trimmed, green tops and white bulbs thinly sliced

¼ cup baby capers, drained

¼ cup finely chopped fresh dill

½ cup finely chopped fresh chives

FOR THE DRESSING

6 anchovy fillets

2 egg yolks (see Tater Tips, page 81)

1 tablespoon Dijon mustard

2 large cloves garlic, crushed

¼ cup extra-virgin olive oil

¼ cup canola oil

1 teaspoon Worcestershire sauce

¼ cup freshly squeezed lemon juice

½ teaspoon cayenne pepper

1 teaspoon coarse sea or kosher salt

½ teaspoon coarsely cracked black peppercorns

1. To make the salad, scrub the potatoes well under running water, cut them in half, and place them in a medium-size saucepan. Cover them with cold water and bring to a boil over medium-high heat. Briskly boil the potatoes, uncovered, until they are just tender but still firm, 12 to 15 minutes. Take care not to overcook the potatoes.

2. Drain the potatoes in a colander and rinse them under cold running water to cool them down. Give the colander a few good shakes to rid the potatoes of excess water, and transfer them to a large bowl. Add the radishes, celery, cucumber, scallions, capers, dill, and chives to the potatoes.

3. To make the dressing, place the anchovy fillets, egg yolks, mustard, and garlic in a blender jar and puree, turning off the blender and scraping the inside of the jar as needed, until smooth. Combine the two oils together in a small bowl. With the blender on low speed, drizzle the oils through the hole in the cover in a steady stream. Once the oils are added, you will have a thick emulsion, which is your own homemade mayonnaise. Add the Worcestershire, lemon juice, cayenne, salt, and peppercorns and pulse the dressing to ensure a smooth mix.

4. Pour the dressing over the salad and give it all a good toss. Serve at room temperature, but because this is a mayonnaise-based salad, do not leave it at room temperature for long periods of time.

"Even the potato has a
low form of cunning."
—Samuel Butler,
Victorian-era English novelist

SMASHED
MASHED
BAKED
FRIED
SHREDDED
ROASTED
BOILED
RICED

African

HARISSA POTATO SALAD

TATER TIP

▲ If you prefer more heat in terms of chiles, increase them by another one or two or use a hotter variety. Habanero chiles pack more intensity with perfumed undertones. I usually add 1 whole habanero instead of the serranos in the recipe. And, of course, you want to make sure you have adequate ventilation over the stove, otherwise I guarantee you a coughing fit from the fumes emanating from the chiles.

Morocco's staple condiment, harissa (an aromatic chile paste used in North African and Middle Eastern cuisines), is my addiction. Typically made from an assortment of bell peppers, chiles, and spices, it provides a pleasing punch to many dishes. My version, with far fewer ingredients, delivers the same intensity, and its inclusion to drape boiled fingerlings makes this a much-talked-about dish at the table. Perfect for picnics and parties, this is a great stand-in for ho-hum mayonnaise-bathed salads. SERVES 6

1 pound fingerling potatoes (use a variety of colors, if available)

2 tablespoons canola oil

1 tablespoon coriander seeds

1 large red bell pepper, stem, ribs, and seeds discarded, cut into 1-inch pieces

2 fresh green serrano chiles (see Tater Tip), stems discarded, coarsely chopped (do not remove the seeds)

Juice from 1 large lime (about 3 tablespoons)

1½ cups finely chopped scallions (green tops and white bulbs)

¼ cup finely chopped fresh mint leaves

¼ cup finely chopped fresh cilantro leaves and tender stems (see Tater Tips, page 86)

1 teaspoon coarse sea or kosher salt

TATER TIPS

▲ If you are a cilantro hater, by all means, use an herb you like better. I find fresh tarragon leaves or even rosemary are a great match for the mint in the recipe.

▲ Preparing the salad a day ahead allows the flavors to meld a bit more. Let it return to room temperature before serving.

1. Scrub the potatoes well under running water. Cut them into 1-inch pieces and put them in a small saucepan. Cover the pieces with cold water. Bring to a boil over medium-high heat and boil, uncovered, until the potatoes are tender when pierced with a fork or knife but still firm, 12 to 14 minutes.

2. As the potatoes cook, heat the oil in a medium-size skillet over medium-high heat. Once the oil appears to shimmer, sprinkle in the coriander seeds, which will immediately start to sizzle, turn reddish brown, and smell nutty with a citrus undertone, 5 to 10 seconds. Add the red bell pepper and chiles and stir-fry the medley to sear and blister the skins, 3 to 5 minutes.

3. Scrape the pepper medley into a blender jar and pour in the lime juice. Puree the vegetables, scraping the inside of the jar as needed, to a smooth, bright red paste. Scrape this into a medium-size bowl.

4. Drain the potatoes in a colander, giving it a good shake or two to rid the potatoes of any excess water. Add the potatoes while still hot to the paste along with the scallions, mint, cilantro, and salt. (The potatoes absorb all those incredible flavors far better while they are still warm.) Give it all a good stir. Serve right away or refrigerate the salad for later consumption.

MOJITO POTATO-POMEGRANATE SALAD

This stunning potato salad, which goes beyond the boundaries of those that are creamy or vinegar based, can be your cocktail for the evening. Boozy, bold, and anything but bland, the flavors in a summery mojito cocktail that appeal to my 5:00 p.m. sensibilities bring these fingerling potatoes to life. Take this to your Fourth of July festivities and watch the fireworks ignite all around you. SERVES 6

1 pound assorted fingerling potatoes (a mix of purple, red, and white)

4 small Key limes, each cut in half, or 1 large lime, cut into 8 wedges

½ cup fresh mint leaves

1 tablespoon unrefined granulated sugar (such as Sugar in the Raw)

2 teaspoons coarsely cracked black peppercorns

1 teaspoon coarse sea or kosher salt

¼ cup white rum (see Tater Tip)

½ cup fresh pomegranate seeds (see Tater Tip, page 89)

1. Fill a small saucepan halfway with water and bring it to a rolling boil over medium-high heat. As

TATER TIP

▲ If liquor isn't your thing, leave it out. I would recommend a tablespoon or two of a fruity extra-virgin olive oil to anoint the mix instead.

SMASHED
MASHED
BAKED
FRIED
SHREDDED
BOILED
ROASTED
RICED

the water comes to a boil, scrub the potatoes under running water. Cut them into 1-inch pieces and add them to the boiling water. Lower the heat to medium and cook the potatoes at a brisk simmer or gentle boil, uncovered, until tender when pierced with a fork or knife but still firm, 10 to 12 minutes.

2. While the potatoes cook, pile the limes, mint, sugar, peppercorns, and salt in a deep mortar. Pound the herbaceous medley with the pestle to release the juices from the limes and the essential oils from the mint. Remove and discard the lime shells. If you don't have a mortar and pestle, squeeze the limes and briefly pulse the herbaceous mix in a food processor. Stir in the rum.

3. As soon as the potatoes are tender, drain them in a colander and rinse under cold running water to cool them down a bit. Leave the potatoes a little warm to the touch, as they will absorb the flavors much better.

4. Transfer the potatoes to a medium-size bowl and scrape the muddled ingredients over them. Add the pomegranate seeds and give it all a good stir.

5. Let the salad stand for an hour or so to allow the flavors to boogie. Serve at room temperature. If you prefer, you can also serve it chilled.

TATER TIP

▲ Everyone has a way of removing the seeds from a fresh pomegranate, some easier than others. I often buy pomegranates (firm, all hues of red, apple-like) by the case, usually six to a box, and peel the fruit to get to the seeds. It takes about an hour of my time but then I am rewarded—and so is my son, who is a fanatic when it comes to the seeds—with a gigantic bowl of juicy, nutty, succulent, ruby-red seeds that both of us can eat by the spoonful. To get the seeds out of a pomegranate, here's what I do: I fill a large, deep bowl halfway with tap water. I cut the fruit in half lengthwise (through that glorious crown stem), and then cut each half in half again lengthwise. Working with one quarter at a time, I turn it inside out under the water in the large bowl, so the seeds and flesh are pushed out, like a puffed-up penguin chest. Using my fingers, I cajole the seeds out of their flimsy off-white cell-like house. The seeds, heavy with sweet juices, sink to the bottom and any papery membranes float to the top. Once finished, I skim off the flotsam from the surface and drain the seeds into a colander.

SMASHED
MASHED
BAKED
FRIED
BOILED
SHREDDED
ROASTED
RICED

TATER TIP

▲ Making the salad a day ahead, refrigerating it, and serving it at room temperature is certainly acceptable—and more flavorful as well.

North American

SKILLET POTATO SALAD

WITH BASIL

Who doesn't love a good potato salad? Sure, there's a time and place for whatever renditions you may concoct of those mayo-doused ones with hard-cooked eggs and mustard. But give me one that's unique, spirited with citrus and herbs, and just the right touch of heat, and I will be your new BFF. This version is all that—plus the textural difference from skillet-roasted potatoes rounds out the experience. SERVES 6

1½ pounds assorted fingerling potatoes (use a mix of colors)

2 tablespoons canola oil

1 tablespoon coriander seeds

¼ cup orange juice (freshly squeezed would be ideal)

½ cup finely chopped fresh basil leaves (see Tater Tip)

½ cup finely chopped fresh cilantro leaves and tender stems

1½ teaspoons coarse sea or kosher salt

1 teaspoon unrefined granulated sugar (such as Sugar in the Raw)

½ teaspoon cayenne pepper

1. Wash the potatoes well under running water. Cut them into 1-inch pieces, drop them in a medium-size bowl, and cover them with cold water. Allow them to soak for 15 to 20 minutes to remove any surface starch. Lay out a clean cotton kitchen towel or several layers of paper towels on the counter for drying the potatoes.

2. Drain the potatoes in a colander and rinse them a bit under cold running water. Give the colander a good shake or two to rid the potatoes of excess water. Spread the potatoes on the towel and dry them well.

3. Heat the oil in a large nonstick skillet over medium heat. Once the oil appears to shimmer, add the potatoes, cover them, and cook them, stirring occasionally, until they are crispy brown on the outside and tender when pierced with a fork or knife without being fall-apart overcooked, 15 to 20 minutes.

4. As the potatoes brown, heat a small skillet over medium-high heat. As soon as the pan is hot, sprinkle in the coriander seeds. Toast the seeds, shaking the pan very often for even browning (more reddish brown actually), about 1 minute. Transfer the seeds to a spice grinder or a clean coffee grinder. Once they are cool, grind them to the consistency of finely ground black pepper. (I guarantee you the escape of a "wow!" when you open that grinder.)

5. Once the potatoes are ready, dump them into a serving bowl, along with any residual oil in the skillet. While they are still warm, add the orange juice, basil, cilantro, salt, sugar, cayenne, and the coriander. Give it all a good stir. Allow the salad to sit for a half hour or so to let the flavors mingle.

TATER TIP

▲ For a prettier mix, chiffonade the basil leaves: Stack a few similar-size leaves (already washed and dried). Roll the stack into a tight log. Slice the log crosswise into very thin slices to yield the desired ribbons.

SMASHED
BOILED
MASHED
BAKED
FRIED
SHREDDED
ROASTED
RICED

TATER TIPS

▲ Slightly bitter stone-hard fenugreek seeds are from a plant that has highly perfumed, clover-like leaves. A choice among lactating mothers in parts of Asia (it's thought to increase milk supply), the seeds can be found in health-food stores and Indian groceries.

▲ If you make this salad a day or so ahead, cover the bowl with plastic wrap and refrigerate it. Bring the salad to room temperature before you serve it.

NEPALESE POTATO SALAD

Even though Buddhist monks were starting to cultivate potatoes at their monasteries in Nepal and neighboring Bhutan in the 1700s, potatoes never really caught on until almost 150 years later, when the government of Nepal stepped in with some support from the Indian government. Now a staple all across Nepal, the tuber makes its way into every home daily.

Chukauni, a yogurt-based potato salad from the hilly region of Palpa in midwestern Nepal, is a favorite of Suraj Pradhan, a young chef who lived in nearby Chittawan for twenty-three years with his mother and brother. The food business ran through his veins as he became involved at a young age helping his maternal uncle and aunt in the family's restaurant. His path led to Sydney, Australia, where a desire to keep Nepali cuisine alive now drives his passion as he makes every attempt to weave in his childhood flavors at his place of work and other venues. He keeps coming back to this salad—creamy with yogurt, assertive with pickling spices such as fenugreek and mustard oil, comforting in taste, slightly bitter, and with a hint of heat from the cayenne. The cooling yogurt makes it possible for this salad to be a summer favorite, a steadfast accompaniment to picnics, family gatherings, and quick office lunches. SERVES 4

1 pound assorted fingerling potatoes

½ cup freshly shelled green peas or frozen peas (no need to thaw)

½ cup finely chopped red onion

2 tablespoons mustard oil, mustard-canola blended oil, or canola oil (see Tater Tip)

1 tablespoon coriander seeds

1 teaspoon cumin seeds

1 teaspoon fenugreek seeds (see Tater Tip, facing page)

½ teaspoon cayenne pepper

¼ teaspoon ground turmeric

1 cup plain Greek yogurt, whisked until smooth

¼ cup finely chopped fresh cilantro leaves and tender stems

1 teaspoon coarse sea or kosher salt

1. Scrub the potatoes under cold running water and cut them into 1-inch pieces. Place them in a small or medium-size saucepan and cover them with cold water. Bring to a boil over medium-high heat. Lower the heat to medium-low, partially cover the pan, and gently boil until the potatoes are tender when pierced with a fork or knife but still firm, 10 to 12 minutes. Fish the pieces out of the water with a slotted spoon and place them in a medium-size bowl.

2. Drop the peas into the potato cooking water and boil them just to warm them up, 1 to 2 minutes. Drain them in a colander, give them a good shake or two to remove any excess water, and add the peas to the potatoes along with the onion.

3. Heat the oil in a small skillet over medium-high heat. Once the oil appears to shimmer and smells quite pungent, sprinkle in the coriander, cumin, and fenugreek seeds. Allow them to sizzle and turn reddish brown, about 1 minute. Remove the pan from the heat and sprinkle in the cayenne and turmeric, staining the oil with their sunny dispositions. Pour most of the oil out over the potatoes and peas, holding back the seeds in the skillet as much as you can. Scrape these seeds into a mortar and pulverize them into a coarse powder with a pestle. Or if you don't have one, transfer them to a spice grinder (like a coffee grinder) and grind them. Scrape this blend into the bowl with the potatoes.

4. Add the yogurt, cilantro, and salt to the potatoes and give it all a good stir. Serve at room temperature.

TATER TIP

▲ Viscous, light brown, and exceptionally bitter, pure mustard oil is used extensively in the northern regions of India and in Nepal as a cooking and finishing oil. Bottles here in the United States are labeled "for external uses only" because of the high amounts of erucic acid (deemed toxic by the FDA). But hey, millions have been using it elsewhere for thousands of years with no health concerns, so you be the judge. Many of India's store-purchased pickles contain mustard oil. It's more common to see blended oils (such as a mustard-canola mix) and, by all means, use that if you prefer. Yes, any oil will do, but I love the intensity of mustard oil.

SMASHED
MASHED
BAKED
BOILED
FRIED
SHREDDED
ROASTED
RICED

SANDRA GUTIERREZ'S PAPAS A LA HUANCAÍNA

In his book *Potato: A History of the Propitious Esculent*, John Reader talks about the formation of the *Centro Internacional de la Papa* (the International Potato Center) in Lima, Peru. The Center was opened in 1971 in Huancayo, as a research and field station, with the goal of increasing food security and lowering poverty rates in the developing world. Another task was to identify and preserve the genetic resources of the potato in its Andean homeland—no easy undertaking, especially when there are more than 3,800 varieties identified in Peru alone. There, the preparation of many of those varieties is simple and often relies on plainly boiling them.

Sandra Gutierrez, a well-respected teacher and author on the foods of South America, shared this recipe, a family favorite and classic Peruvian recipe made slightly hot with the inclusion of indigenous yellow peppers. I love the technique of creating a milk-based dressing with peppers and onion to blanket the potato slices. A creaminess without mayonnaise is great in my book, because I often find the taste of mayo a bit metallic and also prefer the slight heat the peppers deliver. SERVES 6

1½ pounds medium-size Yukon Gold potatoes

4 large eggs

¼ cup canola oil

8 Peruvian yellow peppers (frozen, canned, or jarred), drained (see Tater Tips)

1 small white or yellow onion, coarsely chopped

1 large clove garlic

6 ounces queso fresco, crumbled (about 1½ cups)

2 soda crackers, crumbled (see Tater Tips)

1 can (14 ounces) evaporated milk

1 teaspoon coarse sea or kosher salt

½ teaspoon coarsely cracked black peppercorns

16 pitted black olives, each sliced in half

1. Scrub the potatoes well under running water and place them in a medium-size saucepan. Cover them with cold water and bring to a boil over medium-high heat. Once the water starts to boil, partially cover the pan and lower the heat to medium. Simmer the potatoes vigorously until they are tender when pierced with a fork or knife but still firm, 15 to 20 minutes.

2. As the potatoes boil, place the eggs in a separate medium-size saucepan and cover them with water. Bring to a boil over medium-high heat. Lower the heat to medium-low and gently simmer them, uncovered, until hard-cooked, 10 to 12 minutes. Drain the eggs immediately and run cold water over them until they are cool to the touch. (I usually just place the pan under the tap and let cold water run over them.) Peel the eggs and cut them lengthwise into quarters. Set them aside.

3. Once the potatoes are cooked, drain them in a colander and run cold water over them until they are cool enough to handle. Peel them and cut them into ½-inch-thick slices. Arrange the slices on a serving platter.

4. To make the sauce, pour the oil into a blender jar. Add the yellow peppers, onion, garlic, cheese, crackers, milk, salt, and peppercorns. Puree the ingredients, scraping the inside of the jar as needed, until smooth.

5. Pour the sauce over the potato slices and top them with the olives and the quartered eggs. Serve at room temperature.

VARIATION: For a more colorful presentation, vary the potatoes by incorporating a variety of yellow, red, and purple fingerlings.

TATER TIPS

▲ Peruvian yellow peppers (*aji amarillo*), with an orange tint, are not easy to come by. But it's worth the effort to get them. I found them in the freezer section of a Mexican grocery that also sold quite an assortment of the produce, spices, and goods used in Latin American foods. Melissa's, a well-known fruit and vegetable wholesale and retail company, also stocks them. If you can't find them, use a small red bell pepper as an alternative along with a fresh green serrano chile, stem removed, to create the taste and heat of the yellow peppers.

▲ Use a fine-quality soda cracker—the flavor and thickening ability of that soda cracker provides an essential drape to the sauce.

YUKARI SAKAMOTO'S
JAPANESE POTATO SALAD

Yukari Sakamoto, author of *Food Sake Tokyo*—part of the Terroir Guides series—was born in Tokyo and raised in Minnesota near many potato farms. Trained at the French Culinary Institute (now the International Culinary Center) and the American Sommelier Association (both in New York City), Yukari was the first person who was not a Japanese citizen to pass the rigorous exam to become a "*shochu* advisor" (*shochu* is a distilled beverage made from barley, sweet potatoes, sesame seeds, and a host of other ingredients). She has taught classes on food, wine, and *shochu*, and has conducted culinary tours of Tokyo's shops and markets. She now divides her time among Tokyo, Singapore, and New York City.

I met her years ago at a mutual friend's wedding in Minnesota and then again at numerous conferences of the International Association of Culinary Professionals. With a passion for all things Japanese, she embodies her generation's new way of looking at the foods of Japan. I have always been in awe of Japanese cooking and culture, and the attention paid to the presentation of food and living spaces.

I was instantly drawn to her openness and willingness to share memories of foods from her childhood, and, in particular, this unusual salad that turns the traditional chunky potato salad on its head. Many *izakayas* (Japanese pub-like establishments that also serve food), from inexpensive to high end, have it on their menus. Potato salad can be a side dish in a bento box. It is also used in sandwiches. "Potato salad sandwich, a lot of carbohydrates, but *oishii* (delicious)," says Yukari. I find this potato salad an interesting mix of the garden-variety American creamy style and a German-style offering. SERVES 4

TATER TIP

▲ Multi-color is the new orange! It used to be that carrots came in one color, but now you can get them in a wide range—red, yellow, white, and purple. Look for this carrot rainbow in farmers' markets and large grocery stores, and use them for a more lively presentation.

1 pound russet or Yukon Gold potatoes

1 large carrot, peeled, ends trimmed, cut into long thin slices (see Tater Tip)

1 medium-size to large English or Persian cucumber, unpeeled, ends trimmed, cut in half lengthwise, seeds discarded, and thinly sliced (see Tater Tip, facing page)

8 ounces cooked ham slices, cut into ¼-inch-wide strips

½ cup mayonnaise

¼ cup rice vinegar

1 teaspoon coarse sea or kosher salt

1 teaspoon coarsely cracked black peppercorns

1. Peel the potatoes and give them a good rinse under cold running water. Cut them into quarters, place them in a small saucepan, and cover them with cold water. Bring to a boil over medium-high heat. Partially cover the pan, lower the heat to medium, and boil the potatoes until they are fall-apart tender when pierced with a fork or knife, 10 to 12 minutes.

2. Working in batches if necessary, fish the potatoes out of the water (don't discard the water yet) and place them in a ricer. Push them through into a medium-size to large serving bowl. (If you don't have a ricer, use a potato masher and fluff them with a fork when completely mashed.)

3. Add the carrot slices to the potato water. Briefly boil them to make them a little tender, about 2 minutes. Drain them in a colander and run cold water over them to prevent them from cooking any more. Give the colander a few good shakes to get rid of the excess water. Add the carrots to the potatoes.

4. Stir in the cucumber, ham, mayonnaise, vinegar, salt, and peppercorns. Serve at room temperature or chilled.

VARIATIONS: Many add a hard-boiled egg to the salad or even boiled sweet potatoes to the mix along with regular potatoes. Yukari's friend who owns an *izakaya* adds a smoked hard-boiled egg. Another Tokyo *izakaya* adds apples. There are many variations throughout the city, making it something fun to order to see how each pub makes its own version.

TATER TIP

▲ Some people like leaving the seeds in their cucumbers, but I find it makes the salad very watery. It's easy to discard them—once you slit the cucumber lengthwise, use a teaspoon to scoop out the seeds. That's it.

ENTREES MAINS & FULL PLATES

To be able to travel the world of potatoes and sweet potatoes without leaving your kitchen is nothing short of miraculous. And did I say inexpensive and easy? No need to call in security, unless your parties get out of hand when you make the insanely sensuous Potato Leek Pie, bringing in the flavors of Provence with red potatoes, leeks, and fresh thyme in an oh-so-flaky crust. If Italy is in your dreams, gather a group of friends, pour yourselves a cocktail or a glass of wine, and start rolling out Potato-Basil Gnocchi, so light and tender they melt in your mouth—a great contrast to the hearty cannellini bean sauce they are served with.

If you'd rather wake up to a Persian morning brunch, the Persian-Style Potatoes and Eggs punctuated with chiles and ginger is sure to deliver. Another hands-down favorite is the Moroccan Potato Stew with Saffron Biscuits, an abundance of Yukon Gold potatoes and sweet potatoes accentuated with fresh ground spices and crowned by sun-hued saffron biscuits that are light and glorious. It would be downright insulting if I didn't give a nod to Ireland with her epic love affair and history with potatoes. My tribute to that relationship is Irish Lamb Stew, boozy with stout beer, scented with earthy thyme, and succulent with tender-sweet baby potatoes drenched in roasted lamb juices.

Whatever your country of choice, you can never go wrong with any of these main course offerings.

SMASHED
FRIED
SIMMERED
MASHED
BOILED
SHREDDED
ROASTED
RICED

TATER TIP

▲ Canned unsweetened coconut milk is readily available in most major supermarkets. Just make sure you buy the unsweetened version. Low-fat varieties are also common. I don't see much of a difference in flavor between full-fat and low-fat, so use either. Shake the can well to make sure the cream that rises to the top and the thinner whey-like liquid on the bottom are mixed together.

Thai

CREAMY MASSAMAN CURRY

A seventeenth-century dish originating in the royal courts of Thailand, this curry is reflective of the rich influences of the active spice trade, especially from India. Favorites among the Islamic communities, aromatics such as cinnamon, star anise, and cardamom punctuate this curry with the more pervasive ingredients like lemongrass and lime leaves. Beef (as opposed to pork, a taboo meat among Muslims) and potatoes are a common combination stewed with coconut milk and the complex-tasting curry paste. Given that there are potatoes in the curry, it may surprise you to know that it is enticing served over freshly steamed and fluffed rice. A leafy salad and crusty bread also make perfect partners. SERVES 4

1 pound red potatoes

2 tablespoons canola oil

1 pound boneless beef chuck or stew meat, cut into 1-inch cubes

1 medium-size yellow onion, cut into ½-inch cubes

1 can (13.5 ounces) unsweetened coconut milk (see Tater Tip)

1 teaspoon coarse sea or kosher salt

¼ cup Massaman Curry Paste (recipe follows)

2 tablespoons fish sauce (see Tater Tips, facing page)

1. Fill a medium-size bowl with cold water. Lay out several layers of paper towels on the counter, for drying the potatoes. Peel the potatoes and cut them into 2-inch cubes. Submerge them in the bowl of water to rinse off surface starch and to prevent them from discoloring.

2. Drain the potatoes in a colander, give the colander a good shake or two to rid the potatoes of excess water, and pat the potatoes dry with the paper towels.

3. Heat the oil in a Dutch oven or large saucepan over medium-high heat. Once the oil appears to shimmer, add the beef, onion, and potatoes. Stir-fry the medley to allow the beef to sear and the onion and potatoes to lightly brown around the edges, 5 to 8 minutes.

4. As they brown, whisk together the coconut milk, salt, and curry paste in a medium-size bowl. Pour this over the beef and vegetables and give it all a good stir, releasing any browned bits of meat and vegetables from the bottom of the pan. Reduce the heat to medium-low, cover, and simmer, stirring occasionally, until the beef cubes are very tender when pierced with a fork or knife, the potatoes are cooked but still firm, and the sauce is thick, 1¼ to 1½ hours.

5. Stir in the fish sauce and serve.

VARIATION: For the vegetarian or the vegan, substitute either tempeh or mock duck (compressed wheat gluten) for the beef and use soy sauce or tamari instead of the fish sauce. (But then it won't be gluten-free.)

TATER TIPS

▲ Fish sauce, a fermented liquid similar in color to soy sauce, is polarizing in its aroma. In my opinion the sauce tastes nothing like its smell. It helps provide that umami taste to many of the dishes that it punctuates, and it does so even in small amounts. A good-quality fish sauce is extracted from salted anchovies and water, but I have seen some brands that include shellfish as well (make sure to read the label, especially if you are allergic to shellfish or keep kosher).

▲ Galangal (used in the curry paste, see page 104) is a rhizome (the bulbous stem-end of a plant) and is a close sibling of ginger and turmeric. Very medicinal and menthol-like in its aromas, it is more commonly available in Southeast Asian groceries next to the ginger and fresh herbs. Choose a piece that is very firm, with smooth skin. Yes, it will have the bumps and feel of fresh ginger. Slice the pieces and wash them well before use. Like ginger, there is no need to peel it.

TATER TIP

▲ Bunches of cilantro with their roots attached are not that common in mainstream supermarkets. Southeast Asian groceries, on the other hand, sell them intact. If you have them, cut off the roots and thoroughly wash them before use, since they are very muddy. In terms of flavor, they are extremely mellow, and have no resemblance to the sharpness in the leaves and tender stems. For the cilantro naysayers (the ones who don't like the flavor, as opposed to those who have any allergies associated with them), the roots are noncontroversial in the paste; as long as you don't tell them what's in it, they won't know.

MASSAMAN CURRY PASTE

You will need only ¼ cup of paste for the Creamy Massaman Curry on page 102. Save the remaining paste for other times you wish to repeat the recipe. It freezes brilliantly well for up to four months in a freezer-safe container or sealed zip-top bag. MAKES 1 GENEROUS CUP

1 tablespoon coriander seeds

2 teaspoons cumin seeds

6 dried red chiles (such as cayenne or chile de árbol), stems discarded

Seeds from 3 green or white cardamom pods (see Tater Tips, page 194)

2 whole star anise

1 stick (3 inches) cinnamon, broken into smaller pieces

¼ cup cilantro roots, thoroughly rinsed (see Tater Tip) or tightly packed coarsely chopped leaves and tender stems

2 tablespoons finely chopped lemongrass (see Tater Tips, page 51)

1 large shallot, finely chopped

2 tablespoons finely chopped fresh galangal (see Tater Tips, page 103)

3 medium-size to large lime leaves, the middle bony vein removed (see Tater Tips, page 51)

1. Combine the coriander, cumin, chiles, cardamom, star anise, and cinnamon in a small bowl. Heat a small skillet over medium-high heat. Once the pan is hot (placing your palm close to its base will make you pull it back within 2 seconds), sprinkle in the spice blend. Toast the spices, shaking the pan occasionally, until the seeds crackle and everything smells very aromatic and turns a shade darker than their original colors, 1 to 2 minutes. Transfer to a blender jar.

2. Pile in the cilantro, lemongrass, shallot, galangal, and lime leaves. Drizzle in ¼ cup of water. Puree the ingredients to a smooth paste, scraping the inside of the jar as needed.

VARIATION: Curry Paste the Old-Fashioned Way. If you wish to do this the old-fashioned way, a deep mortar would be perfect as you combine the toasted spices with the "wet" ingredients. Pound the mixture to a pulpy paste. You will not need the water if you use a mortar.

IRISH LAMB STEW

It is said that during the late 1500s, on their way back to Europe from South America, Spanish sailors dumped all the extra uneaten potatoes they had onboard into the harbors of European seaports. This "garbage" was soon picked up by the locals, who then began growing their own potatoes. By 1699, potato cultivation had spread all over Britain and Ireland, where initially potatoes were horse fodder but later were grown for human consumption. However, the British upper class still considered potatoes poor man's food. Stews with meat (usually goat or mutton) and simple vegetables were already part of the Irish culinary repertoire, but the inclusion of potatoes became omnipresent after their pervasive cultivation by the late seventeenth and early eighteenth centuries.

"Before the Irish had the nourishing potato, they ate shamrocks and oats."

—Anonymous

TATER TIP

▲ If possible, buy your lamb roast from a butcher who supports local farmers. If the farmer raises livestock organically on a grass-fed diet, you'll be rewarded with lamb that has a more robust flavor—perfect for this stew.

The aromas that waft from the oven are reason enough to make this stew. Fresh herbs, creamy baby potatoes, and pungent onions all come together to flavor the lamb ever so delicately. Assertive beer and beef stock provide the right braising liquids, and, yes, if you have a bit of that beer left, by all means chug it down as you wait patiently for the stew to finish. SERVES 6

2 pounds baby red potatoes

2 tablespoons canola oil

About 3 pounds bone-in lamb shoulder roast or leg, in 1 piece

1 large yellow or white onion, cut into ½-inch pieces

4 large cloves garlic, finely chopped

1 large carrot, peeled, ends trimmed, cut into 1-inch pieces

¼ cup coarsely chopped fresh thyme leaves and tender stems

1 teaspoon coarse sea or kosher salt

1 teaspoon coarsely cracked black peppercorns

2 cups beef stock (preferably low-sodium)

2 cups dark beer (such as stout)

¼ cup finely chopped fresh curly parsley

1. Position a rack in the lower half of the oven and preheat the oven to 375°F.

2. Scrub the potatoes well under cold running water. Leave the skin on them. Set them aside in a colander.

3. Heat the oil in a Dutch oven over medium heat. Once the oil appears to shimmer, add the lamb and sear the underside to a reddish-brown color, 3 to 5 minutes. Lift the roast with tongs and repeat searing as many other sides as you can, 3 to 5 minutes each side. Remove the lamb from the pan and set it aside on a large plate.

4. Lower the heat to medium-low and add the onion and garlic. (There will be enough fat left behind in the pan; no need to add more.) Stir-fry the medley until the pungent aromas mingle with the roasted perfume from the meaty browned bits, and the onion and garlic brown nicely along the edges, 5 to 8 minutes.

5. Stir in the potatoes, carrot, thyme, salt, and peppercorns. Cook the vegetables, stirring occasionally, to allow the medley to acquire the aroma and flavor of the thyme, 3 to 5 minutes.

6. Pour in the stock and beer, scraping the bottom to release any browned bits of vegetables and meat. Return the lamb to the pan along with any pooled juices. Make sure to anoint the roast with boozy broth if it's not already submerged in it.

7. Place the pot in the oven and braise the roast, uncovered, periodically ladling the liquid over the meat and vegetables to continue to keep them all succulent, until the potatoes are tender when pierced with a fork or knife and the meat is super tender and easy to pull apart or cut, 1¼ to 1½ hours. If the liquid starts to dissipate more quickly than it should, cover the pan. (You want a rich, stew-like consistency to the sauce when done.) Insert an instant-read thermometer into the thickest part of the lamb (not touching the bone) to gauge its internal temperature. For medium-rare, look for a temperature range between 125° and 130°F. For medium, the temperature should be between 135° and 145°F.

8. Lift the roast from the pan onto a clean cutting board. Slice the meat off the bone and transfer the slices to a lipped platter deep enough to cup the stew of potatoes and vegetables as well. Serve while still hot, sprinkled with the parsley.

TATER TIP

▲ During the colder months, I include other root vegetables, such as turnips and rutabagas. Any combination is fair game, as are the herbs. If fresh rosemary and oregano are available, make them part of the ¼ cup along with the thyme.

CANADIAN LAMB-POTATO TOURTIÈRE

BOILED
RICED
SMASHED
MASHED
BAKED
SHREDDED
ROASTED
FRIED

Renowned pastry chef James Dodge, born to a French-Canadian mother and an English father, grew up in the hospitality business and spent a major part of his childhood watching pastry cooks unravel the mysteries of perfect cakes, cookies, pies, and pastries. He went on to become one of the nation's most well-respected pastry chefs, becoming close friends with the likes of Julia Child and James Beard. I feel fortunate I can text him at a moment's notice with questions related to baking. This recipe is adapted from his family's secret stash of never-before-released French-Canadian gems. Potatoes and lamb come together with fresh herbs and spices in a flaky pastry to be the main event at the dinner table. A simple green salad is all you need to leave the table satisfied. SERVES 6

"Potatoes are one of the last things to disappear in times of war, which is probably why they should not be forgotten in times of peace."

—*M.F.K. Fisher, writer*

TATER TIP

▲ Pie crust dough will keep, well wrapped, in the refrigerator for up to a week. On occasion, I have even frozen the dough. Once it's thawed, you will need to add a tiny bit more flour when rolling it out.

FOR THE PASTRY

2½ cups unbleached all-purpose flour

½ teaspoon coarse sea or kosher salt

16 tablespoons (2 sticks) unsalted butter, cut into ½-inch cubes and chilled

About ½ cup ice water

FOR THE FILLING

½ pound russet potatoes

1 tablespoon unsalted butter

½ cup finely chopped red onion

1½ pounds ground lamb

1 small fresh bay leaf

2 tablespoons finely chopped fresh Italian parsley

1 tablespoon finely chopped fresh rosemary leaves

1 teaspoon finely chopped fresh thyme leaves and tender stems

1 teaspoon coarse sea or kosher salt

½ teaspoon coarsely cracked black peppercorns

¼ teaspoon freshly grated nutmeg

1 egg white, slightly beaten (save the yolk; see the Tater Tips on page 211)

1. To make the pastry, combine the flour and salt in the bowl of a stand mixer and attach the paddle. Add the butter cubes and run the mixer on medium speed. Once the color of the flour turns buttery yellow and the mixture resembles coarse bread crumbs, drizzle in the ice water a little at a time. Stop the mixer as soon as the dough comes together into a ball.

2. Lightly dust the clean counter with flour. (A shaker is perfect to do that job, since you do not want a lot of flour; see Tater Tips, page 131.) Transfer the dough to the counter. Lightly sprinkle the top of the dough with flour. Gather the dough gently with your cupped hands and knead it with a shallow movement just to bring it together, no more than 30 seconds if you can help it. It is okay to use a bit more flour from the shaker if you need it. Divide the dough into 2 equal halves. Wrap each half in plastic wrap and refrigerate them until you finish the filling.

3. To make the filling, peel the potatoes and give them a good rinse under cold running water. Cut them up into large chunks, place them in a small saucepan, and cover them with cold water. Bring to a boil over medium-high heat. Partially cover the pan, lower the heat to medium-low, and simmer vigorously until the pieces are fall-apart tender when pierced with a knife or fork, 12 to 15 minutes.

4. As the potatoes cook, melt the butter in a large skillet over medium-high heat. Add the onion and cook, stirring occasionally, until tender, translucent, and light gold around the edges, 3 to 5 minutes. Add the lamb and bay leaf and cook, breaking up the meat into smaller pieces while stirring occasionally, until it starts to brown and exude some of its own fat. Once it is no longer red in the middle but very slightly pink, 10 to 13 minutes, stir in the parsley, rosemary, thyme, salt, peppercorns, and nutmeg. Remove the pan from the heat.

5. When the potatoes are done, drain them in a colander and return them to the same saucepan. Dry them out over medium-low heat, stirring occasionally, until the surface appears dry; some of the pieces will start to break down into smaller morsels. Working in batches if necessary, transfer these to a ricer and press them directly over the seasoned lamb. (If you don't have a ricer, use a potato masher and fluff them with a fork when completely mashed, then spread them over the lamb.) Fold the potatoes into the meat; they will be the binder for the filling. The filling should feel light and moist, not stiff and dry.

6. About 15 minutes before you plan to roll out the dough, remove it from the refrigerator so it softens a little and is easier to roll. While you wait for the dough to soften, position a rack in the lower half of the oven and preheat the oven to 400°F.

7. Again sprinkle the counter with a very little bit of flour. Roll out each piece of dough into an 11-inch circle. Fit 1 circle into a 9-inch pie plate, pressing it gently against the bottom. Add the filling, spreading it out to cover the dough evenly. Place the second circle over the filling and press it onto the rim of the bottom circle. Flute and seal the edge by lifting a bit of the dough and pinching it between your thumb and forefinger. Or, press the edges with the tines of a fork to seal. Brush the top with the beaten egg white. Gently cut slits through the top crust to allow steam to escape. Bake for 10 minutes.

8. Lower the temperature to 375°F and continue baking until the top is golden brown, 30 to 40 minutes.

9. Transfer the pie plate to a wire rack and allow the *tourtière* to cool for about 15 minutes. Slice and serve warm.

TATER TIP

▲ If ground lamb is unavailable or not your cup of tea, use ground beef or pork instead. Their cooking times will be comparable to that of the lamb. For a vegetarian alternative, use crumbled tofu or finely chopped mock duck.

SWEET POTATOES WITH CHICKEN AND LEMONGRASS

> "The potato,
> like man,
> was not meant
> to dwell alone."
>
> —*Sheila Hibben,*
> *food writer and journalist*

Next to California, Minnesota is home to the second-largest Hmong community in the United States—comprised of those who fled Laos, Cambodia, and Vietnam in 1975. More than 66,000 Hmong now call Minnesota home, and a large number of them are farmers who grow the vegetables and herbs of their former homeland. Their dishes are very simple, often with just an ingredient or two boiled together. Hmong emphasize green vegetables during the summer months, while root vegetables such as sweet potatoes are winter fare. This thin-bodied stew primarily showcases lemongrass and sweet potatoes, yet it could not be any more flavorful. SERVES 4

1 pound sweet potatoes
(preferable Japanese because
they add color to the dish)

2 stalks lemongrass
(see Tater Tips, page 51)

2 tablespoons canola oil

1 pound boneless, skinless chicken
breasts, cut into 1-inch cubes

1 teaspoon coarse sea or kosher salt

1 teaspoon coarsely cracked black
peppercorns

Steamed white rice, for serving

TATER TIP

▲ Accompany the stew the way Hmong do: with 10 to 12 thinly sliced fresh green and/or red Thai chiles (do not remove the seeds) that are lightly salted and mixed with a tablespoon of finely chopped fresh ginger and a tablespoon of finely chopped fresh cilantro leaves and tender stems.

1. Fill a medium-size bowl with cold water. Peel the sweet potatoes and give them a good rinse under cold running water. Cut them into 1-inch cubes and submerge them in the bowl of water to prevent them from turning gray.

2. Slice off the root ends of the lemongrass stalks, and the top three fourths of the blade-like greens. All you will use is about 3 inches of the light-colored tightly knotted stalk. Slice these in half lengthwise, then cut each half into thin strips. Stack a few of these strips at a time and cut them crosswise into teeny tiny pieces.

3. Heat the oil in a wok or large saucepan over medium-high heat. Once the oil appears to shimmer, add the chicken cubes and stir-fry to sear them, 1 to 2 minutes.

4. Drain the potatoes in a colander. Add them to the chicken along with 1 cup of water, the lemongrass, salt, and peppercorns. Bring to a boil, reduce the heat to medium-low, and cook the stew, covered, stirring occasionally, until the potatoes are tender and the chicken pieces are cooked through, about 10 minutes. When you cut into a piece of chicken, it should no longer be pink in the middle and the juices will run clear.

5. Serve hot with a bowl of steamed white rice—it's great to have a mellow base to catch all the lemony broth.

BIRD'S NESTS WITH
SHRIMP
& POTATOES

Elegant in presentation, these nests, fashioned from potato shreds, are home to a potato-shrimp stir-fry that sings with flavor. If you wish to appease the vegetarians at the table, use tofu or mock duck, ounce for ounce, instead of the shrimp. Even though it's a fussy recipe, rest assured it is a cinch to make. If you prepare the nests in advance (see Tater Tip, page 117), it's a dish you can execute even on a frenzied weekday. **SERVES 4**

½ pound assorted fingerling potatoes (I use a combination of red Amarosa, Russian banana, and purple)

¼ cup canola oil

4 slices fresh ginger (each about the size and thickness of a quarter; no need to peel first), cut into thin shreds

1 small green bell pepper, stem removed, seeds and ribs discarded, cut into ¼-inch cubes

8 ounces jumbo shrimp (about 8), peeled but tail-on, deveined

1 teaspoon ground Chinese five-spice powder (see Tater Tip)

2 tablespoons soy sauce

1 teaspoon cornstarch

4 Bird's Nests (recipe follows)

1. Thoroughly scrub the fingerling potatoes under running water and pat them dry with paper towels. Cut them into ½-inch pieces. Heat 2 tablespoons of the oil in a large nonstick skillet or a wok over medium-high heat. Once the oil appears to shimmer, add the potatoes and give them a good stir. Cover the pan, lower the heat to medium, and cook the potatoes,

TATER TIP

▲ Chinese five-spice powder is a highly complex-tasting blend that adroitly balances sour, bitter, sweet, pungent, and salty in keeping with age-old traditions. Classic versions contain fennel, cloves, cinnamon, Sichuan peppercorns, and star anise, but I have also seen blends that include cinnamon, ginger, nutmeg, and licorice root (yes, five-spice powder may contain more than five spices). You can make your own by combining equal amounts of the classic five ground spices. Or, of course, any supermarket will carry the blend in the spice aisle, as will Asian groceries.

stirring occasionally, until they turn crispy brown on the surface and are tender but still firm, 5 to 8 minutes. Using a slotted spoon, transfer the potatoes to a plate.

2. Next, pour the remaining 2 tablespoons of oil into the same pan; it will instantly shimmer, thanks to the residual heat. Maintain the heat under the pan at medium-high. Add the ginger and bell pepper and stir-fry the medley so the peppers blister in places and the ginger browns slightly, about 5 minutes. Add the shrimp and continue to stir-fry until the shrimp turn salmon orange and curl up a bit, 2 to 4 minutes.

3. Add the potatoes back to the pan and sprinkle in the five-spice powder. Give it all a good stir. The heat of the pan's contents is just right to cook the spices without burning them. Quickly combine the soy sauce and cornstarch in a small bowl to create a slurry. Pour this over the stir-fry and give it all a good toss. This light brown sheen provides that umami flavor we so desire in a dish like this.

4. To serve, place the nests on a serving platter and divide the stir-fry among them. Serve right away.

BIRD'S NESTS

To make the nests, you'll need a couple of metal sieves with long wooden or stainless-steel handles, one 5 inches in diameter, the other small enough to rest in the larger one. There are also contraptions specifically for making bird's nests; you can find them at fancy houseware stores and online. MAKES 4 NESTS

1 pound russet or Yukon Gold potatoes

¼ cup unbleached all-purpose flour

1 tablespoon cornstarch

Canola oil, for deep-frying

Coarse sea or kosher salt, for sprinkling

1. Fill a medium-size bowl with cold water. Lay out a clean cotton kitchen towel or several layers of paper towels on the counter, for drying the potatoes.

TATER TIP

The potato bird's nests can be made several days in advance. Store the cooked nests in a sealed zip-top bag in the refrigerator. Place them on a wire rack over a cookie sheet and bake at 350°F for 8 to 10 minutes to re-crisp. These nests are a great bowl for everything from scrambled eggs in the morning to fresh berries and a dollop of ice cream at night.

BIRD'S NESTS STEP-BY-STEP

1 Spread one quarter of the potato shreds in the larger oil-coated sieve. Place the smaller oil-coated sieve on top of the shreds and squeeze the sieves together.

2 Submerge the sieves in oil and fry for 5 to 7 minutes, until the nest turns brown and crispy.

3 Remove the sieves from the oil. Carefully lift off the smaller sieve. Turn the larger sieve over and tap lightly until the nest loosens. Let it drain on a cookie sheet fitted with a wire rack or paper towels. Sprinkle with salt.

4 The crispy nests, cooled and ready to be filled.

2. To make the bird's nests, peel the russet potatoes. Shred them through the large holes of a box grater, the fine teeth of a mandoline, or the shredding disk of a food processor. Immediately transfer them to the bowl of water. Soak them for 10 to 15 minutes to rinse off surface starch and to prevent them from discoloring.

3. Drain the shreds in a colander and run cold water through them to rinse off any surface starch. Give the colander a good shake or two to get rid of excess water. Spread the shreds out on the towel and pat them dry. Transfer the shreds to a clean, dry medium-size bowl.

4. Stir the flour and cornstarch together, then place in a fine-mesh sieve (such as a tea strainer) and sprinkle evenly over the shreds. Toss everything well to make sure all the shreds are coated with the flour-starch mix.

5. Line a cookie sheet with several layers of paper towels or a wire rack, for draining the nests of excess oil. Place a plate next to the cookie sheet. Pour oil to a depth of 2 to 3 inches (or high enough to completely submerge the 2 sieves) into a wok, Dutch oven, or medium-size saucepan.

Heat the oil over medium heat until a candy or deep-frying thermometer inserted into the oil (without touching the pan bottom) registers 375°F (see Tater Tips, page 18).

6. Immerse the 2 sieves in the hot oil to coat them. Remove them from the oil and set the smaller sieve on the plate. With the larger sieve still over the oil (so the oil continues to drip into the pan) or cookie sheet, spread one quarter of the shreds in it to fashion a bird's nest. Place the smaller sieve on top of the shreds. Squeeze the 2 sieves together securely to hold the shreds in place. Submerge this contraption in the hot oil and fry until the nest turns caramel brown and crispy, 5 to 7 minutes. Remove from the oil, gently lift out the smaller sieve, and turn the nest out onto the paper towels or rack to drain. (You might need to tap the larger sieve lightly on the towels to loosen the nest.) Sprinkle it with a little salt. Repeat with the remaining shreds.

PERSIAN-STYLE POTATOES AND EGGS

Eggs and potatoes are the proverbial love and marriage among the Parsi community in western India. Originally from Persia (Iran), the Parsis fled around the tenth century after being persecuted by the Muslim rulers because they were followers of the prophet Zarathustra. They were welcomed in India, where they set up new roots and flourished as businessmen in the centuries that followed. Perinne Medora (her son, Zubin, is my webmaster), a Parsi from Mumbai now settled in California, talked about the prevalence of potatoes (called *seb-i-zaminee*, which literally translates to "apples of the earth," just like the French *pommes de terre*) and eggs at every meal. This recipe, a family favorite over the years, is comfort food whenever Zubin stops by for a visit to Perinne's home. **SERVES 4**

2 pounds russet or Yukon Gold potatoes

2 tablespoons canola oil

1 small red onion, cut in half lengthwise and thinly sliced

8 slices fresh ginger (each about the size and thickness of a quarter; no need to peel first), finely chopped

1 or 2 fresh green serrano chiles, stems discarded, finely chopped (do not remove the seeds)

1 teaspoon coarse sea or kosher salt

½ teaspoon ground turmeric

¼ cup finely chopped fresh cilantro leaves and tender stems

8 large eggs

TATER TIP

▲ Forget your usual three-egg omelet brunch. Here, the lovely nested eggs let the gorgeous potatoes take center stage. Weekends just got even better.

TATER TIP

▲ If you'd like a bit of bright red in the skillet, add a small red bell pepper cut into thin strips, just like the onion. Stir-fry it along with the onion-ginger-chiles medley.

1. Fill a medium-size bowl halfway with cold water. Peel the potatoes. Shred them through the large holes of a box grater, the fine teeth of a mandoline, or the shredding disk of a food processor. Immediately transfer the shreds to the bowl of water to rinse off some of their surface starch and to prevent them from discoloring due to oxidation.

2. Heat the oil in a large skillet over medium heat. Once the oil appears to shimmer, add the onion, ginger, and chiles and cook them, uncovered, stirring occasionally, until the onion slices are light brown around the edges and the chiles smell pungent, 5 to 8 minutes.

3. As the onion medley cooks, drain the potato shreds in a colander and give them a good rinse under cold running water to wash off the starch. Spread out several layers of paper towels on the counter, for drying the potatoes. Give the colander a good shake or two to rid the potatoes of excess water. Spread out the shreds on the towels and pat them dry, to make for splatter-free pan-frying.

4. Stir the salt and turmeric into the onions. Add the potato shreds and give it all a good stir. Cover the pan and cook without stirring to allow the underside to brown lightly, 5 to 8 minutes. Flip the potatoes over (use two spatulas, one on either side—or if you have one large spatula, that works great, too) and cook, covered, on the other side for an additional 5 to 8 minutes.

5. Break up the browned potatoes with a spatula to expose the softer, creamier shreds within. Sprinkle on the cilantro. Make 8 little concave "nests" in the potato surface. Crack an egg into each of these nests. Cover the pan and allow the eggs to cook, without stirring, until the whites are soft-steamed and the egg yolks are set but still sun yellow under the film of white, 3 to 5 minutes.

6. Either set the whole skillet on the table as is, or gently scoop out a portion of potatoes along with 2 eggs per person. Serve warm.

CHORIZO-STUFFED HASH BROWNS

SHREDDED
SMASHED
MASHED
BAKED
BOILED
ROASTED
FRIED
RICED

This is one of those complete all-in-one breakfasts that make life easy even with minimal coffee in the morning. I often serve this for Sunday brunch, a tradition that I love but don't get a chance to follow much. I sometimes crack an egg on top of each hash brown cake, cover them, and let the egg steam as the potatoes finish cooking, for a more complete experience. Looks gorgeous as well. SERVES 4

2 pounds russet potatoes

¼ cup canola oil

8 ounces fresh Mexican chorizo, removed from casing (see Variations)

1 small red onion, cut in half lengthwise and thinly sliced

2 fresh green serrano chiles, stems discarded, cut in half lengthwise then into thin strips (do not remove the seeds)

8 ounces fresh spinach leaves, thoroughly rinsed, dried, and coarsely chopped

1½ teaspoons coarse sea or kosher salt

1 teaspoon smoked paprika

1 teaspoon dried oregano

2 large eggs (see Variations)

1. Fill a medium-size bowl halfway with cold water. Peel the potatoes. Shred them through the large holes of a box grater, the fine teeth of a mandoline, or the shredding disk of a food processor. Immediately transfer the shreds to the bowl of water to rinse off some of the surface starch and to prevent them from discoloring due to oxidation.

TATER TIP

▲ There are several ways to shred potatoes, but I do love the mandoline for the neat, uniform shreds it gives me. Of course you don't need one, but if you're a kitchen gadgeteer like me, you'll enjoy its usefulness not only when shredding, but when slicing fruits and vegetables—particularly potatoes for french fries (page 175) and potato crisps (page 225).

Fabulous on their own, the potato cakes taste even more luxurious when topped with a poached or fried egg.

2. Heat 2 tablespoons of oil in a large skillet over medium heat. Once the oil appears to shimmer, add the chorizo, onion, and chiles and cook them, uncovered, stirring occasionally, until the meat is cooked through and light brown, the onion is soft, and the chiles smell pungent, 8 to 10 minutes.

3. Crank up the heat to medium-high or high. Stir in handfuls of the spinach until all the leaves wilt, 2 to 4 minutes. Stir in ½ teaspoon of the salt, the paprika, and oregano. Remove the pan from the heat.

4. When you're ready to make the hash browns, lay out a clean cotton kitchen towel or several layers of paper towels on the counter, for drying the potatoes. Drain the potato shreds in a colander and give them a good rinse under cold running water to wash off the starch. Give the colander a good shake or two to rid the potatoes of excess water. Spread the shreds on the kitchen towel and dry them well, to make for splatter-free frying.

5. Rinse any starch out of the bowl and dry it. Crack the eggs into the bowl and beat them lightly. Stir in the potato shreds and the remaining teaspoon of salt.

6. Drizzle the remaining 2 tablespoons of oil into a large nonstick skillet or on a large griddle (the kind that sits atop two burners) over medium heat. Once the oil appears to shimmer, spoon in one eighth of the potato shreds with some egg, forming a roughly 4-inch pancake-like base. Repeat with three more portions, making sure there is enough space between them to be able to lift each with a spatula. Spread a fourth of the chorizo-spinach filling on each of the hash brown cakes. Top them with the remaining potato shreds, spreading them with a spatula to cover the filling and form a stuffed cake.

7. Cook the undersides, uncovered, until crispy brown, 5 to 7 minutes (lift an edge with the spatula to check). Carefully flip each cake over and cook the second side to crispy brown, an additional 5 to 7 minutes. The egg in the potato shreds will help bind everything together.

8. Serve them while they are still crispy on the outside.

VARIATIONS:

▲ For the vegetarians at the table who are okay with eggs, use a cup of cooked, drained kidney beans or black beans instead of the chorizo. If you are using canned beans, rinse them before using. In this instance, sauté the onion with the chiles before you add the beans. Continue with the recipe at Step 3.

▲ For the vegans, in addition to swapping in beans for the chorizo, I usually use a vegan egg substitute equivalent to 2 beaten eggs (the package tells the comparable amount). I also don't rinse off the surface starch in Step 4, as the starch helps to bind the cakes. If you feel you need more binding, add up to 2 tablespoons of potato starch.

SMASHED
MASHED
SIMMERED
BAKED
BOILED
FRIED
ROASTED
RICED

MOROCCAN POTATO STEW
WITH SAFFRON BISCUITS

In Morocco, stews slow-cooked in tagines—rich with root vegetables, spices, meats, and legumes—are served alongside plates of pearl-like couscous and dollops of fiery harissa. This version incorporates both regular and sweet potatoes, punctuated with assertive spices. But what makes the presentation sing is the dollop of saffron biscuit batter atop each portion that puffs and bakes with a sunny glow. Not native, but you won't complain! SERVES 6

1 pound Yukon Gold potatoes

8 ounces sweet potatoes

2 tablespoons canola oil

1 cup finely chopped yellow or white onion

4 medium-size cloves garlic, finely chopped

2 tablespoons coriander seeds

1 teaspoon cumin seeds

1 stick (3 inches) cinnamon, broken into smaller pieces

1 teaspoon sweet paprika

1 teaspoon smoked paprika

1 teaspoon cayenne pepper

1 teaspoon coarse sea or kosher salt

¼ teaspoon ground turmeric

2 cups canned diced tomatoes (including any juices)

2 cups water

2 cans (15 ounces each) chickpeas (garbanzo beans), drained and rinsed

1 pound fresh baby spinach leaves, thoroughly rinsed and dried

Saffron Biscuits (optional; recipe follows)

½ cup finely chopped fresh cilantro leaves and tender stems

½ cup thinly sliced scallions (green tops and white bulbs)

About 4 tablespoons (½ stick) salted butter, melted, for brushing the biscuits

1. Peel all the potatoes and give them a good rinse under cold running water. Cut them into 1-inch cubes and pile them into a medium-size bowl. Cover them with cold water to prevent them from oxidizing and turning gray.

2. Heat the oil in a Dutch oven over medium-high heat. Once the oil appears to shimmer, add the onion and garlic and stir-fry until they are light brown around the edges, about 5 minutes.

3. Meanwhile, grind the coriander, cumin, and cinnamon in a spice grinder (or a clean coffee grinder) to the consistency of finely ground black pepper. Tap the spices into a small bowl and stir in the sweet and smoked paprikas, cayenne, salt, and turmeric to create a potent and highly aromatic blend.

4. Stir the spice blend into the onion and garlic. The heat of the pan's contents is just right to cook the spices without burning them, barely 15 seconds. Quickly pour in the tomatoes, water, and chickpeas. Drain the potatoes and add them to the mélange. Bring the stew to a boil. Lower the heat to medium-low, cover the pan, and simmer, stirring occasionally, until the potatoes are tender when pierced with a fork or knife and

the stew is slightly thick, about 25 minutes. If you are making biscuits to top the stew, now is the time to prepare them.

5. As the stew simmers, position a rack in the center of the oven and preheat the oven to 475°F.

6. Once the potatoes are tender, add the spinach and cover the pan again. The steam will wilt the leaves in 3 to 5 minutes. Add the cilantro and scallions and give it all a good stir. You can serve the soup as is or continue on to Step 7 if serving it topped with biscuits.

7. Leave the stew in the Dutch oven or ladle it into a baking dish. If you transfer it to a baking dish, place the dish on a cookie sheet to catch any spills when the stew is in the oven.

8. Cover the top of the stew with the prepared unbaked biscuits. Brush the tops of the biscuits with melted butter. Place the lidless Dutch oven or baking dish in the oven and bake until the biscuits are sunny brown with an orange-yellow hue and slightly crusty, about 25 minutes.

9. Serve the stew hot from the oven.

SAFFRON BISCUITS

Although you can serve the potato stew without the biscuit topping, why would you? These are so easy to prepare and are the crown on this queen of stews. **MAKES 6 OR 7 BISCUITS**

½ cup heavy (whipping) cream

½ teaspoon saffron threads

2 cups cake flour

2 teaspoons baking powder

½ teaspoon coarse sea or
    kosher salt

4 tablespoons (½ stick) salted butter,
    cut into slices and chilled

1 cup buttermilk

Unbleached all-purpose flour,
    for dusting

1. Warm the heavy cream in a small saucepan over medium heat or in a microwave-safe bowl. (No need to bring it to a boil.) Stir in the saffron threads. The warmth of the cream will allow the threads to unleash their beautiful aroma and sunny orange-yellow disposition. Transfer this to the freezer to chill it quickly.

2. Combine the flour, baking powder, and salt in a medium-size bowl. Add the chilled butter and cut it in, using a pastry cutter or a fork, until you end up with pea-size pellets. Pour in the buttermilk and chilled saffron cream and stir them in with a wooden spoon. The batter will be quite wet.

3. Cover a cookie sheet with wax paper or parchment paper. Dump some all-purpose flour into a medium-size bowl. Flour your hands. Scoop out about a ⅓-cup portion of the batter into the bowl of flour. Gently roll it around to coat it completely with flour. Shape it into a biscuit with your floured hands and place it on the prepared cookie sheet. Repeat until all the biscuits are formed (you should have 6 or 7). Refrigerate while you wait for the stew to be ready for its biscuit topping.

European and North American

POTATO LEEK PIE

Think beyond the classic French potato-leek soup, vichyssoise, hot or cold, I challenged myself. I love a good bowl of soup, mind you, but I wanted something that would appeal to my textural senses. A perfect pie crust, flaky and crispy, with an herbaceous medley of potatoes and leeks, was just the ticket. To round out the experience, I make a creamy jalapeño sauce to serve alongside. **SERVES 6**

FOR THE CRUST

1 cup unbleached all-purpose flour, plus more for rolling (see Tater Tips)

½ teaspoon coarse sea or kosher salt

4 ounces cream cheese, chilled

8 tablespoons (1 stick) unsalted butter, chilled

3 tablespoons ice water

1 teaspoon white distilled vinegar

FOR THE FILLING

1½ pounds red potatoes (see Tater Tips)

1 pound leeks, beards and tough dark green leaves trimmed

2 tablespoons unsalted butter

¼ cup finely chopped fresh thyme leaves

1 teaspoon coarse sea or kosher salt

1 teaspoon coarsely cracked black peppercorns

½ cup shredded cheese (such as Gruyère, mozzarella, sharp cheddar, Havarti, or a blend)

Creamy Jalapeño Sauce (recipe follows), for serving

1. To make the crust, combine the flour and salt in a food processor. Cut the cream cheese and butter into large cubes and add them to the flour. Pulse to break up the cubes into smaller pea-size pellets.

TATER TIPS

▲ I usually keep some flour in a confectioners' sugar shaker (a little can with small holes in the top and a handle on the side). When it comes time for rolling out dough, a few shakes ensure a stick-free roll without too much added flour.

▲ I use both red-skinned and red-fleshed potatoes in this recipe. The red-skinned varieties are easy to find, but not so the red-fleshed. If your market sells them, do buy them for this pie.

2. Drizzle in the water and vinegar through the feeding chute and continue to pulse the machine until the dough comes together into a fairly cohesive ball. It will still be a bit loose. Scrape the dough onto a clean cutting board or counter. Gather the clumps into a tight ball, compressing it. Do not knead it, as you do not want to form a lot of gluten, which will make the crust chewy. Pat it down into a disk about 1 inch thick. Wrap the dough in plastic wrap and refrigerate it while you make the filling.

3. Fill 2 medium-size bowls three-quarters full with cold water. Lay out two piles of paper towels on the counter, for drying the potatoes and leeks.

4. To make the filling, peel the potatoes, give them a good rinse under cold running water, and cut them into ½-inch cubes. Submerge the cubes in one of the bowls of water.

5. Cut the leeks in half lengthwise and thinly slice them crosswise. Dunk them in the other bowl of water. Leeks are inherently muddy, so you will need to wash them a few times. (Trust me when I say grittiness is not a desired texture in this pie.) Scoop the leeks out of the water into a colander, and dump the water out of the bowl. You will notice the bottom of the bowl is muddied from the leeks; rinse out that mud. Drop the leeks back into the bowl and fill it up again with cold water. Repeat the dunk, rinse, scoop, and dump a few times until the water is clear when the leeks have been removed. Drain the leeks in the colander and pat them dry with one set of paper towels. (Alternatively, you can spin them dry in a salad spinner.)

6. Drain the potatoes in the colander and give the colander a good shake or two to rid the potatoes of excess water. Pat the potatoes dry with the other set of paper towels.

7. Melt the butter in a Dutch oven or large skillet over medium heat. Once the butter starts to foam, add the leeks and stir-fry them until they soften up a bit, 5 to 7 minutes. Stir in the potatoes, cover the pan, and cook the potatoes and leeks, stirring occasionally, until they are barely tender, 8 to 10 minutes. Stir in the thyme, salt, and peppercorns and remove the pan from the heat.

8. Position a rack in the center of the oven and preheat the oven to 400°F.

9. Lightly flour a clean countertop (see Tater Tips, page 131). Roll out the crust to a 12-inch circle. Keep dusting the crust lightly with flour as needed to ensure a stick-free crust. Place the rolled-out crust in a 9-inch pie plate, pressing it gently against the bottom and sides. Flute the edge by lifting a bit of the rim of the crust and pinching it between your thumb and forefinger; do this all around the edge. Alternatively, press the tines of a fork into the dough all around the edge to create ridges.

10. Stir the shredded cheese into the potato-leek filling. Spoon and spread this into the prepared crust. Place the pie on a cookie sheet to catch any dripping fat from the crust. Bake the pie until the crust at the edge is crispy brown and the potatoes and leeks in the filling have a well-tanned appearance, 30 to 40 minutes.

11. Transfer the pie plate to a wire rack and allow the pie to cool for 15 minutes before slicing it into wedges and serving with the sauce.

CREAMY JALAPEÑO SAUCE

I love a little saucy heat alongside the Potato Leek Pie. A great balance is essential in terms of a satisfying mouthful. Here is a simple sauce to put together as the pie bakes. MAKES ABOUT 1 CUP

1 or 2 fresh green jalapeño chiles

½ teaspoon cumin seeds

¼ cup heavy (whipping) cream

1 medium-size tomato, cored and coarsely diced

½ teaspoon coarse sea or kosher salt

1. Blister the jalapeños in a small dry skillet (I usually use a cast-iron pan) over medium-high heat, making sure you flip them occasionally for a relatively even blister, 5 to 7 minutes. Cut off and discard the stems. Transfer the chiles to a blender jar.

2. Sprinkle the cumin seeds into the hot pan and allow them to toast until they smell nutty, barely 5 seconds. Add them to the chiles. Pour in the cream and add the tomato and salt. Puree the medley into a smooth sauce, scraping the inside of the jar if needed to ensure an even blend.

TATER TIP

▲ If you have any extra sauce left, serve it as a dip with the Ultimate French Fries (page 175)—so much more satisfying than ketchup—or even with a bowl of potato chips.

BAKED
SMASHED
MASHED
BOILED
FRIED
SHREDDED
ROASTED
RICED

TWICE-BAKED POTATOES WITH BACON

"The merriest-eyed potatoes, nursed in gloom / Just resurrected from their cradle-tomb."

—*Will Carleton, American poet*

Christmas in Minnesota during my earlier years was always a bit forlorn, filled with self-pity for being in a foreign land, away from family and friends for the first time. But that changed the holiday I was introduced to my partner's parents, who lived in a small town in rural Minnesota. They welcomed me with open arms, their curiosity—as well as mine—bridging cultural gaps through the medium of food. Though we had nothing in common in terms of spicing techniques, we all agreed on the goodness of the potato. I was asked to go to the chilled garage and unearth, from a cardboard box covered by a heavy blanket, an armful of fall-dug potatoes. Way ahead of the game in terms of organics, Dad Erickson was proud of his garden patch that yielded enough vegetables to feed his wife and visiting kids all summer and fall.

This was my introduction to the beauty of potatoes stored in mud (for a prolonged shelf life) then scrubbed, rinsed, and cooked simply, their inherent creaminess punctuated with locally churned butter. Terry, my partner, was well versed in cooking from his culinary training and showed me how to make twice-baked potatoes—or "double-stuffed," as his mom and dad called them. I was hooked. Every holiday it became my task to make them, now adding my own twist of sautéed onions and peppers with an abundance of cream and cheese.

Mom insisted I make a double batch so she could stretch out their goodness well after the holiday had passed. This remains a tribute to their memory, with gratefulness to them for giving me a loving home to call my own. SERVES 8

Coarse sea or kosher salt,
    for smothering the potatoes

4 large russet potatoes
    (each about 1 pound)

6 tablespoons (¾ stick) salted butter
    (or 2 tablespoons if using the
    bacon fat; see Tater Tip)

1 cup finely chopped onion

4 large cloves garlic, finely chopped

1 medium red bell pepper, stem,
    ribs, and seeds discarded,
    finely chopped

½ cup heavy (whipping) cream

½ cup buttermilk

1 cup shredded cheese
    (such as cheddar, Gruyère, pepper
    Jack, or fontina,
    or an assortment)

¼ cup finely chopped chives

6 strips bacon, cooked until crisp,
    and crumbled (see Tater Tip)

1. Position a rack in the center of the oven and preheat the oven to 375°F. Spread a thick layer of salt on a large plate.

2. Scrub the potatoes well under running water. While they are still wet, pierce them in multiple spots with a fork or knife to enable them to vent steam as they bake. Cake each damp potato all over with salt, forming a white-speckled blanket. Place the potatoes directly on the oven rack and bake them until tender, about 1 hour. If you wish, you may place a cookie sheet on the rack below if you have a fear that the salt will fall off—but it really won't.

3. As the potatoes bake, melt 2 tablespoons of butter in a large skillet over medium-high heat. Once the butter foams, stir-fry the onion and garlic until they become light brown around the edges, 3 to 5 minutes. Add the bell pepper and cook the vegetables, stirring occasionally, until the pepper softens, 2 to 4 minutes. Remove the pan from the heat and add the remaining 4 tablespoons of butter or the fat saved from the cooked bacon.

4. Once the potatoes are done, transfer them to a cutting board and allow them to cool enough so you can handle them. Leave the oven on if you will be serving the potatoes soon. Slice off a ¼-inch-thick slice from the top along the length of each potato. (They're

TATER TIP

▲ Cooking the bacon is a no-brainer. On the stovetop is fine, but since you have the oven turned on for the potatoes, just lay out the strips on a rimmed cookie sheet and bake them until crusty brown. At that temperature you should have crispy strips in 8 to 10 minutes. Flip them halfway through so they cook evenly. Once the bacon strips are cool, crumble them into bits. If you wish, save the bacon fat and add it to the riced potatoes instead of the extra butter.

TATER TIP

▲ Use the leftover filling to stuff and bake mini peppers. Or if fresh figs are in season, cut them in half, pipe a bit of the filling on each half, and bake them until just warm. A Sunday brunch favorite: Gather a tablespoon of the filling, flatten it into a disk, roll it in panko bread crumbs, and pan-fry in a bit of oil until crispy brown on both sides (a nonstick skillet or well-seasoned cast-iron pan works best for this).

for nibbling—the cook's bonus as you finish the dish!) With a teaspoon, scoop out as much of the tender insides as you can without boring a hole through the potato, and set them aside in a medium-size bowl. (I usually leave a ¼-inch-thick layer of potatoes around the inside wall to avoid any possibility of leaks.) As you handle the potatoes, you will experience some of the salt crust falling apart on the board. Just save some of it for later inclusion.

5. Working in batches if necessary, place all the scooped-out whites in a ricer and push them through and back into the same bowl. (If you don't have a ricer, use a potato masher and fluff them with a fork when completely mashed.) Scrape the pepper-onion medley over the fluffy potatoes and pour in the cream and buttermilk. Add about 1½ teaspoons of salt and the cheese, chives, and bacon, and fold it all until just mixed.

6. Spoon as much of the filling as you possibly can into each potato shell. (You will, in all likelihood, have filling left over. Do yourself a favor and save it for later! See Tater Tip for some ideas.) At this point you can refrigerate the potatoes, covered, and bake them in a day or two.

7. When you are about ready to serve the potatoes, make sure the oven is preheated to 375°F. Line a cookie sheet with parchment paper or aluminum foil and place the stuffed potatoes on it. Bake them until some of the filling oozes out onto the sides and the top is speckled brown, 35 to 45 minutes.

8. Slice each in half and serve hot.

BAKED POTATOES
WITH WHITE BEANS
& BÉARNAISE

have always loved the concept of loaded baked potatoes on restaurant menus but have despised that cheesy fake sauce that drenches the overcooked potatoes. Oh, and wrapping potatoes in aluminum foil to "bake" them is really not baking, but steaming. Once I stepped off my high horse, I decided to do something about that travesty. So I created my own version and fell in love with the notion once again, along with its execution: A sophisticated homemade béarnaise cloaks white beans and asparagus over salt-crusted baked potatoes. I've included a vegan version, which I adapted from Miyoko Nishimoto Schinner's book *The New Now and Zen Epicure*. SERVES 4

TATER TIP

▲ If you know my spice preachings from previous books, it should come as no surprise that I like my spices freshly ground. Whole coriander seeds, when pulverized in a spice grinder (or a clean coffee grinder), add astonishing citrus-like aromas and flavors to this recipe, as the essential oil within has just been released and is at its full potential. Surely you have 2 seconds to spare in the kitchen to do this, don't you?

"Comedy just pokes at problems, rarely confronts them squarely. Drama is like a plate of meat and potatoes, comedy is rather the dessert, a bit like meringue."
—*Woody Allen*

FOR THE POTATOES

Coarse sea or kosher salt,
for smothering the potatoes

4 large russet potatoes
(each about 1 pound)

½ cup clarified butter (see Tater
Tips) or 8 tablespoons (1 stick)
whole unsalted butter

1 cup finely chopped onion

4 large cloves garlic, finely chopped

1 can (15 ounces) white kidney beans,
drained and rinsed

Tips from 8 ounces fresh asparagus
(see Tater Tips), chopped into
¼-inch pieces

2 teaspoons coriander seeds,
ground (see Tater Tip, page 137)

1 teaspoon crushed red pepper flakes

FOR THE BÉARNAISE

¼ cup white wine vinegar

¼ cup dry white wine

¼ cup finely chopped shallots

2 large egg yolks, slightly beaten
(see Tater Tips, page 81,
for information on pasteurized
eggs; reserve the whites for
another use)

2 tablespoons finely chopped fresh
tarragon

1 teaspoon coarsely cracked black
peppercorns

1. Position a rack in the center of
the oven and preheat the oven to
375°F. Spread a thick layer of salt
on a large plate.

2. Scrub the potatoes well under
running water. While they are
still wet, pierce them in multiple
spots with a fork or knife to
enable them to vent steam as
they bake. Cake each damp potato
all over with the salt, forming a
white-speckled blanket. Place the
potatoes directly on the oven rack
and bake them until tender, about
1 hour. If you wish, you may place
a cookie sheet on the rack below
if you have a fear that the salt will
fall off, but it really won't.

3. As the potatoes bake, melt 2
tablespoons of clarified butter in
a large skillet over medium-high
heat. Once it appears to shimmer,
stir-fry the onion and garlic until
they become light brown around
the edges, 3 to 5 minutes. Add the
beans, asparagus, coriander, red
pepper flakes, and ½ teaspoon
salt. Give it all a good stir. Lower
the heat to medium-low, cover the
pan, and allow the asparagus to
steam, stirring occasionally, until
they are tender but still firm, 5 to
7 minutes. Keep the cover on after
you have turned off the burner so
the filling stays warm.

4. To make the béarnaise, bring
the vinegar, wine, and shallots
to a boil in a small saucepan
over medium-high heat. Boil
the mixture, uncovered, stirring

TATER TIPS

▲ How deeply do you clarify
butter? Melt unsalted butter
over low heat and allow the
milk solids to separate and
sink to the bottom. Strain
through cheesecloth or a very
fine-mesh sieve. Indians take
it a step farther, first skimming
as much foam as possible
from the melted butter, then
continuing to cook it until
it's amber in color (about 20
minutes). Once amber, it is
strained through cheesecloth
so that no milk solids remain.
The clear, light amber-colored
fluid is called "ghee."

▲ How much of the asparagus
stalk is good for this recipe?
First, choose a bunch with
stem ends that are not dried
up. And don't pick a bunch
that has thick stalks, since
they can be woody. The
thinner they are, the more
tender they are. Cut off the
top 2 to 3 inches from the
stalks to use in this recipe.
You can still use much of the
remaining stalks, sans the
woodiest inch from the stem
ends, to steam and eat when
your heart desires.

occasionally, until the liquid is reduced by half, 5 to 7 minutes. Allow the reduction to cool (it should be just warm to the touch but not hot), 2 to 4 minutes. Pour this into a blender jar and add the egg yolks. Melt the remaining 6 tablespoons clarified butter. (I usually put it into a microwave-safe glass measuring cup and warm it 30 seconds at a time until it's hot.) With the blender running on low speed, slowly drizzle in the hot butter. This creates the emulsion needed to make a smooth sauce. Pour and scrape the sauce into a small bowl or the measuring cup that you melted the butter in. Fold in the tarragon and the peppercorns. Keep the sauce near the stove so it stays warm.

5. Once the potatoes are tender, transfer them to a cutting board and allow them to cool enough so you can handle them. Slice off a ¼-inch-thick slice from the top along the length of each potato. (They're for nibbling—the cook's bonus as you finish the dish!) With a teaspoon, scoop out as much of the tender insides as you can and stir them into the asparagus and beans. Leave a thin layer of flesh on the bottom of each potato and try not to bore a hole through the skin. (I usually leave about a ¼-inch-thick layer of potatoes around the inside wall to avoid any possibility of leaks.)

6. Fill each potato with as much of the filling as you can (mound it, if necessary, to use it all) pour the béarnaise sauce over each, and serve immediately. The caked-on salt on the potato's surface provides a delectable layer, rounding out the whole experience in one well-balanced mouthful at a time.

VEGAN BÉARNAISE SAUCE

To make about 1 cup of the sauce, discard the stems from 2 ounces fresh shiitake mushrooms and finely chop the caps. Transfer these to a small saucepan and add ¼ cup dry white wine, ¼ cup white wine vinegar, and 1 finely chopped medium-size shallot. Boil this on medium-high, uncovered, stirring occasionally, until the liquid is reduced to half the initial amount, 5 to 7 minutes. Transfer this to a blender jar. Drain 2 ounces silken tofu of all excess water, gently pat it dry, and add it to the blender. Puree the medley to a smooth sauce, stopping the machine and scraping the inside of the jar when necessary. With the blender running on low speed, drizzle in ¼ cup canola oil to create a smooth emulsion. Scrape the sauce into a medium-size bowl and fold in 2 tablespoons finely chopped fresh tarragon leaves, ½ teaspoon coarsely cracked black peppercorns, and ¼ teaspoon coarse sea or kosher salt.

SMASHED
ROASTED
MASHED
BAKED
BOILED
FRIED
SHREDDED
RICED

Italian

MOZZARELLA POTATO STACKS

I have always been a fan of a simple but well-executed eggplant parmesan, those layered crisped eggplant slabs smothered with a tomato sauce and cheese. So this rendition with potatoes as the star made total sense to me. A perfect weekday meal, there is enough for leftovers to use on a day you may have no desire to step into the kitchen. SERVES 6

2 large russet potatoes
   (each about 1 pound)

1 cup buttermilk

1½ cups panko bread crumbs

1 tablespoon dried basil

2 teaspoons dried oregano

2 teaspoons dried rosemary

1 teaspoon crushed red pepper flakes

1 teaspoon coarse sea or kosher salt

Extra-virgin olive oil, for drizzling

4 cups tomato pasta sauce
   (store-purchased or homemade)

8 ounces fresh buffalo or regular
   mozzarella, cut into thin slabs
   or slices

½ cup freshly shredded Parmigiano-
   Reggiano cheese

¼ cup thinly shredded fresh basil
   leaves (chiffonade; see Tater Tips,
   page 91)

1. Position a rack in the center of the oven and preheat the oven to 375°F. Line a cookie sheet with parchment paper.

"Why should the work of a potato planter be less interesting or less noble than any other activity?"

—*Jean-François Millet, painter,* The Potato Planters

Instead of the bread crumbs (unless you can find or make them with vegan bread), try using ground almonds as a great alternative. I love the nutty crunch they deliver. Yes, of course, you have to use a vegan cheese instead of the mozzarella to maintain vegan status!

2. Peel the potatoes and rinse them under cold running water. (If you wish to leave the skin on, for a healthier component, make sure you scrub the potatoes well before use.) Using a chef's knife or a mandoline, slice the potatoes lengthwise into ¼-inch-thick planks. Place them in a baking pan and pour the buttermilk over them to soak a bit and also to prevent them from discoloring.

3. Thoroughly mix together the bread crumbs, basil, oregano, rosemary, red pepper flakes, and salt in a medium-size bowl. Place a potato plank, still coated with buttermilk, in the seasoned crumbs, making sure it gets well cloaked. Place this on the prepared cookie sheet. Repeat, using up all the potato planks and crumbs. If you pack the planks close together, you should be able to fit them all on 1 cookie sheet. Wash and dry the baking pan and set aside.

4. Liberally drizzle olive oil over the planks—don't skimp on oil. It is essential not only to provide good flavor, but also to turn the slices crispy brown. Place the cookie sheet in the oven and roast the planks, flipping them periodically to ensure even browning, until they are crispy all over and tender when pierced through the crackly shell with a fork or knife, about 45 minutes. Remove the cookie sheet from the oven.

5. Cover the bottom of the baking pan with about 1⅓ cups of the sauce. Place a layer of the crisped potato planks on the sauce and top them with another 1⅓ cups of the sauce. Spread half the mozzarella slices over the sauce, followed by another layer of the baked potato planks. Spread the remaining sauce over this layer. Cover the baking pan with aluminum foil and bake until the sauce is bubbly, about 30 minutes.

6. Remove the foil and sprinkle the Parmigiano-Reggiano evenly over the sauce, followed by the remaining mozzarella slices. Return the pan to the oven, uncovered, to melt the cheesy topping, about 5 minutes.

7. Remove from the oven, sprinkle with the fresh basil, and serve.

CREAMY
BOW TIE PASTA
WITH POTATOES AND BASIL

Many cultures outside the United States don't think twice of combining two or more starches in one dish. Pizza crusts and pastas are fair game in Italy for incorporating the potato in all its varied incarnations. This pasta embraces the bounty of summer. When tomatoes and basil overflow vegetable baskets at farmers' markets alongside just-dug potatoes, bring them all home for a synergistic meal. **SERVES 8**

1 pound purple or red potatoes

2 tablespoons extra-virgin olive oil

4 medium-size cloves garlic, finely chopped

1 teaspoon coarse sea or kosher salt

2 cups vegetable stock

4 ounces cream cheese, cut into chunks

1½ teaspoons coarsely cracked black peppercorns

1 teaspoon crushed red pepper flakes

8 ounces uncooked bow tie pasta (see Tater Tip, page 144)

8 ounces fresh green or yellow wax beans, stem ends trimmed, cut into 2-inch pieces

6 grape tomatoes, sliced in half

2 scallions, beards trimmed, green tops and white bulbs thinly sliced

1 cup finely chopped fresh basil leaves

Freshly shredded Parmigiano-Reggiano cheese, for serving (optional)

1. Fill a medium-size bowl with cold water. Lay out a clean cotton kitchen towel or several layers of paper towels on the counter, for drying the potatoes. Peel the potatoes and cut them into 1-inch cubes. Submerge them in the bowl of water to rinse off some of the surface starch.

TATER TIP

▲ Don't feel limited to bow tie pasta. Vary the dish by using fusilli, penne, or any other shape that's similar in size and that suits your fancy.

2. Drain them in a colander and rinse them under cold running water. Give the colander a good shake or two to rid the potatoes of excess water. Spread out the cubes on the towel and pat them dry.

3. Heat the oil in a large skillet over medium heat. Once the oil appears to shimmer, add the potatoes, garlic, and ½ teaspoon of the salt. Cover the pan and cook the potatoes, stirring occasionally, until they are three-quarters cooked, about 10 minutes. Don't worry about the garlic burning, since the potatoes will cushion it (actually, it turns a medium caramel brown).

4. While the potatoes cook, bring the stock and cream cheese to a boil in a small saucepan over medium-high heat. Once the stock comes to a boil, whisk the two to make sure the stock gets an evenly creamy appearance. Stir in the peppercorns and red pepper flakes and keep the sauce warm on the lowest heat possible as you finish with the potatoes.

5. Also as the potatoes cook, fill a medium-size saucepan three-quarters full with water and bring it to a rolling boil over medium-high heat. Add the pasta, reduce the heat to medium, and

boil, uncovered, until it is just tender but not overcooked (al dente), according to the package instructions. As soon as the pasta is tender, drain it and give the colander a good shake or two. (Never rinse pasta, since the cooking water clinging to it provides essential starch to give the sauce a more viscous body.)

6. After the potatoes have cooked for about 10 minutes, add the green beans and sprinkle in the remaining ½ teaspoon of salt. (Adding salt in stages provides for a deeper flavor, in my opinion.) Cover the pan again and continue to cook the potatoes and beans until they are just tender when pierced with a fork, about 5 minutes. Keep the vegetables warm on low heat if the pasta isn't ready.

7. Add the pasta and creamy sauce to the vegetables and crank up the heat under the skillet. The sauce will thicken as it boils, 3 to 5 minutes.

8. Stir in the tomatoes, scallions, and basil and serve right away, while it's still hot. If you wish for a burst of nutty saltiness, sprinkle each serving with Parmigiano-Reggiano.

Italian

POTATO LASAGNA

A good lasagna is satisfying, but a great one is lusty. I am the first to admit this is a production, but the promise of leftovers for those nights when all you want to do is reheat a portion after a long workday makes it worthwhile. Even though I go to the effort of making my own sauce and ricotta (give it a try, page 148), you can opt out and use store-purchased versions. SERVES 8

FOR THE SAUCE

4 pounds grape tomatoes

Extra-virgin olive oil, for drizzling

1 teaspoon coarse sea or kosher salt

1 teaspoon coarsely cracked black peppercorns

FOR THE RICOTTA

2 cups ricotta cheese (recipe follows)

Zest from 1 large lemon

2 large eggs, slightly beaten

1 cup finely chopped fresh basil leaves

1 teaspoon crushed red pepper flakes

½ teaspoon coarse sea or kosher salt

FOR THE VEGETABLE MEDLEY

1½ pounds Yukon Gold potatoes

2 tablespoons extra-virgin olive oil

1 medium-size yellow onion, finely chopped

1 large red bell pepper, fresh finely chopped

8 large cloves garlic, finely chopped

8 ounces stem, ribs, and seeds discarded, baby spinach, thoroughly rinsed and dried

1 teaspoon coarsely cracked black peppercorns

½ teaspoon coarse sea or kosher salt

FOR THE PASTA AND ASSEMBLY

Cooking spray, for greasing the pan

12 ounces fresh lasagna sheets (see Tater Tip)

12 ounces shredded Italian cheese blend

TATER TIP

▲ Fresh lasagna sheets are common in the refrigerated section of supermarkets that carry numerous varieties of pasta. They don't need to be precooked before baking. If you are using dried lasagna sheets, cook them according to the package directions before using them in the recipe.

TATER TIP

1. Position a rack in the lower third of the oven and preheat the oven to 375°F. Line a large baking pan with parchment paper.

2. To make the sauce, place the tomatoes in a large bowl and anoint them with enough olive oil to give them a glistening coat. Sprinkle the salt and peppercorns over them and give it all a good toss. Spread the tomatoes in the baking pan and roast, stirring them once in a while, until their skins shrivel and they are brown, 45 to 50 minutes.

3. Remove the tomatoes from the oven and lower the temperature to 350°F. Transfer the tomatoes to a blender jar and puree them until smooth, scraping the inside of the jar as needed. If you are okay dispensing the sauce from there when assembling the lasagna, just leave it in the jar. If not, pour and scrape it into a bowl.

4. Place the ricotta in a medium-size bowl and stir in the lemon zest, eggs, basil, red pepper flakes, and salt.

5. To make the vegetable medley, scrub the potatoes well under cold running water. Fill a medium-size bowl with cold water. Slice the potatoes into ⅛-inch-thick planks with a chef's knife or mandoline.

Submerge the planks in the bowl of cold water to prevent them from graying and to remove excess surface starch. Allow them to soak while you work on the vegetables.

6. Heat the oil in a large skillet over medium heat. Once the oil appears to shimmer, add the onion, red bell pepper, and garlic and stir-fry the medley until the onion and red pepper are light brown around the edges, 7 to 10 minutes. Add half the spinach leaves and cover the pan. The steam will wilt them in 2 to 3 minutes. Pile in the remaining leaves and cover the pan to wilt them, an additional 2 to 3 minutes. Sprinkle in the peppercorns and salt and give it all a good stir.

7. Drain the potatoes in a colander and run them under cold running water to rinse off any surface starch. Give the colander a good shake or two to rid the potatoes of excess water.

8. Now you are ready to assemble the lasagna (finally!). Spray the inside of a 13-by-9-inch baking pan with cooking spray. (A clear glass pan will certainly look pretty.) Pour in enough sauce to thinly coat the bottom. Place one third of the pasta sheets (4 ounces) to cover the bottom.

Spread half of the ricotta over the sheets. Arrange a layer of half the potatoes on the ricotta. A little overlapping of potato planks is okay, but not much. Follow this by half of the vegetable medley. Pour and spread some of the remaining sauce, then sprinkle on one third of the cheese. Place another third of the lasagna sheets on top and repeat the layering, using up all the ricotta, potatoes, and vegetables, and half of the remaining sauce and cheese. Place the last of the sheets over this, followed by the remainder of the sauce. Cover the pan with aluminum foil and place it on a cookie sheet in case the cheese and sauce spill a bit during baking.

9. Bake the lasagna until the sides look bubbly and the center of the lasagna, when pierced with a knife, reveals a hot, cheesy, bubbly interior, 1 to 1¼ hours.

10. Sprinkle the remaining shredded cheese on top and return the uncovered pan to the oven. Let the cheese melt, about 2 minutes. If you wish for a deeper brown color, turn on the oven broiler and place the pan under it. The cheese will melt and also acquire that reddish-brown color that makes it so appealing.

11. Transfer the pan to a wire rack and allow the lasagna to cool and set a bit, about 15 minutes. Slice the lasagna into portions and serve warm.

HOMEMADE RICOTTA CHEESE

Housemade ricotta cheese served under a light pool of extra-virgin olive oil is all the rage in restaurants. Now you can impress your friends by making your own. My way of making it is as easy as boiling milk. The right temperature and the right amount of acid yield incredibly creamy curds. If you drain them in a fine-mesh sieve, you won't need cheesecloth. If your mesh isn't fine, line it with damp cheesecloth. Save the whey and use it as the liquid in dough. Both curds and whey will keep, refrigerated, for up to four days. MAKES 2 CUPS

½ gallon whole milk

¼ cup white distilled vinegar

Pour the milk into a Dutch oven or large heavy saucepan and heat it over medium heat, stirring regularly. Stick a candy thermometer into the milk; when it registers around 175°F, pour in the vinegar and give it a good stir. The milk will start to curdle and soon the curds will separate, leaving behind a watery greenish-gray whey. Place a fine-mesh sieve in a colander in the sink or over a deep bowl and scoop the curds out of the pot into the sieve. Allow the curds to drain for about 30 minutes before using.

FRIED
SMASHED
MASHED
BOILED
RICED
SHREDDED
BAKED

Greek

POTATO MOUSSAKA

This version of a moussaka is a layered infatuation that captures the essence of Greece and its seasonal produce. Some of the traditional moussakas include ground meat such as lamb with the eggplant, but this vegetarian rendition incorporates potatoes in two forms: one sliced and pan-fried crisp, the other boiled and riced, then folded into a rich béchamel sauce dotted with nutmeg. Keep in mind that Greece was a key player in the world spice trade so this classic is scented with cumin and oregano. The recipe appears daunting but it really is a simple one to execute. When accompanied with a green salad, this main course offering can be your ticket to a gratifying dinner any weekday or weekend. **SERVES 8**

FOR THE VEGETABLE LAYERS

2 pounds eggplant

2½ pounds Yukon Gold potatoes

Extra-virgin olive oil, for pan-frying and greasing the baking pan

2 cans (14.5 ounces each) diced tomatoes, juices drained

1 tablespoon dried oregano leaves (preferably Greek)

2 teaspoons cumin seeds, ground

1 teaspoon crushed red pepper flakes

1 teaspoon coarse sea or kosher salt

FOR THE BÉCHAMEL SAUCE

1 pound russet potatoes

3 tablespoons unsalted butter

3 tablespoons unbleached all-purpose flour

2 cups whole milk

1 large egg, slightly beaten

1 teaspoon freshly grated nutmeg

½ teaspoon coarse sea or kosher salt

1 cup shredded kefalotyri or Parmigiano-Reggiano cheese (see Tater Tip)

TATER TIP

▲ Kefalotyri is a light yellow, very firm cheese made from sheep's or goat's milk. Salty in its taste with a slight nuttiness, it is available in gourmet cheese stores and in Greek neighborhoods. Ideal for shredding, use it just as you would Parmigiano-Reggiano. In fact, if it is difficult to procure kefalotyri where you live, by all means use Parmigiano-Reggiano as a perfect stand-in.

1. To make the vegetable layers, lop off the stem end of each eggplant. Stand them up on their cut surface and slice them into ¼-inch-thick planks.

2. Fill a medium-size bowl halfway with cold water. Peel the Yukon Gold potatoes and give them a good rinse under cold running water. Slice them lengthwise into ¼-inch-thick planks. Submerge them in the bowl of water to rinse off surface starch and to prevent them from discoloring.

3. Drizzle 2 tablespoons of oil into a large skillet and heat it over medium heat. Once the oil appears to shimmer, arrange as many eggplant planks as you can in a single layer, without overlapping. Allow the underside to brown and soften, 2 to 3 minutes. Flip the planks and repeat on the other side for an additional 2 to 3 minutes. Lift them out of the skillet with tongs and place them in a stack on a large cookie sheet. Brown the remaining eggplant planks, adding more oil as needed. Add them to the stack on the cookie sheet when they're done.

4. Lay out several layers of paper towels or a clean cotton kitchen towel on the counter. Drain the potato planks in a colander and give them a good rinse under cold running water to remove any residual surface starch. Give the colander a good shake or two to rid the potatoes of excess water. Pat the potatoes dry on the paper towels. Pour another 2 tablespoons of oil into the skillet and heat over medium heat until it shimmers. Arrange a single layer of potato planks, without overcrowding. Once the underside browns slightly and the top looks opaque, 2 to 3 minutes, flip them over and repeat on the other side for an additional 2 to 3 minutes. Lift them out of the skillet and set them in their own stack, on the same cookie sheet as the eggplant. Brown the remaining potato planks, adding them to their stack.

5. Combine the tomatoes, oregano, cumin, red pepper flakes, and salt in a medium-size bowl.

6. To start the béchamel sauce, peel the russet potatoes, cut them into quarters, and give them a good rinse under cold running water. Place them in a medium-size saucepan and cover them with cold water. Bring to a boil over medium-high heat. Lower the heat, cover the pan, and gently boil the potatoes until the pieces fall apart quite easily

TATER TIP

▲ If you have 2 large skillets and are adept at managing both at one time, by all means brown the eggplant and potatoes simultaneously. That way, you can lower your active cooking time.

when pierced with a fork, 20 to 25 minutes.

7. While the potatoes boil, melt the butter in a small saucepan over medium heat. Spoon in the flour and whisk it into the butter, making sure there are no lumps. Continue to cook the flour, whisking constantly, so the flour cooks evenly but does not start browning, about 1 minute. Pour in ½ cup of the milk, whisking to ensure a lump-free sauce. Slowly whisk in the remaining 1½ cups of milk. Simmer the sauce over medium heat, uncovered, whisking occasionally, until it starts to thicken and bubble, 3 to 5 minutes. Remove from the heat.

8. Whisk a few tablespoons of the sauce into the beaten egg to warm it. Pour the egg mixture into the sauce along with the nutmeg and salt and give it all a good whisking. Set the béchamel sauce aside.

9. Once the potatoes are ready, drain them into a colander and return the pieces to the dry pan. Return the pan to the burner, and over low heat, dry the potatoes of any residual water that may cling to their surfaces, about 30 seconds.

10. Working in batches if necessary, transfer the potatoes to a ricer and press them through directly into the béchamel. (If you don't have a ricer, use a potato masher and fluff them with a fork when completely mashed, then add them to the sauce.) Sprinkle in the cheese and fold the potatoes and cheese into the béchamel.

11. Now you are ready to assemble the moussaka. Position a rack in the center of the oven and preheat the oven to 350°F. Lightly grease a 13-by-9-inch baking pan with some oil.

12. Arrange half of the potato planks as the bottom layer. (A little overlapping is fine.) Spoon on half of the seasoned tomatoes and top with a layer of half of the eggplant. Repeat with the remaining potatoes, tomatoes, and eggplant. Top it off with the béchamel sauce, spreading the sauce evenly with a spatula.

13. Bake the moussaka, uncovered, until bubbly and the top is lightly browned, about 1 hour. Cut into squares and serve hot.

TATER TIPS

▲ Pouring all the milk into the butter-flour mixture at one time makes it difficult to ensure there will be no lumps. Hence the gradual addition.

▲ Whisking a little of the hot sauce into the egg is called "tempering": The egg comes up to a warmer temperature that more closely matches that of the sauce. Then the egg won't cook and curdle when added to the rest of the hot sauce. A few tablespoons of the sauce will do the trick.

SMASHED
MASHED
BAKED
FRIED
SHREDDED
ROASTED
BOILED
RICED

Polish

POTATO PIEROGIES

TATER TIP

▲ To freeze uncooked pierogies, lay them out in a single layer on a cookie sheet and place the sheet in the freezer. Once they are frozen, transfer them to a zip-top bag. They will keep for up to 3 months. No need to thaw them before you boil them. Just allow for an extra minute or two of cooking time.

Meredith Deeds, a close friend, colleague, cookbook author, and teacher, knows her pierogies. And she knows my love for potatoes. Her birthday gift to me during my landmark fiftieth year was to throw a potluck gathering where all the invited guests were asked to bring a potato dish. Now that's a true friend. Having lived in a Polish community in Cleveland, she learned the correct way to make and shape the potato-filled dumplings. The dough is smooth and pliable without being dry, and my inclusion of decadent crème fraîche (instead of her sour cream) in both the dough and the filling fashions an experience that can only be called opulent and indulgent. MAKES ABOUT 60 PIEROGIES

FOR THE FILLING

1½ pounds russet potatoes

⅓ cup crème fraîche

6 ounces shredded sharp cheddar cheese

1 teaspoon coarse sea or kosher salt

1 teaspoon coarsely cracked black peppercorns

½ teaspoon freshly grated nutmeg

FOR THE DOUGH

4 large eggs

1 teaspoon coarse sea or kosher salt

1 cup crème fraîche

4¼ cups unbleached all-purpose flour, plus more for rolling the dough

1. To make the filling, peel the potatoes and give them a good rinse under cold running water. Cut them into chunks, place them in a medium-size saucepan, and cover them with cold water. Bring to a boil over medium-high heat. Lower the heat to medium-low, cover the pan, and boil the potatoes until they are tender when pierced with a fork or knife, 25 to 30 minutes. Scoop out and save about ½ cup of the cooking water. Drain the potatoes in a colander.

2. Working in batches, transfer the potatoes to a ricer and press them through into a medium-size bowl. (If you don't have a ricer, use a potato masher and fluff them with a fork when completely mashed.) Spoon in the crème fraîche and sprinkle in the cheese, salt, peppercorns, and nutmeg. Fold these into the potatoes, mixing just until they're incorporated.

3. To make the dough, crack the eggs into the bowl of a stand mixer, sprinkle in the salt, and spoon in the crème fraîche. Attach the whisk. On medium speed, whisk everything until well combined and slightly frothy, 2 to 4 minutes. Undo the whisk attachment and replace it with the dough hook. On medium-low speed, gradually sprinkle in the flour until a soft dough starts to come together. You may have to stop the mixer

and scrape the flour off the sides of the bowl and into the dough. Continue to knead it until the dough starts to feel silky smooth and not sticky. If it still feels a bit sticky, sprinkle just enough flour to bring it to that desired consistency. If it feels dry, drizzle in a bit of the cooking water and continue to knead it. Undo the dough hook and remove the bowl from the mixer. Cover the bowl with plastic wrap and allow the dough to rest about 10 minutes.

4. Divide the dough into 2 equal halves. Work with one half at a time, keeping the other one covered to prevent it from drying out. Sprinkle some flour onto the counter and roll out the dough to an even ⅛-inch thickness (the shape doesn't matter). Using a 2-inch biscuit cutter, cut out rounds. Stack them up. Make sure there is a liberal amount of flour between the rounds to prevent them from sticking to one another. Repeat with the other half of the dough. Lightly cover the stacks with plastic wrap to prevent them from drying out.

5. Thoroughly flour a cookie sheet. One at a time, hold a dough round in the palm of one hand and spoon about ½ tablespoon of the filling close to the center

"Only two things in this world are too serious to be jested on, potatoes and matrimony."

—*Irish saying*

PIEROGIES STEP-BY-STEP

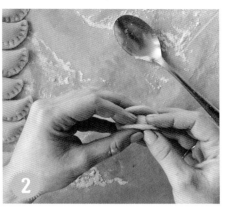

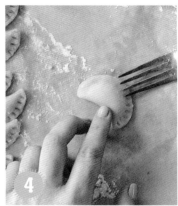

1 Spoon ½ tablespoon of the filling onto a 2-inch dough round.

2 Fold the dough in half around the filling.

3 Pinch the edges of the pierogi closed.

4 Use the tines of a fork to further seal the edges—you don't want filling leaking out when you boil the pierogies.

of the circle. Fold over the dough and pinch the edges shut to fashion a well-sealed half-moon. Press the edges with the tines of a fork to doubly secure the filling. Lay the pierogies on the prepared cookie sheet in a single layer. Make sure the pierogies don't touch one another as you set them aside, or they might stick. If you run out of room, cover the first layer with parchment paper; then you can stack another layer on top.

6. Fill a medium-size saucepan halfway with water and bring to a boil over medium-high heat.

Turn down the heat to keep the water at a gentle boil, just above a simmer. Carefully submerge a few of the pierogies, without overcrowding the pan. Allow them to cook, stirring very gently once or twice with a slotted spoon to prevent them from sticking to one another. Once they appear a bit opaque and lose that raw dough look, 5 to 8 minutes, lift them out of the water carefully with the spoon, let them drain briefly, and place them on a platter. Cook only as many pierogies as you are planning to serve at that time. They are best eaten right away. (See Tater Tip, page 153, for how to freeze extras.)

VARIATIONS: Serving pierogies is a matter of taste. To gild the lily (and your arteries), you can serve them with some crème fraîche or applesauce on the side.

◆ Most people prefer to serve them with onions sautéed in butter to a nice brown. Heat 4 tablespoons of butter (½ stick, salted or unsalted) in a large skillet over medium heat. Once the foam subsides, stir-fry 4 cups thinly sliced yellow or red onion until they are deep brown and look caramel-sweet (and are almost candy-like when tasted), about 20 minutes. Stir in ½ cup finely chopped fresh chives along with ¼ cup finely chopped fresh dill and ½ teaspoon coarse sea or kosher salt. Toss your pierogies with the onions just to warm them, or you can continue cooking the pierogies in the pan of onions until the pierogies are crispy.

◆ Another way to cook the pierogies is similar to the way you make potstickers. Heat 2 tablespoons of canola oil in a large nonstick skillet over medium heat. Once the oil appears to shimmer, place a single layer of uncooked pierogies (either fresh or frozen) in the oil without overcrowding. Allow the underside to brown, 2 to 3 minutes. Flip them over and brown the other side for an additional 2 to 3 minutes. Pour in ½ cup water, which will instantly bubble and generate steam that you entrap by covering the pan. Allow the water to be absorbed. As soon as the dumplings appear swollen with juicy goodness, 2 to 4 minutes, serve them warm with the onions above.

POTATO-BASIL GNOCCHI

In Italy, potato dumplings have been around since as early as the seventeenth century. The perfect dumpling should be light, and you should still be able to taste the delicacy of the floury potatoes. If you consume a batch and wind up feeling lead-bellied, you have not experienced the right texture.

Most commonly you see these dumplings tossed with browned butter and sage as a side dish, but my version makes them an entree with the inclusion of legumes and vegetables. **SERVES 4**

1 pound russet potatoes

1 large egg

1 teaspoon coarse sea or kosher salt

2 tablespoons finely chopped fresh basil leaves

About 1½ cups unbleached all-purpose flour

Hearty Vegetable Sauce (recipe follows)

Freshly shredded Parmigiano-Reggiano cheese, for sprinkling

1. Peel the potatoes and give them a good rinse under cold running water. Cut them into quarters, place them in a small saucepan, and cover them with cold water. Bring to a boil over medium-high heat.

Partially cover the pan, lower the heat to medium-low, and simmer vigorously until the potatoes are fall-apart tender when pierced with a fork or knife, 12 to 15 minutes.

2. Drain the potatoes in a colander and return them to the saucepan. Dry them out over medium-low heat, stirring occasionally so they don't stick to the bottom of the pan, until the surface appears dry. Some of the pieces will start to break down into smaller morsels. Working in batches if necessary, transfer these to a ricer and press them directly onto a cookie sheet in a flat layer. (If you don't

> "Money is the root of all evil, and yet it is such a useful root that we cannot get on without it any more than we can without potatoes."
>
> *—Louisa May Alcott, American novelist and poet*

TATER TIP

▲ If you are a gadget geek like I am, you can buy a gnocchi board that looks like a small wooden cutting board with a handle and a surface of lined grooves. Gently roll each piece of dough along the grooves to get the gnocchi groove marks onto the dough.

have a ricer, use a potato masher and fluff them with a fork when completely mashed. Spread them lightly on the cookie sheet.) Place the potatoes in the freezer to chill quickly, about 5 minutes.

3. Remove the cookie sheet from the freezer, gather the potatoes into a ball, and place it on a clean cutting board or wide bowl. Make a well in the center of the potatoes, crack the egg into it, and top it off with the salt and basil. Use a bench scraper or a large spatula to lift the potatoes up and over the egg, working all around the mound of potatoes and cutting into it to incorporate the egg and basil. The potatoes will turn a light yellow speckled with jade green. Sprinkle half the flour over the potatoes and blend it in with the bench scraper. (This is a great way to incorporate the flour into the eggy potatoes without handling the flour too much, which can toughen up the gnocchi.) If it's too wet, once it comes together to form dough—it will feel incredibly sticky—sprinkle on a bit more flour and repeat. You may not need to add all the flour. Once you've got the right dough consistency, soft and a bit smooth (not dry, not sticky), knead it for 30 seconds to smooth it out completely. Transfer the dough to a bowl, cover the bowl with

plastic wrap, and refrigerate it for 30 minutes to firm it up.

4. Clean and dry the cutting board. Sprinkle it very lightly with flour. Line a clean cookie sheet with wax paper or parchment paper.

5. Cut the dough into 6 pieces. Roll each on the cutting board into a rope about ½ inch thick. Sprinkle each rope with flour to prevent anything from sticking. (I use a shaker so the flour addition is minimal; see Tater Tips, page 131.) Cut each rope into ½-inch-long dumplings.

6. Roll each dumpling away from you against the tines of a fork to make grooves, or use a gnocchi board (see Tater Tip). The grooves in the dough help capture the sauce, making the eating experience more succulent. As you shape each dumpling, set it on the prepared cookie sheet, keeping them in a single layer. Dust a little flour on the finished gnocchi and cover them loosely with plastic wrap as you prepare the sauce. At this point you can freeze them on the cookie sheet. Once frozen, store them in a zip-top bag for up to 3 months.

7. Fill a large saucepan halfway with water and bring it to a rolling boil over medium-high heat. Add all the gnocchi and lower the heat to allow them to boil gently, uncovered. Initially they will sink to the bottom, but once they are fully cooked, they will float to the top, 5 to 8 minutes. Gently skim them off with a slotted spoon.

Give it a good tap or two against the pan's lip to rid the gnocchi of excess water. Place them in a serving platter or bowl and add the vegetable sauce. Gently toss them to coat with the sauce. Serve immediately, with the cheese.

HEARTY VEGETABLE SAUCE

Any beans will work in this stew-like sauce, if cannellini are not your game. I particularly love the nutty bravado of garbanzos (chickpeas) as well. Start preparing the sauce about 30 minutes before serving. MAKES ABOUT 3 CUPS

2 tablespoons extra-virgin olive oil

4 medium-size cloves garlic, finely chopped

½ cup shelled pistachio nuts, coarsely chopped (see Tater Tip)

1 can (14 to 15 ounces) diced tomatoes (including juices)

1 can (15 ounces) white cannellini beans, drained and rinsed

8 ounces fresh baby spinach, thoroughly rinsed and dried

1 teaspoon coarse sea or kosher salt

½ teaspoon coarsely cracked black peppercorns

½ teaspoon crushed red pepper flakes

1. Heat the oil in a medium-size saucepan over medium heat. Once the oil appears to shimmer, stir-fry the garlic and pistachios until the garlic is lightly brown and the nuts are fragrant, 1 to 2 minutes.

2. Pour in the tomatoes, including the juices, and the beans. Stir once or twice. Bring the sauce to a boil, stirring occasionally. Pile in the spinach, cover the saucepan, and allow the greens to wilt in the rising steam, without stirring, about 5 minutes.

3. Stir in the salt, peppercorns, and red pepper flakes. Lower the heat to allow the sauce to simmer, uncovered, about 15 minutes.

TATER TIP

▲ Shelled pistachio nuts, salted or unsalted, are easy to come by in the supermarket. Pulse them in a food processor or mini chopper to break them down to the consistency of bread crumbs. Pine nuts are a great alternative in this recipe. Use them whole.

STUFFED CRISPY FLAUTAS

TATER TIP

▲ Cotija cheese from Mexico, a product of the milk from grass-eating cows, is salty, crumbly like feta, and maintains its granular texture even when warmed. It possesses a sharpness pleasing to the palate. If you can't find it, by all means substitute the more available feta or even Parmigiano-Reggiano, ounce for ounce. Mexican *queso fresco* also works well in this recipe.

I have sampled *flautas*—interchangeably called *taquitos*—with a multitude of fillings ranging from cheese to meats to potatoes, wrapped in both corn and flour tortillas. These are a perfectly satisfying lunch, especially when I serve them with avocado, cheese, and lettuce. The crispy shells and warm, creamy potato-oregano filling are a great contrast to the chilled lettuce and buttery avocado. SERVES 4

8 ounces russet or Yukon Gold potatoes

¼ cup finely chopped fresh cilantro leaves and tender stems

2 tablespoons finely chopped fresh oregano leaves

1 fresh green serrano chile, stem discarded, finely chopped (do not remove the seeds)

1 teaspoon coarse sea or kosher salt

8 corn tortillas (6-inch rounds)

Canola oil, for pan-frying

1 large Hass avocado, finely chopped (see Tater Tip, page 27)

¼ cup Mexican crema (homemade or store-purchased; see Tater Tip, page 161)

2 ounces Cotija cheese, crumbled (see Tater Tip)

1 cup shredded lettuce (preferably romaine or red leaf)

Avocado Salsa (recipe follows)

1. Peel the potatoes and give them a good rinse under cold running water. Cut them into quarters, place them in a small saucepan, and cover them with cold water. Bring to a boil over medium-high heat. Partially cover the pan, lower the heat to medium, and boil the potatoes until the pieces are fall-apart tender when pierced with a fork or knife, 10 to 12 minutes.

2. Drain the potatoes in a colander and give the colander a good shake or two to rid the potatoes of excess water. Return them to the pan. Dry them out over medium heat, stirring occasionally so they don't stick to the bottom of the pan, until the surface appears dry, about 30 seconds. Working in batches if necessary, transfer the potatoes to a ricer and press them into a medium-size bowl. (If you don't have a ricer, remove the pan from the heat, use a potato masher, and fluff them with a fork when completely mashed.) Sprinkle in the cilantro, oregano, chile, and, salt. Mix until just incorporated. Place a large sheet of parchment paper on the counter. Divide the filling into 8 equal portions and place them on the parchment. Set a wire rack over a cookie sheet, for draining the flautas of excess oil.

3. Warm a small skillet on the stove over medium heat.

4. Drop a tortilla into the skillet. Allow it to warm up on both sides, about 30 seconds each side. (This makes the tortilla supple and pliable to fill and fold.) Place the tortilla on a plate or a cutting board and spoon a portion of the potato filling along the lower third. Starting from the filled side, fold and roll it, flute-like (*flautas*, get it?). A toothpick through the flauta helps hold it together. Set the flauta aside on a large plate as you repeat with the remaining tortillas and filling.

5. Heat a medium-size skillet over medium heat. Pour oil to a depth of ½ inch into the skillet. Once the oil appears to shimmer, place 4 of the flautas in the oil, seam side down. Allow them to sizzle and brown on the underside, 2 to 3 minutes. Flip the flautas to brown the remaining parts, an additional 2 to 3 minutes. Lift them out of the pan with tongs and place them on the rack to drain as you pan-fry the remaining flautas.

6. Remove the toothpicks and place the flautas on a serving platter. Top them off with the avocado, drizzle with the crema, sprinkle on the cheese, and garnish with the lettuce. Serve while they're still warm, accompanied by the Avocado Salsa.

TATER TIP

▲ Mexican crema is a cultured cream with a runnier consistency than rich French crème fraîche or American store-purchased sour cream. It's available at upscale supermarkets and Latin American groceries, if you happen to have one in your city. If crema is hard to come by, use sour cream or even crème fraîche as alternatives. Or, make your own crema—it's easy.

Bring 1 cup of heavy cream to a boil in a small saucepan over medium heat, stirring it frequently to prevent scorching. Remove it from the heat and let it cool down to about 100°F. Whisk in 2 tablespoons of cultured buttermilk with active bacteria. Pour it into a jar, screw on the lid, and set it in a warm spot for a few hours or even overnight. You will end up with a somewhat sweet, slightly sour pourable crema. Keep it refrigerated, and it will last for at least a month.

AVOCADO SALSA

Aperfect accompaniment to some of the potato cakes, tortillas, and *flautas* in the book, the avocado is a superfruit, chock-full of nutrients. The beauty of its buttery spread is its ability to soak up assertive-tasting ingredients such as chiles to produce that umami taste we all crave for a satisfying experience. MAKES ABOUT 2 CUPS

1 teaspoon cumin seeds

2 dried red chiles (such as cayenne or chile de árbol), stems discarded

½ teaspoon coarse sea or kosher salt

¼ cup finely chopped fresh cilantro leaves and tender stems

1 medium-size tomato, cored and finely chopped (no need to discard the seeds)

2 scallions, beards trimmed, green tops and white bulbs thinly sliced

Juice from 1 medium-size lime (about 2 tablespoons)

1 large ripe Hass avocado (about 8 ounces), cut into ¼-inch pieces (see Tater Tips, page 27)

1. Heat a small skillet to hot over medium-high heat. Sprinkle in the cumin seeds and chiles and toast them, shaking the pan regularly to ensure the seeds are evenly reddish brown and aromatic and the chiles blacken slightly, 1 to 2 minutes. Transfer the medley to a spice grinder, a clean coffee grinder, or a mortar and grind to the consistency of finely ground black pepper.

2. Transfer the spice blend to a medium-size bowl and add the salt, cilantro, tomato, scallions, lime juice, and avocado. Give it all a good stir. Refrigerate until you're ready to serve. I usually press a layer of plastic wrap directly on the salsa's surface to make sure there's an air-free seal; this prevents the avocado from oxidizing and turning black.

POTATO-STUFFED CHILES RELLENOS

SMASHED
BOILED
MASHED
RICED
FRIED
SHREDDED
ROASTED
BAKED

The *chiles rellenos* in Mexican restaurants often contain plenty of salty cheese filling in roasted poblanos that are dipped in an egg-flour batter and fried. Not that there is anything wrong with them—I do love a good dose of indulgence. But when you can execute a healthier rendition with creamy potatoes and an eggless batter, it allows you to enjoy them guilt-free. **SERVES 4**

1 pound russet or Yukon Gold potatoes

4 large cloves garlic, peeled

8 dried guajillo chiles (see Tater Tip)

2 cups boiling water

4 large poblano chiles (see Tater Tips, page 165)

¼ cup finely chopped fresh oregano leaves

2 tablespoons finely chopped fresh cilantro leaves and tender stems

2½ teaspoons coarse sea or kosher salt

1 teaspoon smoked paprika

2 tablespoons canola oil, plus extra for deep-frying

1 cup finely chopped onions

1 cup chickpea flour (see Tater Tips, page 164)

1. Peel the potatoes and cut them into quarters. Give them a good rinse under cold running water, place them in a medium-size saucepan, and cover them with cold water. Throw in the garlic cloves. Bring it to a boil over medium-high heat. Turn down the heat to medium-low, cover the pan,

TATER TIP

▲ Almost leathery in their dryness, blood-red guajillos are commonly available in Latin American groceries and in some supermarkets that stock a variety of chiles. Long, stout, and mild in heat, these are prized in Mexican kitchens for their musky flavor, low heat from capsaicin, and deep red color.

TATER TIPS

▲ The ability of chickpea flour to have that egg-like quality of binding is uncanny. Rich in fiber and proteins, it is available in the flour section of most moderately sized grocery stores. If the flour appears a bit clumped up—perhaps because it has been exposed to too much humidity or moisture—break up the clumps with a fork to return it to its powdery state. Or tap them through a fine-mesh sieve.

▲ If you wish to alter the chiles you use and don't mind the punch of capsaicin, by all means, try using a fresh jalapeño or two or a habanero. I still blister the skin in a dry skillet or even on a grill before mincing them. But don't turn on the grill just for this task. At the tail end of summer, when chiles are abundant at the farmers' market, I grill them all and freeze them in zip-top bags for later use.

and gently boil the potatoes and garlic until the potato pieces fall apart quite easily when pierced with a fork or knife, 15 to 20 minutes.

2. While the potatoes cook, place the guajillo chiles in a medium-size bowl and pour the boiling water over them. They will float at first because they are very light when dry, but as they absorb water and start to soften, they will sink. Allow them to soak for about 15 minutes.

3. Meanwhile, prepare the poblano chiles. Slit each from the stem end down, halfway through its length, without cutting through (make sure to leave the stem intact). You want to create a slit wide enough so you can reach in with your fingers and scoop out as much of the seeds and ribs as possible to fashion a cavity.

4. Once the potatoes are ready, scoop out 1 cup of the potato cooking water and set aside. Drain the potatoes and garlic in a colander and give it a good shake or two to get rid of excess water. Working in batches if necessary, transfer the potatoes and garlic to a ricer and press them through into a medium-size bowl. (If you don't have a ricer, use a potato

masher and fluff them with a fork when completely mashed.) Sprinkle in 2 tablespoons of the oregano, all the cilantro, and 1 teaspoon of the salt, and fold to incorporate them.

5. Fish out each guajillo from the soaking liquid (it should be tepid enough to handle the chiles) and yank out the stems. The stems will separate easily along with the ribs and some of the seeds. Discard these. Reserve the soaking liquid. Transfer the guajillos to a blender jar, sprinkle in the remaining 2 tablespoons oregano and the paprika, and pour in ½ cup of the soaking liquid. Set the jar aside.

6. Pour 2 tablespoons of oil into a medium-size skillet and heat it over medium-high heat. Once the oil appears to shimmer, add the onions and stir-fry them until they start to turn light brown around the edges, 3 to 5 minutes. Scrape the onions into the blender jar and add 1 teaspoon of the salt. Pour another ¾ cup of the guajillo soaking liquid into the onion skillet to dislodge any remaining bits.

7. Puree the guajillo-onion mélange to a smooth paste, scraping down the inside of the jar as needed. Stop the machine, pour in the liquid from the skillet, and give the blender another whirl. (If you were to pour that into the blender earlier, the total liquid in the jar would have been too much to create a smooth puree. Hence the addition in batches.)

8. Divide the potato filling into 4 equal portions and stuff 1 portion into each poblano cavity.

9. Combine the chickpea flour and the remaining ½ teaspoon salt in a medium-size bowl. Pour ½ cup of the potato cooking water over the flour and whisk it in, making sure that there are no lumps and that the batter is the consistency of thick pancake batter. If it is too thick, thin it a bit with a few more tablespoons of the reserved liquid.

10. Pour oil to a depth of 2 to 3 inches into a wok, Dutch oven, or medium-size saucepan. Heat the oil over medium heat until a candy or deep-frying thermometer inserted into the oil (without touching the pan bottom) registers 350°F.

11. Line a large plate or a cookie sheet with several layers of paper towels. Once the oil is hot, dunk a poblano into the batter, making sure it is completely coated. Gently slide it into the hot oil. Coat and add a second poblano to the oil. Deep-fry the poblanos, periodically turning them with tongs until they are reddish brown and crispy, 5 to 8 minutes. Transfer them from the oil to the paper towels to drain. Repeat with the remaining poblanos and batter.

12. To serve, ladle a few tablespoons of the guajillo sauce on each serving plate. Place a warm poblano on it and ladle a generous ½ cup of the sauce over the top. Serve right away.

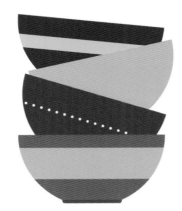

TATER TIP

▲ If you wish for a more tender poblano, first pan-fry them whole in a bit of oil in a large pan over medium-high heat, turning them occasionally, until they blister and become slightly soft to the touch but still firm, 5 to 8 minutes. Once they are cool, slit them as described in the recipe and proceed to stuff, batter, and deep-fry them.

SMALL PLATES & SIDE DISHES

The main course really doesn't always have to be the diva at the dinner table at home or in a restaurant. A meal composed of several sides, to my mind, makes for a much better experience than having one entree. In fact, as I noted in the intro to this book, when I go to restaurants, I usually check out the sides before I peruse the menu for the full plates.

If that appeals to you, too, try the Roasted Potatoes with Spinach Sauce, replete with aromatic spices and a bit of velvety cream. Enhance them with a stack of shredded purple Potato Tortillas speckled with chiles and cilantro. Or serve Potato-Habanero Biscuits piled high with a generous smear of butter to cut down on the heat from the habanero chiles. When dunked in the sauce that cloaks Patatas Bravas, dramatic as it sounds, they make me swoon.

Of course, the purpose of sides is to tastily set off the entree. When I go to my favorite hometown Chinese restaurant, I order a double side of Shredded Potatoes with Pepper and Chiles punctuated with a hint of rice vinegar. The chiles, blackened in oil, provide smoke and heat to the barely cooked potato shreds. I had to include my version here. The same with Ultimate Mashed Potatoes—riced potatoes, creamy and piled high, studded with coarse cracked black peppercorns and livened up with a shower of chives. A must at every holiday table! And yes, when I serve a burger, Ultimate French Fries, crispy on the outside, creamy on the inside, never fail to make me happy.

"Since I happen to have some cream and butter, I am just going to add them to my potatoes."

—*Julia Child, cookbook author and cooking teacher*

The World

ULTIMATE MASHED POTATOES

The secret to perfect mashed potatoes lies in the right floury potato (the russet), a potato ricer, and, of course, indulgent fats like cream and butter. Single-handedly the most comforting of foods (no wonder it was touted as an effective cure for hangovers), this cloud-soft fluff is the perfect bed for any and all kinds of herbs, spices, sauces, meats, and even vegetables. **SERVES 6**

2 pounds russet potatoes

½ cup heavy (whipping) cream

4 ounces cream cheese, cut into chunks

4 tablespoons (½ stick) salted butter

1½ teaspoons coarse sea or kosher salt

1½ teaspoons coarsely cracked black peppercorns

½ cup finely chopped fresh chives

1. Peel the potatoes and give them a good rinse under cold running water. Cut them into quarters, place them in a medium-size pan, and cover them with cold water. Bring to a boil over medium-high heat. Lower the heat, cover the pan, and gently boil the potatoes until they fall apart quite easily when pierced with a fork, 20 to 25 minutes.

2. While the potatoes cook, pour the cream into a small saucepan and add the cream cheese, butter, salt, and peppercorns. Simmer over medium heat, uncovered, whisking occasionally, until the

Add-Ins

MASHED POTATOES AROUND THE WORLD The cloud-soft texture of mashed russets is the perfect bed for a world of flavors. You may want to try any or all of these combinations.

▲ Swirl 2 tablespoons finely chopped fresh rosemary and 2 tablespoons finely chopped fresh mint leaves into the just-heated cream.

▲ Add ½ cup finely chopped fresh basil leaves just before you fold the liquid into the potatoes.

▲ As you boil the potatoes, add 3 or 4 large cloves of garlic and a small onion, coarsely chopped. Rice them all together for an earthy base.

(continued on next page)

▲ Toast 3 or 4 dried red chiles (such as chile de árbol; stems discarded and seeds left intact) and a tablespoon of coriander seeds in a tablespoon of oil in a small skillet over medium-high heat. Once the chiles blacken slightly and the coriander seeds are reddish brown, 2 to 3 minutes, transfer them, oil and all, to a mortar and pound the mix to an intoxicating but simple blend. Fold this into the cream as it simmers instead of the peppercorns.

▲ Toast a jalapeño or two over an open flame, holding them with tongs and turning them around to blister the skin on all sides. Discard the stems and add the chiles to the potatoes as they boil. Do not discard the seeds from the jalapeños; mashed potatoes are an excellent medium for modulating the heat of the capsaicin in the chiles. Rice the potatoes and chiles together for a pleasant green color and some smoky heat.

cream bubbles, the cheese softens and becomes smooth, and the butter melts, 5 to 8 minutes. Keep the cream warm over very low heat until the potatoes are done.

3. Drain the potatoes in a colander and give it a gentle shake to remove excess water. Return the potatoes to the pan. Dry them out over low heat until the surface appears dry, stirring occasionally so they don't stick to the bottom of the pan, about 1 minute.

4. Working in batches, if necessary, transfer the potatoes to a ricer and press them through into a serving bowl. (If you don't have a ricer, use a potato masher and fluff them very thoroughly with a fork when completely mashed.) Pour the pepper-speckled cream over the potatoes and sprinkle with the chives. Fold together with a spatula just until the liquid is incorporated. Don't overmix it.

5. Serve hot. A guaranteed crowd pleaser!

"New Hampshire polling data are unreliable because, when you call the Granite State's registered Republicans and independents in the middle of dinner and ask them who they're going to vote for, they have a mouth full of mashed potatoes and you can't understand what they say."

—*P. J. O'Rourke,
American journalist and
political satirist*

SMASHED
MASHED
BAKED
FRIED
SHREDDED
ROASTED
BOILED
RICED

Danish

BURNING LOVE

DANISH MASHED POTATOES
WITH ONIONS AND PORK BELLY

Growing up in Copenhagen, Mette Nielsen—now a remarkable food photographer settled in the Twin Cities of Minneapolis and St. Paul—was the pickiest of eaters. She did not care for potatoes at all, not even the freshly dug new potatoes from her parents' kitchen garden. This was a huge concern for her mother, Lizzi Nielsen, as potatoes played a part almost daily at the dinner table. Lizzi even took Mette to the doctor with this concern, as Mette was thin as a rail. The doctor, a rather portly man, looked her in the eye and said: "Mrs. Nielsen, do not worry. She will be fine. I do not eat potatoes either!"

Lizzi had grown up in the 1960s as a child of parents who were teenagers during the German occupation of Denmark in the Second World War. Because of food rationing, nothing went to waste in her childhood home. So she learned how to stretch any small amount of meat to make the most memorable dish. The portion sizes were small, but the food was substantial. There was one potato dish Mette liked, actually loved, and it was this one, her mother's mashed potatoes, the silkiest of mash, all done by hand with a whisk. A few slabs of darkly dense rye bread accompanied these potatoes, ensuring no desire for

TATER TIP

▲ It will initially appear you are stewing the onions since they are overcrowded, but as they start to cook down and the liquid evaporates, the sugars will start to release a bit. Let the onions color lightly. You want to reach the stage called *bløde løg* in Danish ("soft onions"). All this takes a while, so patience is a good virtue.

dessert. Rich-tasting (with the inclusion of pork belly and butter), sweet, and fluffy, this dish is great any time of the day. SERVES 6

2 pounds russet or Yukon Gold potatoes

6 tablespoons (¾ stick) salted butter

2 large yellow or white onions, cut in half lengthwise and thinly sliced

1 pound rind-on pork belly

1 cup whole milk

1½ teaspoons coarse sea or kosher salt

1 teaspoon coarsely cracked black peppercorns

1. Peel the potatoes, cut them into quarters, and give them a good rinse under cold running water. Place them in a medium-size saucepan and cover with cold water. Add 2 tablespoons of the butter. Bring it to a boil over medium-high heat. Lower the heat, cover the pan, and gently boil the potatoes until the pieces fall apart quite easily when pierced with a fork, 20 to 25 minutes. Remove the pan from the heat and leave the potatoes in the water.

2. While the potatoes cook, melt the remaining 4 tablespoons of butter in a large skillet over medium heat. Once the foam subsides, add the onions and cook, uncovered, stirring occasionally, until they turn a light caramel color, 20 to 25 minutes. Remove the pan from the heat.

3. As the potatoes and onions cook, cut the pork belly lengthwise into ½-inch-thick slices. Working in batches if necessary so there's no crowding, lay them out in a single layer in another large skillet. Cook the slices over medium heat, turning them occasionally to ensure even browning and slight crispiness, 15 to 20 minutes. Remove them from the pan with tongs and stack them on a plate. Drain off the fat and set it aside. Cook the remaining slices. Add them to the stack and add the fat to the already reserved fat.

4. Bring the milk to a boil in a small saucepan over medium-high heat. Stir in the salt and peppercorns. Remove the pan from the heat.

5. Drain the potatoes in a colander. Return them to the saucepan. Dry them out over medium heat, stirring occasionally so they don't stick to the bottom of the pan, until the surface appears dry, 1 to 2 minutes. Working in batches if necessary, transfer the potatoes to a ricer and press them through into a large serving bowl. (If you don't have a ricer, use a potato masher and fluff them with a fork when completely mashed.) Pour the hot milk over the potatoes. If you wish, add up to ¼ cup of the reserved pork fat. Fold everything together until just mixed. Spoon the onions over the potatoes and top with the pork belly slices. Or cut the slices into smaller pieces and place them over the top.

6. Serve right away. Make sure you spoon through all the layers for each serving.

BOILED
SMASHED
RICED
BAKED
MASHED
SHREDDED
ROASTED
FRIED

European

VEGETABLE-FILLED
POTATO
KNISHES

Sandra Mandel, the mother of my friend Dr. Jeff Mandel, rarely made potato knishes, since she found them to be too bland and simple, a tasteless memory from her childhood days. Home cooking was an important daily ritual and everything, even simple weekday meals, was fashioned from the best raw ingredients. Weekend meals and family gatherings warranted special dishes that took effort and brought comfort to body and soul. Jeff wanted to doctor up the knish of his mother's childhood and punctuate it with fresh herbs and aromatic spices, ingredients that populate his own refrigerator and pantry. This lively rendition is an homage that brings comfort to Sandra, who now loves its inclusion at any family dinner. **SERVES 6**

1 pound russet or Yukon Gold potatoes

1 small yellow onion, coarsely chopped

2 large cloves garlic, coarsely chopped

1 stick (3 inches) cinnamon

4 whole cloves

1½ teaspoons coarse sea or kosher salt

½ teaspoon freshly grated nutmeg

1½ teaspoons coarsely cracked black peppercorns

2 tablespoons canola oil, plus extra for brushing

2 large carrots or parsnips, peeled, ends trimmed, finely chopped

½ cup finely chopped fresh dill

4 phyllo sheets (18-by-14-inch), thawed

1. Peel the potatoes and give them a good rinse under cold running water. Cut them into quarters. Place them in a small saucepan, add the onion, garlic, cinnamon, and cloves, and cover everything with cold water. Bring to a boil over medium-high heat. Partially cover the pan, lower the heat to medium, and boil the potatoes until the pieces are fall-apart tender when pierced with a fork or knife, 10 to 12 minutes.

2. As the potatoes cook, position a rack in the lower third of the oven and preheat the oven to 375°F. Line a cookie sheet with parchment paper or grease it lightly with oil.

3. Once the potatoes (and onion and garlic) are tender, drain them in a colander and give them a good shake or two to get rid of excess water. Fish out and discard the cinnamon stick and whole cloves. Transfer everything back to the pan. Dry out the vegetables over medium-low heat, stirring occasionally so they don't stick to the bottom of the pan.

4. Working in batches if necessary, transfer everything to a ricer and press into a medium-size bowl. (If you don't have a ricer, use a potato masher and fluff with a fork when completely mashed.) Fold in 1 teaspoon of the salt, nutmeg, and peppercorns.

5. Heat the oil in a medium-size skillet. Once the oil appears to shimmer, add the carrots and stir-fry them until they are tender but still crisp, 3 to 5 minutes. Stir in the remaining ½ teaspoon of salt and the dill. Remove the pan from the heat.

6. Gently place a sheet of the phyllo on a clean counter or a cutting board with the wider end toward you. Brush the pastry with oil. Place a second sheet on top of the first sheet and brush with oil. Repeat twice more with the remaining two sheets, brushing each sheet with oil. Spread half of the mashed potatoes along the lower third of the stacked sheets as close to the edges as you can. Spoon on and spread out the dilled carrots over this bed. Top them off with the remaining mashed potatoes. Shape the filling into a somewhat cohesive log. Lift the edge of the pastry closest to you and roll up everything tightly into a log. Transfer this log to the prepared cookie sheet and brush the whole surface with oil, rolling it over as necessary. You want to end up with the seam on the bottom. Tuck in the ends of the phyllo.

7. Bake the log until the crust is flaky, sunny brown, and crispy, 30 to 40 minutes.

8. Gently transfer the log to a wire rack and allow it to sit until it's cool enough to handle, about 15 minutes. Transfer it to a cutting board and slice it into 6 knishes. Serve warm.

ULTIMATE FRENCH FRIES

While the Incas invented many techniques for preparing potatoes, frying was not one of them. They either baked or boiled or made flour from them. Until after the arrival of the Europeans, the New World had no cooking oil. But in Europe, with lard and olive oil, frying was a common mode of cooking.

Fried potato recipes began to evolve around the late 1700s and early 1800s. Fritters, pancakes, latkes, hash browns, home fries, and rosti were made under various names around the world. Cottage and home fries became breakfast fare, but deep-frying was mastered in France (Belgians would beg to differ) during the late eighteenth century and the resulting dish was called *pommes de terre frites*, *pommes frites*, or *pomfrits*. In *Potato: A Global History*, author Andrew Smith notes that in 1801 President Thomas Jefferson brought a French chef to the White House and made a note of a recipe for *pommes de terre frites à cru, en petites tranches* (raw potatoes cut into small strips and fried).

What makes mine Ultimate? The proper technique of cutting the potatoes into the right width, the double frying method (the

For Serving

There are so many ways you can serve fries.

▲ I often sprinkle fries with finely chopped fresh herbs, a burst of citrus zest, and a pinch of cayenne pepper.

▲ Any sauce is fair game, including good-quality ketchup, mustard, or just malt vinegar.

▲ For a change of pace, serve them with the Creamy Jalapeño Sauce (page 133) or the Black Bean-Queso Dip (page 179).

▲ Try a homemade buffalo sauce: Combine 1 cup vinegar-based bottled hot sauce (such as Frank's) with 1 tablespoon white distilled vinegar and a few dashes of Worcestershire sauce in a small saucepan. Heat it over medium heat. Once it starts to simmer, add 2 tablespoons cold butter and whisk to create a quick little emulsion. Toss a batch of the fries with the buffalo sauce as soon as they come off the fryer. Serve as is or topped with crumbled blue cheese.

▲ Serve poutine as they do in Québecois Canada: with a light brown gravy and cheese curds.

second frying after being dusted with cornstarch), and the perfect temperatures during both frying stages deliver the crispy-on-the-outside and tender-on-the-inside fry. SERVES 4

1 pound large russet potatoes

Canola oil, for deep-frying

1 tablespoon cornstarch

Coarse sea or kosher salt, for sprinkling

Coarsely cracked black peppercorns, for sprinkling (optional)

1. Fill a large bowl with cold water. Scrub the potatoes well under cold running water. Peeling them or leaving the skin on is a personal preference. (I love them both ways but then I love potatoes every way, so that really should not surprise you.) Slice the potatoes lengthwise into ¼-inch-thick planks. Stack a few planks and cut them lengthwise into ⅛- to ¼-inch-wide fingers. (Alternatively, you can use a mandoline with its french-fry blade in place or the french-fry disk on a food processor.) Submerge the cut potatoes immediately in the bowl of water to prevent them from discoloring and to rid them of excess surface starch.

2. As the potatoes soak, pour oil to a depth of 2 to 3 inches

into a wok, Dutch oven, or large saucepan. Heat the oil over medium heat until a candy or deep-frying thermometer inserted into the oil (without touching the pan bottom) registers 325°F. (I cannot emphasize too much the importance of a thermometer if you wish to make perfect fries.) Line a cookie sheet with several layers of paper towels and set a wire rack on top, for draining the partially cooked potatoes of excess oil.

3. Lay out a clean cotton kitchen towel or several layers of paper towels on the counter, for drying the potatoes. Drain the potatoes in a colander and rinse them a bit under cold running water. Give the colander a good shake or two to rid the potatoes of excess water. Spread out the potatoes on the towel and dry them well.

4. Divide the potatoes into 4 equal portions. Drop a portion gently into the oil. You will notice the temperature dip down 30°F or so. Allow the potatoes to cook at that temperature, stirring a couple of times, until they appear a bit soft and pale brown, about 5 minutes. Do not let them sit any longer in the oil. Lift them out with a slotted spoon and transfer them to the rack to drain. Return the oil to 325°F and repeat with the

"Some people are chocolate and sweets people. I love French fries. That and caviar."
—*Cameron Diaz, actress*

THE STORY OF FROZEN FRENCH FRIES

They are an important piece of our history, since they're eaten throughout the world. Manufacturing frozen french fries for mass production was a concept introduced by the J. R. Simplot Company in the 1940s. Twenty years later, Ray Kroc of McDonald's fame contracted the company to produce frozen fries for all their outlets, replacing the fresh-cut ones McDonald's shops were used to serving. A need for uniformity and quality took over and the decision stuck.

The year 1957 heralded the entry of two brothers into the world of frozen potatoes. Their company, McCain Foods in Florenceville, New Brunswick, Canada, was a family-run business with ancestral roots deeply embedded in potato farming. A vision to see growth in frozen french fries pushed them to expand from their inaugural plant across the Atlantic to the United Kingdom, followed by the United States, Australia, France, and eventually the rest of the world.

Allison McCain stood next to me in his kitchen in Florenceville, peeling potatoes as I busied myself getting the spinach-scallion stuffing spiced for the potato cakes (my adaptation is on page 57) I planned to serve to his family and guests. Shepherding the current company as its unpretentious, quiet, and deeply introspective chairman, he shared with me his family's commitment to the french fry business and their foray into diverse product lines. Deeply appreciative of their humble beginnings, he chose to return to live in Florenceville with his wife, Clare, and his son, Brian, after years abroad.

Brian, the voice of the future, works as the night shift manager, learning the ropes from the ground up. He handed me a hard hat and goggles as he guided me through one of their main plants in town, walking me through the receiving of perfectly sized potatoes from nearby farms. The just-unearthed potatoes went through a scrubbing cycle followed by a deep steam and quick ice shock to rid them of their jackets in one easy move. Precision cuts, a hot-water poach, an initial lower-temperature fry in hot oil, followed with an immediate freeze, produce the perfectly frozen french fry, packed and shipped to all corners of the world. McCain products can be found in thousands of restaurants and supermarket freezers in more than 160 countries. One in every three french fries in the world is a McCain fry.

remaining potatoes. When you're done, turn off the heat.

5. Once the potatoes have all had a chance to drip excess oil, transfer them to a medium-size bowl and sprinkle the cornstarch over them, snow-like. Toss to coat the potatoes well with the starch. Remove the paper towels from the cookie sheet and give it a wipe to clear off any remaining oil. Transfer the potatoes back to the cookie sheet, spread them out in a single layer, and place them in the freezer to chill for about 10 minutes. (You can let them freeze at this point. Once frozen, move them to a zip-top bag. They'll keep, frozen, for up to a month.)

6. When you are ready to eat, line a medium-size bowl with several layers of paper towels. Crank up the heat under the oil (the same oil if you're continuing right away, fresh oil if you had frozen the potatoes) until the thermometer registers 400°F. Carefully drop one-quarter of the chilled (or frozen) fries into the oil. The temperature will drop to around 375°F. Make sure the heat under the pan is adjusted to maintain this temperature. As soon as the fries are caramel brown and crispy, 2 to 3 minutes, fish them out of the hot oil with a slotted spoon and drop them into the paper towel-lined bowl. Toss them gently to remove excess oil. Sprinkle the salt and peppercorns, if desired, over them, and toss again. Repeat frying, draining, sprinkling, and serving the remaining potatoes in 3 more batches.

TATER TIP

▲ No, do not wait to serve the fries until all of them are fried. They are best devoured as soon as you sprinkle them with salt and pepper. Have any dips or condiments at the ready.

BLACK BEAN-QUESO DIP

I have always been a fan of textural differences within any recipe. *Queso fundido*, creamy molten cheese, often houses little morsels of sautéed peppers and onion with a wisp of heat from chiles. But this version folds in black beans and tomatoes for a deeper contrast not only of texture, but of color as well. The habanero breathes fire, and also perfumes the creamy concoction for one addictive dip. Serve the dip warm and bubbly with a heaping portion of Ultimate French Fries or Potato Tortillas (page 216). MAKES 4 CUPS

2 tablespoons canola oil

1 cup finely chopped red onion
(about 2 onions)

3 large cloves garlic, finely chopped

1 teaspoon cumin seeds, ground

½ teaspoon coarse sea or kosher salt

1 can (15 ounces) black beans,
drained and rinsed

1 package (8 ounces) cream cheese

1 habanero chile, stem discarded,
finely chopped (do not remove
the seeds)

1 cup shredded cheese
(I use a packaged mix)

¼ cup finely chopped fresh cilantro
leaves and tender stems

1 medium-size tomato, cored and
finely chopped (no need to
discard the seeds)

1. Heat the oil in a medium-size saucepan over medium-high heat. Once the oil appears to shimmer, add the onion and garlic and stir-fry until the edges are light brown and the raw smell dissipates, 3 to 5 minutes.

2. Stir in the cumin and salt. The heat of the pan's contents is just right to cook the spice without burning it, about 10 seconds. Add the black beans, cream cheese, and chile and cook, stirring occasionally, to soften the cheese, 3 to 5 minutes.

3. Stir in 1 cup of water. The result will appear curdled and slightly unruly. The water will quickly come to a boil. Cook the queso, stirring occasionally, until the sauce appears smooth and curdle-free, 3 to 5 minutes.

4. Stir in the shredded cheese, cilantro, and tomato. As soon as the cheese melts, remove from the heat and serve.

Chinese

KUNG PAO POTATOES

Around the early 1600s, the Dutch introduced the potato to China, where it was referred to as "earth bean," "ground nut," or "tuber with many children." It wasn't until the mid-1980s that the Chinese government made concerted efforts to increase crop production; now China is the world's biggest producer of potatoes. All this still comes as a surprise to Guanghe Luo, a 61-year-old immigrant to Minnesota, via California, from the southwestern city of Chengdu in Sichuan province. Growing up there, he and his family never ate much of the tuber at home as it was very much considered poor man's food. Even as a trained master chef and successful restaurateur in China, potatoes never played a role in his culinary offerings. But now he finds unique ways to serve them, including this rendition that he whipped up for me in his busy restaurant kitchen. Each bite of the dish was a perfect balance of crunch, heat, salty soy, and nutty peanuts. SERVES 6

TATER TIP

▲ The number of chiles may sound alarming, but keep in mind they are left whole. The heat will be wispy but the smokiness from having been blackened in oil will provide an essential dimension to the potatoes.

1½ pounds russet potatoes

Canola oil, for deep-frying

½ cup cornstarch

½ cup blanched raw peanuts

12 to 16 whole dried red chiles (such as chile de árbol or chile japones; see Tater Tip)

8 slices fresh ginger (each about the size and thickness of a quarter; no need to peel first), cut into thin shreds

¼ cup soy sauce

2 tablespoons rice vinegar

2 teaspoons unrefined granulated sugar, such as Sugar in the Raw

2 teaspoons toasted sesame oil

½ cup finely chopped fresh chives

1. Fill a medium-size bowl with cold water. Peel the potatoes. Slice them into ½-inch-thick planks. Stack a few planks at a time and cut them into ½-inch-wide strips, just as you would for french fries. (A mandoline or food processor with the appropriate slicing attachment works great.) Submerge the potatoes in the bowl of water to rinse off surface starch and to prevent them from discoloring.

2. Pour oil to a depth of 2 to 3 inches into a wok, Dutch oven, or large saucepan. Heat the oil over medium heat until a candy or deep-frying thermometer inserted into the oil (without touching the pan bottom) registers 350°F (see Tater Tips, page 18).

3. When the oil is almost hot enough, line a cookie sheet with several layers of paper towels. Drain the potatoes in a colander and give the colander a good shake to rid the potatoes of excess water. (A little water clinging to the strips is just fine.) Wipe out most of the water from the bowl and return the potatoes to it. Add the cornstarch and toss to completely cloak the potato strips with the starch.

4. Once the oil is ready, gently drop about one fourth of the potato strips into the hot oil. Fry, turning them occasionally with a slotted spoon, until they are caramel brown and crisp all over, about 5 minutes. Remove them with the spoon and spread them on the paper towels to drain. Repeat until all the potatoes have been fried and drained. You may need to adjust the heat to maintain the oil's temperature at 350°F.

5. Heat a wok or large skillet over medium-high heat. Remove 2 tablespoons of the hot oil used for deep-frying and add it to the wok. The oil will instantly appear to shimmer. Add the peanuts, chiles, and ginger and stir-fry them until the peanuts turn sunny brown, the chiles blacken, and the ginger is a light caramel color and smells fragrant, 1 to 2 minutes.

6. Pour in the soy sauce, vinegar, and sugar, all of which will bubble immediately. Add the fried potatoes and toss well to coat. The sauce will cling to the potatoes, thanks to the cornstarch. After a minute, when the potatoes are warm again, stir in the sesame oil and chives. Serve immediately.

TATER TIP

▲ If you plan to stir-fry the final dish right after the potatoes are fried, the potatoes will retain a crispy texture. If you plan on doing it later, refrigerate them in a sealed zip-top bag. A 2-minute dunk in the oil used for deep-frying heated to 350°F will re-crisp the potatoes before you stir-fry them.

SMASHED
MASHED
BAKED
BOILED
FRIED
SHREDDED
ROASTED
RICED

TATER TIP

Australian

POTATO GRATIN

WITH VANILLA CARAMELIZED ONIONS

Potatoes arrived in Australia with the early European settlers during the late 1700s. Never really a huge culinary influence, potatoes are now grown all over Australia with the exception of the far northern areas, where temperatures exceed the optimum growing conditions for potatoes.

This melt-in-your-mouth gratin, with layers of root vegetables from two different families (potatoes from the nightshade clan and sweet potatoes from the morning glory fraternity), cheese, and vanilla-seasoned caramelized onions, is an adaptation of a recipe from colleague Natasha MacAller, who authored the beautiful *Vanilla Table: The Essence of Exquisite Cooking from the World's Best Chefs*. Natasha is a former professional dancer who's now a chef, and her ballet with vanilla and caramelized onion in this gratin is nothing short of genius. She divides her time between Australia and the US, and this recipe is a favorite. The kumara, a variety of New Zealand sweet potato used in the original recipe, has a delicate balance of potato and sweet potato in its sweetness and flavor. Because it can be difficult to find in North America, here is my variation that includes the two varieties as an alternative.

Serve this gratin hot out of the oven, as Natasha recommends, as an accompaniment to roast chicken or a grilled pork chop. SERVES 4

8 ounces Yukon Gold potatoes

8 ounces sweet potatoes (preferably Japanese or Stoke's purple)

1 small vanilla bean (see Tater Tip, facing page)

4 tablespoons (½ stick) salted butter, plus extra for greasing the ramekins

2 large onions, cut in half lengthwise and thinly sliced

4 ounces freshly shredded Parmigiano-Reggiano cheese

4 ounces freshly shredded Gouda cheese

Coarse sea or kosher salt, for sprinkling

Coarsely cracked black peppercorns, for sprinkling

1 cup heavy (whipping) cream

1. Fill a medium-size bowl with cold water. Peel the potatoes and sweet potatoes and give them a good rinse under cold running water. Cut them lengthwise into ⅛-inch-thick planks with a mandoline or chef's knife. Submerge them in the bowl of water to prevent them from discoloring. Lay out a clean cotton kitchen towel or several layers of paper towels on the counter, for drying the potatoes.

2. Split the vanilla bean in half lengthwise.

3. Melt the butter in a Dutch oven over medium heat. Once the foam subsides, add the onions. Scrape the vanilla bean seeds into the onions, then drop in the pod. Cook them, uncovered, stirring occasionally, until the onions are a deep caramel brown and the vanilla aroma is intensely profound, 20 to 25 minutes. Fish out and discard the vanilla bean pod.

4. As the onions brown, position a rack in the center of the oven and preheat the oven to 350°F. Grease the insides of 4 medium-size ramekins (each should hold 8 to 10 ounces) with some butter and set them on a cookie sheet.

5. Once the onions are ready, drain the potatoes in a colander and give them a good rinse to get rid of any excess surface starch. Give the colander a good shake or two to rid all the potatoes of excess water. Spread the potatoes on the towel and dry them well.

6. Combine the two cheeses in a medium-size bowl. Make 2 overlapping circles—one on top of the other—of Yukon Gold potatoes and sweet potatoes in each ramekin. Sprinkle with a bit of salt and peppercorns. Spread the potatoes with some of the caramelized onions, then sprinkle on some of the cheese mixture. Repeat layering until all the Yukon Golds, sweet potatoes, onions, and cheeses have been used up. Make sure you end with a top layer of cheese.

7. Drizzle ¼ cup of the cream on top of each gratin and let it bathe the gratin, seep down, and pool at the bottom of the ramekin.

8. Bake the gratins on the cookie sheet until the cheese is bubbly, the top is caramel brown, and the potato slices are tender when pierced with a knife, about 1 hour.

9. Transfer the gratins to a wire rack to cool and set for about 15 minutes. Serve warm.

SMASHED
MASHED
BOILED
FRIED
SHREDDED
ROASTED
BAKED
RICED

French

CHEESY POTATO GRATIN
WITH ROSEMARY

To witness the French work with *pommes de terre* ("apples of the earth") is downright enchanting. They have raised the bar in creating such iconic pièces de résistance as potato galettes, potatoes Anna, vichyssoise, and even the ubiquitous hash browns. This gratin, fashioned with layers of thinly sliced potatoes and an herbaceous cream sauce with an abundance of cheese, is an excellent accompaniment to a piece of simply grilled fish or even a robust steak au poivre. **SERVES 6**

8 tablespoons (1 stick) salted butter, chilled

2 pounds potatoes (a mix of russets, purple, and red)

1¼ cups heavy (whipping) cream

¼ cup finely chopped fresh rosemary leaves (see Tater Tip, facing page)

2 tablespoons finely chopped fresh thyme leaves

1 teaspoon coarsely cracked black peppercorns

½ teaspoon coarse sea or kosher salt

2 cups shredded cheese (such as Gruyère, mozzarella, sharp cheddar, Havarti, or a blend)

1. Preheat the oven to 375°F. Grease the inside of a 10½-inch cast-iron skillet or a round 10-by-2-inch baking dish with a little of the butter. Slice the remaining butter into small pieces and keep them chilled as you prepare the gratin.

2. Fill a large bowl with cold water. Lay out a clean cotton kitchen towel or several layers of paper towels on the counter, for drying the potatoes. Scrub and rinse the potatoes well under cold running water. Slice them lengthwise with a chef's knife or mandoline into long planks, about ⅛ inch thick. Submerge them in the bowl of water to prevent them from discoloring.

3. Bring the cream, rosemary, and thyme to a simmer in a small saucepan over medium heat. Once the cream is hot, 2 to 3 minutes, remove it from the heat.

4. Drain the potatoes in a colander and give the colander a good shake or two to rid the potatoes of excess water. (You don't want to dilute the cream later.) Spread the potatoes on the kitchen towel and dry them well.

5. Arrange a layer using one quarter of the potato planks to cover the bottom of the prepared pan, slightly overlapping them. Sprinkle the potatoes with one quarter each of the peppercorns and salt. Pour one third of the herbed cream over this. Sprinkle one third of the shredded cheese over the cream. Repeat with another layer of the potatoes, peppercorns, salt, and half of the remaining cream and cheese. Top with a third layer of potatoes, peppercorns, salt, the remaining cream, and the final portion of cheese. Arrange the remaining potato slices on top of this and sprinkle the remaining peppercorns and salt over them. Scatter the butter pieces on top and cover the pan with aluminum foil.

6. Place the pan on a cookie sheet and bake until the sauce is bubbly, the potatoes on top are blistered and brown, and the interior potatoes are tender when you pierce the layers with a knife or fork, about 1 hour.

7. Allow the gratin to cool a bit before you slice it and serve. I usually cut it into wedges, like pizza slices.

TATER TIP

▲ It's easy to strip the leaves off a rosemary twig. Hold the stem in one hand. With the fingers of the other, slide them top down, in the opposite direction of the leaves. The leaves not only come off easily but the scent of rosemary oil perfumes your fingers for hours.

BAKED
SMASHED
MASHED
BOILED
FRIED
SHREDDED
ROASTED
RICED

"To me
[potatoes]
are glamorous,
unique, and
special;
an aristocrat
among
vegetables."

—James Beard,
chef, author, and teacher

French

POMMES DE TERRE ANNA

WITH CARDAMOM & NUTMEG

Napoleon III's chef created this dish for one of Napoleon's beloveds. Although each layer is drenched with butter, the natural starchiness of the thinly sliced potatoes holds them all together in a cohesive pie, crispy on the outside and creamy-tender within. A wedge, rich beyond words, is great as a side to any meat or vegetable protein. My rendition flavors the butter with two aromatic spices: cardamom and nutmeg. **SERVES 6**

8 tablespoons (1 stick)
   salted butter, melted

1½ teaspoons flaky salt
   (such as fleur de sel)

1 teaspoon coarsely cracked
   black peppercorns

½ teaspoon freshly grated nutmeg

½ teaspoon cardamom seeds,
   ground (see Tater Tips, page 194)

3 pounds russet potatoes

1. Preheat the oven to 450°F. Grease the inside of a 10½-inch cast-iron skillet, round baking pan, or tart pan with a removable bottom with a little of the butter.

2. Make the spice blend by combining the salt, peppercorns, nutmeg, and cardamom in a small bowl.

3. Peel the potatoes and rinse them well under cold running water. Cut them lengthwise into ⅛-inch-thick planks with a mandoline or chef's knife. Working quickly so the potatoes do not oxidize and discolor, arrange a layer of one quarter of the planks in concentric circles, slightly overlapping them to cover the bottom of the pan. Liberally brush the potatoes with melted butter and sprinkle with one quarter of the spice blend. Repeat with another layer of the potatoes, going the opposite direction from the first circle (just to make it look pretty), brush again with butter, and follow with another sprinkle of the spice blend. Repeat twice more, using up the potatoes, butter, and spice blend. Loosely cover the pan with aluminum foil.

4. Place the skillet on a cookie sheet and bake to partially cook the potatoes with steam trapped within, about 30 minutes.

5. Remove the foil and bake until the potatoes are tender when you pierce the layers with a knife or fork and the top layer looks crusty and brown, about 45 minutes.

6. Allow the spiced Ms. Anna to cool off a bit before you slice it and serve. I usually cut it into wedges.

TATER TIP

▲ The starch that clings to the surface is essential to hold things together as the dish bakes. So do not soak the potatoes, as you normally would to prevent discoloration. Of course, in this case you need to work quickly and start assembling the layered dish as soon as you slice the potatoes.

PRESCRIBING POTATOES

The French populace couldn't be bothered with the common tater even during the earlier part of the eighteenth century. The potato owes its current popularity in France to the single-handed efforts of a pharmacist, Antoine-Augustin Parmentier, who was personally convinced of the nutritional value of the potato because he experienced its life-sustaining effects as a prisoner of war over a period of five years. When the grain harvest failed in France in 1769, he wrote a treatise on potatoes. He won the attention, years later, of Benjamin Franklin, who commissioned him to create a multiple-course dinner, all with potatoes. As the unofficial publicist of potatoes, one of Parmentier's brilliant ways to convince the peasantry to grow potatoes to feed their families—as opposed to their livestock—was to grow potatoes in fenced patches guarded by the soldiers 24 hours a day. The perception that the soldiers were guarding something valuable was intriguing enough for people to steal and plant the potatoes in their own gardens. (Of course, with no ramifications for the theft.) Soon the tuber took root in the community. When he assumed power, Napoleon awarded Parmentier the Legion of Honor.

The origin of the word *pothole* refers to the shallow space in the dirt floor of an Irish cottage where a pot of potatoes was placed for mashing.

Irish

IRISH
COLCANNON

No other country in the world was more deeply affected by the potato blight in the mid-nineteenth century than Ireland. The potato famine ended in 1851 when the Irish farmers discovered potato varieties that were more blight resistant—but by then and for years to come, many Irish emigrated to other countries. By 1900 the population of Ireland was just 4 million, half the number that it was in 1841.

The lucky folks who had milk, cream, or butter added them, along with assorted vegetables, to create variety in their pots of boiled potatoes. This more modern rendition of the Irish classic (also called bubble and squeak by the British because of the noises the ingredients make while cooking) includes kale in addition to cabbage, and is my tribute to the memory of those who perished during the famine. I find this a far more substantive side than a simple bowl of mashed potatoes (not that there is anything wrong with that!). SERVES 8

1 pound assorted fingerling potatoes (red, purple, and white) or Yukon Gold potatoes

2 or 4 tablespoons salted butter

12 ounces green cabbage, shredded (2 cups)

8 ounces kale, tough stems discarded, leaves finely chopped (2 cups)

1 cup half-and-half

4 ounces soft creamy cheese (such as Boursin, plain or flavored)

1 teaspoon coarse sea or kosher salt

1 teaspoon coarsely cracked black peppercorns

½ teaspoon freshly grated nutmeg

1. Scrub the potatoes well under cold running water. Cut them into quarters and place them in a medium-size saucepan and cover with cold water. Bring to a boil over medium-high heat. Lower the heat to medium, cover the pan, and boil the potatoes until they are fall-apart tender, 15 to 20 minutes.

2. As the potatoes cook, melt 2 tablespoons of butter in a large skillet over medium-high heat. Once the foam subsides, pile in the cabbage and kale, cover the pan, and allow them to wilt, stirring occasionally, 5 to 7 minutes.

3. Pour in the half-and-half and add the cheese, salt, peppercorns, and nutmeg. Give it all a good stir and re-cover the pan. Allow the cheese to melt, stirring the contents occasionally, about 5 minutes.

4. Once the potatoes are tender, drain them in a colander. Give the colander a good shake or two to rid the potatoes of excess water. Transfer the potatoes to a large bowl. Mash them with a potato masher. Stir in the cheesy cabbage and kale medley. Dollop the colcannon with an extra 2 tablespoons of butter, if you like, and let it melt and pool on the bumpy surface. Serve hot.

TATER TIP

▲ I like using a variety of potatoes for color and flavor in many of my potato dishes. Against a backdrop of cabbage and kale, they make an especially pretty picture.

TATER TIP

▲ You want the bottoms of the Hasselback Potatoes to stay whole to support the fanning of the slices as they roast. If it's hard for you to slice the potato because it is rocky, slice a small, thin section off the bottom so you have a stable base. This will help you cut more evenly without worrying about the potato moving. Placing a chopstick on either side of the potato before you slice it also prevents you from cutting through (the knife will be stopped by the chopsticks before you cut completely through).

Swedish

HASSELBACK POTATOES
WITH CARDAMOM BUTTER

Created in the eighteenth century by a chef at the Swedish restaurant Hasselbacken, this accordion display of the common potato is perfumed with cardamom (a spice often incorporated in Christmas fare in Sweden) in my take on the classic. Crispy on the outside with a crackly pork-like skin, the creamy insides make for a delectable contrast in textures. SERVES 4

4 large russet or Yellow Finn
    potatoes (each ¾ to 1 pound)

4 tablespoons (½ stick) salted butter,
    at room temperature

4 bay leaves (optional)

4 large cloves garlic, finely chopped

8 green or white cardamom pods,
    smashed (see Tater Tips,
    page 194)

2 tablespoons finely chopped fresh
    lemon thyme (see Tater Tips,
    page 194)

1 teaspoon coarse sea or kosher salt

1 teaspoon coarsely cracked black
    peppercorns

1. Position a rack in the lower half of the oven and preheat the oven to 375°F. Line a baking pan or pie plate with parchment paper if you don't want to deal with any cleanup mess.

2. Scrub the potatoes well under cold running water. Wipe them dry with paper towels. Slice each potato crosswise into ¼-inch-thick slices, making sure you do not cut through the bottom (see Tater Tip). You want all the slices to stay attached. Grease the potatoes all over with a bit of the butter and place them in the baking pan. Slip a bay leaf between 2 of the slices in each of the potatoes, if desired.

TATER TIPS

▲ Green or white cardamom pods are available in the spice aisle of any supermarket. Considered the second most expensive spice (after saffron), they are a close sibling to the ginger and turmeric plant family. To release some of the seeds and their essential oils, place a pod on the cutting board, and with the blade of the knife resting flat on it, whack the knife to smash open the pod. The black seeds within are much more potent than the exterior pod, and if you wish for a more intense cardamom presence in the potatoes, remove the seeds from the pod (discarding the pod) and grind them in a mortar. A "wow" will escape your lips as you are drawn into the earthy allure. You will also realize you should never again purchase relatively insipid-smelling preground cardamom.

▲ Lemon thyme is a common herb, found in the produce section of the supermarket. If all you find are regular thyme sprigs, use those and add the zest of a small lemon to the chopped herb.

3. Roast the potatoes until the slices open out a bit, exposing more of the potato flesh, about 20 minutes.

4. As the potatoes roast, melt the remaining butter in a small skillet over medium heat. Once the butter foams, add the garlic and cardamom. Allow the two to flavor the butter with their pungent and sweet presence, 1 to 2 minutes. Remove the pan from the heat and sprinkle in the thyme, salt, and peppercorns. Give it all a good stir.

5. Once the potatoes have opened up a bit after the initial roast, brush them liberally with the spiced butter. Continue to roast the potatoes, brushing and basting them periodically, until the potato slices fan out and the insides are tender when pierced with a knife, an additional 45 to 50 minutes. Make sure to use up all the butter.

6. Serve the potatoes while they are still hot.

BOILED
SMASHED
MASHED
BAKED
SHREDDED
FRIED
ROASTED
RICED

Spanish

PATATAS BRAVAS

In the early 1930s in Spain, *patatas bravas*, wedges of roasted potatoes drenched in a hot chile sauce punctuated with garlic, onion, and vinegar, was concocted at Las Bravas restaurant in Madrid. Now tapas joints all across the world plate up this classic, and this version, with its multicolor fingerling potatoes, delivers the same assertive flavors.

I love serving these potatoes as an accompaniment to a simply grilled, herb-brushed Pacific halibut. For a tapas-like meal, make it a tater-love day and offer small plates of Spinach-Stuffed Potato Cakes (page 57), Mojito Potato-Pomegranate Salad (page 87), and wedges of Potato Leek Pie (page 131). SERVES 4

Around 1532, Pedro Cieza de Leon, a Spanish conquistador known for chronicling the history of Peru, came upon the Peruvian locals eating *papas*. He referred to them as "roots similar to truffles."

1½ pounds assorted colored fingerling potatoes

5 tablespoons extra-virgin olive oil

1½ teaspoons coarse sea or kosher salt

1 large yellow or white onion, finely chopped

3 large cloves garlic, finely chopped

2 cups canned diced tomatoes (including any juices) or 2 large fresh tomatoes, cored, peeled, and coarsely chopped

1 tablespoon red wine vinegar

1 tablespoon unrefined granulated sugar, such as Sugar in the Raw

1 teaspoon smoked paprika

1 teaspoon crushed red pepper flakes

1 to 2 teaspoons bottled hot sauce (such as Tabasco or another favorite brand), to taste

1. Scrub the potatoes under cold running water. Cut them into 1-inch pieces. Place them in a medium-size saucepan and cover them with cold water. Bring to a rolling boil over medium-high heat. Lower the heat, cover the pan, and simmer the potatoes briskly only until partially cooked, about 5 minutes. They should not give in and fall apart when you try to pierce them with a fork. Drain the potatoes in a colander and give the colander a good shake or two to rid the potatoes of excess water.

2. Heat 3 tablespoons of olive oil in a large nonstick skillet over medium heat. Once the oil appears to shimmer, add the potatoes and sprinkle them with ½ teaspoon of the salt. Cook the potatoes, uncovered, 8 to 10 minutes, and then covered, stirring occasionally, until they are crusty brown on the outside and tender inside when pierced with a fork or knife, an additional 8 to 10 minutes.

3. As the potatoes cook, heat the remaining 2 tablespoons of oil in a medium-size saucepan over medium-high heat. Once the oil appears to shimmer, add the onion and garlic and stir-fry until they are softened and earthy brown, 10 to 12 minutes.

4. Stir in the tomatoes, vinegar, sugar, paprika, red pepper flakes, hot sauce, and the remaining teaspoon of salt. The liquid from the tomatoes will help loosen any stuck-on bits of onion and garlic from the bottom of the pan, effectively deglazing it and creating that desired depth of flavor. Lower the heat to medium and gently boil the chunky sauce, uncovered, to allow the flavors to meld and to slightly thicken the sauce, about 10 minutes. Stir it occasionally as it boils.

5. If you have an immersion blender (also called a stick blender), puree the sauce in the pan until smooth. If not, allow the sauce to cool just a bit, then transfer it to a blender jar. Puree it until smooth, scraping the inside of the jar as needed. Pour the sauce into a serving bowl.

6. Toss the potatoes with the sauce and serve immediately.

TATER TIP

▲ The textural difference between the crispy potatoes and the smooth, smoky hot sauce is wonderful. If you let the potatoes sit in the sauce for a long time, the crustiness softens. Oftentimes I will wait to marry the two until just before serving. I keep the sauce warm over very low heat and hold the potatoes, uncovered, on a cookie sheet in a 200°F oven.

MASHED
ROASTED
BAKED
SIMMERED
BOILED
FRIED
SHREDDED
RICED

Potatoes are used in oil-well drilling, in making penicillin, and for hundreds of other industrial applications. Oh, and let's not forget vodka!

Indian

ROASTED POTATOES

WITH SPINACH SAUCE

To say that I love a good curry is an understatement. (What do I know? Check out my book *660 Curries* for a recipe or two!) This curry—think saucy, not curry powder in a jar—captures the beauty of three ingredients the Spanish and Portuguese took to India from the New World in the sixteenth century: potatoes, tomatoes, and chiles. A great side to any main course, this is also perfect for Sunday brunch, if you wish to make something other than the perfunctory hash browns. **SERVES 4**

1 pound Yukon Gold potatoes

2 tablespoons canola oil

1 small red onion, coarsely chopped

4 slices fresh ginger (each about the size and thickness of a quarter; no need to peel first)

1 or 2 fresh green serrano chiles, stems discarded

2 tablespoons ghee (see Tater Tip, page 38) or unsalted butter

1 teaspoon cumin seeds

1 tablespoon coriander seeds, ground

1 teaspoon coarse sea or kosher salt

½ teaspoon cayenne pepper

¼ teaspoon ground turmeric

1 large tomato, cored and finely chopped

1 pound fresh spinach leaves, thoroughly rinsed and dried (see Tater Tip, facing page)

¼ cup heavy (whipping) cream

1. Fill a medium-size bowl halfway with cold water. Peel the potatoes and give them a good rinse under cold running water. Cut them into 1-inch cubes. Submerge them

in the bowl of water to prevent them from discoloring and to rid them of the surface starch. A half hour is usually plenty, but even 10 minutes will suffice.

2. Lay out a clean cotton kitchen towel or several layers of paper towels on the counter, for drying the potatoes. Drain the potatoes in a colander and rinse them again under running water. Give the colander a good shake or two to rid the potatoes of excess water. Spread the potatoes on the kitchen towel and dry them well.

3. Heat the oil in a large nonstick skillet or a well-seasoned cast-iron pan over medium heat. Once the oil appears to shimmer, add the potatoes and cover the pan. Roast the potatoes, stirring them occasionally to brown evenly, until they give easily without falling apart when pierced with a fork, 12 to 15 minutes. Remove the pan from the heat.

4. Combine the onion, ginger, and chiles in a food processor and pulse until minced.

5. Melt the ghee in a large saucepan over medium-high heat. Once it is hot, sprinkle in the cumin seeds. Allow them to sizzle, turn reddish brown, and smell nutty, 5 to 10 seconds. Immediately add the minced medley and stir-fry until the onion is light brown around the edges and the chiles smell pungent, 5 to 7 minutes.

6. Stir in the coriander, salt, cayenne, and turmeric. The heat of the pan's contents is just right to cook the spices without burning them, 10 to 15 seconds. Add the tomato and cook, uncovered, stirring occasionally, until it softens but is still chunky, about 3 minutes.

7. Add the spinach, in batches if it won't all fit, stirring until it is wilted, 4 to 6 minutes. Once all the spinach has wilted, the water it releases will loosen up all the stuck-on brown bits of goodness, effectively deglazing the pan.

8. Stir in the roasted potatoes, cover the pan, and simmer, stirring occasionally, until the potatoes are warmed through, 2 to 3 minutes.

9. Fold in the cream and warm it through, 1 to 2 minutes. Serve warm.

TATER TIP

▲ I often will replace the spinach in this recipe with mustard greens, collards, Swiss chard, radish greens, or even beet greens. The darker the green, the richer the nutrients and iron. Use a combination of greens if you have a little bit of each left in the refrigerator or if you come back from the farmers' market with a variety because they all looked so pretty piled up on the stand.

"Pray for peace and grace and spiritual food, for wisdom and guidance, for all these are good, but don't forget the potatoes."

—*Rev. J. T. Pettee*

Chinese

TEA-INFUSED POTATOES

I have always been a fan of tea-smoked chicken in Chinese homes and restaurants that showcases an unusual technique of smoking food with black tea leaves. The resulting flavor can be highly smoky and overpowering, especially with potatoes. So I infused them instead by boiling them in brewed tea and then tossed them with aromatic spices and fresh ginger. The potatoes were delicious—buttery, with a fine balance from the pungent ginger and tart lemon juice and an unexpected sweet smokiness from the five-spice powder. Prepare this recipe with the new potatoes that herald the appearance of spring; the flavors and textures will be superior. It is a great side to a simply grilled piece of fish speckled with seasonal herbs. **SERVES 6**

¼ cup black tea leaves or 4 tea bags

2 pounds small red new potatoes

2 tablespoons plus 1 teaspoon coarse sea or kosher salt

2 tablespoons salted butter

4 slices fresh ginger (each about the size and thickness of a quarter; no need to peel first), finely chopped

2 teaspoons Chinese five-spice powder (see Tater Tip, page 115)

½ teaspoon red cayenne pepper

Juice from 1 large lemon

4 scallions, beards trimmed, green tops and white bulbs thinly sliced

1. Bring 4 cups of water to a rolling boil in a medium-size saucepan over medium-high heat. Turn off the heat. Sprinkle in the tea leaves and allow them to steep and color the water light brown, about 3 minutes. Strain the tea leaves from the brew and return the tea water to the pan. Alternatively, if you are using tea bags, drop them in the water and allow them to brew,

discarding the tea bags after about 3 minutes.

2. Scrub the potatoes well under cold running water. Place them in the tea water. Sprinkle in 2 tablespoons of the salt and bring the water to a boil over medium-high heat. Partially cover the pan, lower the heat to medium-low, and continue to gently boil the potatoes, until they are just tender when pierced with a knife but still firm looking, 12 to 15 minutes.

3. As the potatoes cook, melt the butter in a small skillet over medium heat. Once it melts and the foam subsides a bit, add the

ginger and stir-fry until it is light brown, 1 to 2 minutes. Turn off the heat under the pan and sprinkle in the five-spice powder and cayenne. The heat in that butter is just right to cook the spices without burning them.

4. Once the potatoes are ready, drain them in a colander. Give the colander a good shake or two to rid the potatoes of excess water, and transfer them to a medium-size bowl. Scrape in the spiced butter, the remaining 1 teaspoon salt, lemon juice, and scallions. Toss the potatoes so they are all coated in the spicy butter and serve while they are still hot.

BREAKFAST HASH WITH BASIL

ROASTED
SMASHED
MASHED
BAKED
BOILED
FRIED
SHREDDED
RICED

Once a week, usually on the weekend when I happen to be home, I reach into my pottery bowl that is rarely ever out of potatoes and set about making myself a skillet-full of savory tater love: Hash browns, pan-fried chunks, or potato cakes usually call my name. If my refrigerator bin has a handful of vegetables that need to be used up *tout de suite* (that means "immediately" in French, y'all), all the better for a guilt-free breakfast. This hash works on so many levels. It is chock-full of colorful ingredients and certainly meets the daily requirements of vegetable consumption. A balance of color, texture, and taste, this comes alive with the freshness of sweet basil perked up with a little punch from red pepper flakes. The day I created them, I also served toasted baguette slices smeared with just-ripe avocado with a sprinkling of coarse sea salt and a shower of coarsely cracked black peppercorns. **SERVES 4**

1½ pounds assorted colored fingerlings (I use red Amarosa and white Russian banana)

4 ounces broccoli with stalks, thick ends trimmed and discarded

1 large carrot

1 medium-size red bell pepper, stem, ribs, and seeds discarded, cut into ½-inch cubes

2 tablespoons canola oil

1 small red onion, cut into ½-inch cubes

1 teaspoon coarse sea or kosher salt

½ teaspoon crushed red pepper flakes

½ cup finely chopped fresh basil

1 cup shredded cheese (cheddar, mozzarella, colby, or Parmigiano-Reggiano) optional

1. Fill a medium-size bowl with cold water. Scrub the fingerling potatoes and cut them (unpeeled) diagonally into ¼-inch-thick slices. Plunk them into the bowl of water to rid them of excess surface starch and prevent them from discoloring.

2. Cut the broccoli tops into 1-inch florets and set them aside. Peel the stalks and slice them diagonally into ¼-inch-thick slices. Pile them separately from the florets. Peel the carrot and slice it diagonally into ¼-inch-thick slices. Add them to the broccoli florets along with the bell pepper.

3. When you're ready to make the hash browns, lay out a clean cotton kitchen towel or several layers of paper towels on the counter, for drying the potatoes. Drain the potatoes in a colander and give them a good rinse under cold running water to remove any excess starch. Shake the colander a few times to rid the potatoes of excess water. Pile them on the towel and pat them dry.

4. Heat the oil in a large nonstick skillet over medium heat. As the oil starts to shimmer, add the potatoes, broccoli stalks, and onion to the pan. Give them all a good stir and cover the pan. Allow the vegetables to cook a bit, stirring them occasionally, until they start to brown, about 5 minutes.

5. Now add the carrots, broccoli florets, red bell peppers, and salt to the skillet and give it all a good mix. Cover the pan and continue to roast the vegetables, stirring occasionally, until they are fork tender, 8 to 10 minutes.

6. Remove the cover and stir in the red pepper flakes and basil. Serve warm, sprinkled with the cheese, if using. The heat from the vegetables is enough to evenly melt the cheese shreds.

TATER TIP

▲ Think of those vegetables as a delectable bed for anything you wish to top them with. If eggs are your deal, break open 4 large eggs directly onto the vegetables in the pan after they have finished cooking. Cover the pan and continue to steam the eggs until they are cooked to your desired degree of doneness, usually 3 to 5 minutes.

Swiss

ROSTI

This Swiss classic is all about technique and, of course, the magic of butter. Often salt and pepper are the only additions, but the presence of fresh herbs (tarragon, chives, and lemon thyme in this case) and onion makes for great flavor. The butter helps crisp the exterior while the inside gets creamy and soft. Not soaking the shreds before use (because you need the starch to hold them together) and not stirring the rosti as it browns are critical to the recipe's success. **SERVES 4**

1 medium-size yellow onion, finely chopped

¼ cup finely chopped fresh tarragon leaves

2 tablespoons finely chopped fresh lemon thyme leaves (see Tater Tips, page 194)

2 tablespoons finely chopped fresh chives

1 teaspoon coarsely cracked black peppercorns

2 pounds russet potatoes

1 teaspoon coarse sea or kosher salt

8 tablespoons (1 stick) salted butter, cut into tablespoon-size pieces, at room temperature

Hunan Pepper Sauce (recipe follows)

1. Combine the onion, tarragon, thyme, chives, and peppercorns in a large bowl.

2. Peel the potatoes and give them a good rinse under cold running water. Shred them through the large holes of a box grater, the fine teeth of a mandoline, or the shredding disk of a food processor. Immediately add them to the herby onions. Sprinkle in the salt and give it all a good mix.

3. Heat 2 medium-size nonstick skillets over medium heat. Once the pans are hot, drop 2 tablespoons of the butter into each pan. The butter will instantly melt. Once

TATER TIPS

▲ I'm sure you are wondering why I use 2 pans. There's a simple reason: It is easier to flip the rosti in one clean swoop. If you have a large enough skillet or a griddle to accommodate 2 rostis next to each other, by all means, go for it.

▲ Tien Tsin chiles are much smaller and thinner than chiles de árbol, and can deliver a hotter punch. You can use fewer if it's an issue—just remember this is a condiment and is meant to pack strong flavors in minimal bites.

▲ The Asian section of your supermarket may have jars or cans of Chinese brown bean sauce. If not, you will definitely find them in any Asian grocery. These fermented beans give that salty umami-richness to the sauce and to any dish they drape.

it foams a bit, place half of the potato mélange into each pan, forming them into a mound, then pressing them down gently into a pancake-like round about 2 inches thick. Cover the pans and, without stirring, allow the underside to crisp up and turn rusty brown, 8 to 10 minutes.

4. Spread another 2 tablespoons of the butter on the top of each of the rostis. Re-cover the pans to melt the butter, about 15 seconds. Remove the lids and flip the rostis with a sturdy spatula. Cover the pans and once again, without stirring, let the rostis crisp on the underside, 8 to 10 minutes.

5. Serve while still hot with Hunan Pepper Sauce.

.... Chinese ....

HUNAN PEPPER SAUCE

Americans have become familiar with the fiery flavors of Sichuan cooking, but this hot sauce is from its neighboring province, Hunan. Whenever my friend and colleague Phyllis Louise Harris makes it, she makes a double batch for me because she knows I eat it by the spoonful. Adapted from a recipe from the ultimate teacher of Chinese cooking, Florence Lin (a dear friend), it appeals to my well-balanced palate (I'd like to think I have one) with hot, salty, and umami tastes in every little drop. This absolutely wonderful hot sauce can be used almost anywhere a chili sauce is desired—with Rosti, for example.

Interestingly, peppers are not indigenous to China, but were introduced by Spanish and Portuguese traders in the seventeenth century (along with potatoes) when they started bringing foods from the New World to trade for rice, tea, and spices. MAKES ABOUT 1½ CUPS

30 whole dried small chiles
(such as cayenne, chile de árbol,
or Tien Tsin), stems discarded
(see Tater Tips, facing page)

½ cup boiling water

6 tablespoons canola oil

2 large cloves garlic, finely chopped

1 pound red bell peppers, stems,
ribs, and seeds discarded,
finely chopped

¼ cup Chinese brown bean sauce
(see Tater Tips, facing page)

1. To reconstitute the chiles, place them in a small heatproof bowl and cover them with the boiling water. Allow them to soak for at least 30 minutes, or even overnight. They will float initially, but once they start to absorb the water, they will sink.

2. Once the chiles are soft and swollen, fish them out of the water and finely chop them, seeds and all. Save the water.

3. Heat the oil in a medium-size skillet over medium-high heat.

Once the oil appears to shimmer, add the garlic, bell pepper, and the chopped chiles. Stir-fry the medley until the bell pepper pieces brown around the edges and the chiles blacken, offering a visually stunning contrast of pinks, reds, and browns, 10 to 12 minutes. (Oh, and the aromas are not bad, either! But coughing-worthy for sure, so adequate ventilation will do you good.)

4. Stir in the bean sauce and the reserved soaking water. Bring to a boil and cook, uncovered, stirring occasionally, until all the liquid evaporates and a layer of spiced oil starts to separate from the thick, dark chocolate-colored sauce, 8 to 10 minutes.

5. Remove from the heat and allow to cool. Store in covered containers in the refrigerator for several weeks or freeze even longer. Be sure a film of oil covers the top of the sauce to help prevent spoilage.

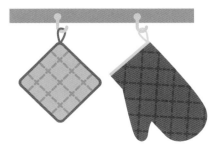

SHREDDED
SMASHED
MASHED
BAKED
BOILED
ROASTED
FRIED
RICED

TATER TIP

▲ Chinese black vinegar (actually more amber) is much more acidic than rice vinegar and slightly musky, and is hardly ever found in mainstream supermarkets (they usually only stock the clear Japanese rice variety). Your Asian grocery will probably carry the dark vinegar. Use it in a heartbeat instead of the clear variety.

Chinese

SHREDDED POTATOES
WITH PEPPER AND CHILES

This is one of those dishes that had such an impact on me the first time I ate it, I could not stop thinking about it. In fact, it was the first recipe I developed for this book. I ate it at my favorite Chinese restaurant in town, Grand Szechuan, where Guanghe Luo is the chef. I marveled at how perfectly long and noodle-like the potatoes were, with an underlying smokiness that can only come from high heat and quick cooking. Some renditions of this dish from the southern region of China include the blackened heat of dried red chiles and the numbing quality of Sichuan peppercorns. If imbalanced in the hands of a cook, that would be a disaster. I have tried it in several other restaurants and have not been happy. So my version keeps to the original rendition I fell in love with, a perfect balance of hot, smoky, acidic, and salty. I love eating the blackened chiles between mouthfuls of the potatoes; it gives me the benefit of wispy heat masked by the starchiness of the potatoes and the acidity of Chinese black vinegar. SERVES 4

1 pound russet potatoes

1 large green bell pepper

¼ cup canola oil

4 dried red chiles (such as chile de árbol), stems discarded

4 teaspoons rice vinegar or Chinese black vinegar (see Tater Tip)

1 teaspoon toasted sesame oil

1 teaspoon coarse sea or kosher salt

1. Fill a medium-size bowl with cold water. Peel the potatoes and give them a quick rinse under cold running water. Shred them with a mandoline, box grater, or a julienne peeler (see Tater Tip) along the length of the potato. You want the shreds to be like long, thin matchsticks. Submerge them immediately in the bowl of water to rinse off excess surface starch. Usually 30 minutes is a good amount of time to soak them, but I have been known to soak them overnight in the refrigerator.

2. Cut the bell pepper in half lengthwise and discard the stem, seeds, and ribs. Thinly cut the pepper halves lengthwise into matchstick-like shreds. Ideally they should be the same thickness as the potato shreds.

3. Lay out a clean cotton kitchen towel or several layers of paper towels on the counter, for drying the potatoes. Drain the potatoes in a colander and give them a quick rinse under cold running water. Give the colander a few shakes to rid the shreds of excess water. Spread the shreds out on the towel and pat them completely dry.

4. Heat 2 tablespoons of oil in a wok or large skillet over medium-high heat. Once the oil appears to shimmer, drop in 2 of the chiles and stir them around until they blacken and smell smoky, 5 to 10 seconds. Add half of the potatoes and half of the bell pepper to the smoky oil. Stir-fry them vigorously, without stopping, to briefly cook the shreds but still make sure they maintain their toothsome quality, 2 to 3 minutes. Scrape everything into a serving bowl. Wipe out the pan with paper towels before you repeat with the remaining oil, chiles, potatoes, and bell pepper. Add them to the batch in the bowl, stir in the vinegar, sesame oil, and salt, and serve immediately.

TATER TIP

▲ Sporting a long handle with an edge that looks like a razor blade with grooves, a julienne peeler is a nifty little gadget that is readily available through mail-order outlets that specialize in kitchen gadgetry, and also at retail stores that appeal to the cook in us. I've found them at a much cheaper price in Asian groceries. They may be plastic instead of swanky stainless steel, but they work.

BOILED
SMASHED
RICED
MASHED
SHREDDED
ROASTED
BAKED
FRIED

North American

POTATO= HABANERO BISCUITS

A great biscuit is all about technique and temperature. Chilled butter, cold flour, no excessive handling or kneading of the dough, and a slightly higher baking temperature than the usual 350°F ensure the perfect exterior crunch with the right flakiness and an interior that is moist, light, and almost creamy. The potatoes in this recipe, cloud-like in their texture after being riced and cooled, still maintain their taste, even in a biscuit punctuated with the heat of habanero chiles and the aroma of oregano. And slathering the biscuits with butter and honey certainly won't hurt. **MAKES 8 BISCUITS**

8 ounces russet potatoes

2 cups unbleached all-purpose flour, plus extra for dusting

1 tablespoon baking powder

1 tablespoon white granulated sugar

1 teaspoon coarse sea or kosher salt

8 tablespoons (1 stick) unsalted butter, cut into ½-inch cubes and chilled

1 medium-size habanero chile, stem discarded, seeds removed or left in (see Tater Tips), finely chopped

2 tablespoons finely chopped fresh oregano leaves

1¼ cups heavy (whipping) cream, chilled

1 large egg white, slightly beaten (save the yolk; see Tater Tips)

TATER TIPS

▲ That addictive and fragrant member of the capsicum family, the second-hottest of cultivated chiles, the habanero chile (translates as "chile from Havana") is also at times labeled "Scotch bonnet," even though the latter chile is a different variety of the same species. If you wish for a less intense heat, discard the vein, ribs, and seeds within its capacious cavity. And you thought only quality cigars came from Havana!

▲ People often toss the egg yolk (or the white) if they are using only one part of the egg in a recipe. Better to save the yolk for another recipe or use it to make a batch of the béarnaise sauce (page 137). To save it, place it, covered, in a small glass bowl and refrigerate it for up to 2 days.

1. Peel the potatoes and cut them up into large chunks. Place them in a small saucepan and cover them with cold water. Bring to a boil over medium-high heat. Partially cover the pan, lower the heat to medium-low, and simmer vigorously until the pieces are fall-apart tender when pierced with a knife or fork, 12 to 15 minutes.

2. Drain the potatoes in a colander and return them to the saucepan. Dry them out over medium-low heat, stirring occasionally so they don't stick to the bottom of the pan, until the surface appears dry, about 1 minute. Some of the pieces will start to break down into smaller morsels. Working in batches if necessary, transfer the potatoes to a ricer and press them directly onto a cookie sheet in a single layer. (If you don't have a ricer, use a potato masher and fluff them with a fork when completely mashed, then spread them on the cookie sheet.) Place the sheet into the freezer to quickly chill the potatoes as you get the dough ready.

3. Pour the flour into a food processor and add the baking powder, sugar, and salt. Pulse to mix everything. Add the butter and pulse a few times to incorporate the fat, until the mixture is the consistency of coarse bread crumbs. Add the habanero and oregano and pulse once or twice to quickly mix them in.

4. Transfer this mélange to a large bowl. Add the chilled potatoes and fold them in. Drizzle in the cream and stir just until everything comes together to form a wet dough. Do not knead it. Cover the bowl with plastic wrap to prevent drying and refrigerate the dough until you are ready to form and bake the biscuits.

5. Position a rack in the center of the oven and preheat the oven to 375°F. Line a cookie sheet with parchment paper. Dump some flour into a small bowl. Flour your hands, remove one eighth of the dough, and gently drop it into the bowl of flour. Roll it around to coat it completely. Shape it into a biscuit roughly 2 inches in diameter and 1 inch thick. Place it on the cookie sheet. Repeat with the remaining dough, making sure to leave some space between the biscuits to allow for a generous rise when baking.

6. Brush the tops lightly with egg white and bake until the tops are glistening brown, 25 to 30 minutes. Rotate the pan front to back at least once during baking for even browning and baking.

7. Transfer the biscuits to a wire rack to cool a bit. Serve while still warm.

SMASHED
MASHED
BOILED
RICED
BAKED
SHREDDED
ROASTED
FRIED

Norwegian

LEFSE

Living in the Twin Cities of Minneapolis and St. Paul, I am fortunate to be among immigrants from the Scandinavian countries of Norway, Sweden, Finland, and Denmark. I have consumed massive quantities of *lefse*. Often rolled with butter and brown sugar, stacks of *lefse* are served for an afternoon snack as coffee flows freely. An amazing *lefse* is paper thin, and when you eat it piping hot, it tastes like snow-light floury potatoes. Adding too much flour and kneading too much yield tough flatbreads, so the goal is to make sure you do neither. A *lefse*-making griddle is standard equipment in Scandinavian homes; if you invest in a good one with all the accessories, you can easily spend $150, but it's well worth it, in my opinion.

As a teacher I yearn to learn, and if time permits, I love taking cooking classes. So when I was on a *lefse* mission, I signed up for a class with David and Martha Dovart, a husband-and-wife team who have been teaching for years at the well-known Scandinavian hot spot in town, Ingebretsen's. Their love for the craft of making the perfect *lefse* shows, and this recipe, which they have been using for thirty years, made me realize what the hoopla is all about. Note that you do have to start the recipe the day before you plan to serve the *lefse*. MAKES 8 LEFSE

TATER TIP

▲ A *lefse* griddle, usually electric, is about 16 inches in diameter. The evenness of heat transfer is an essential prerequisite for a well-cooked *lefse*. The griddle kit often includes a corrugated rolling pin that comes with a cloth cover for easy washing; a cloth-covered rolling board; and a long, thin, flat wooden spatula (similar to those mixing sticks in paint stores) for transferring the rolled-out dough from the board to the griddle, and to flip the *lefse* during cooking. Of course, you can make *lefse* on a regular griddle, but if you invest in a kit, follow the instructions for seasoning the griddle and for flouring the board and rolling pin cover.

TATER TIP

⚠ Rubbing in flour to dry out the rolling board is essential. Sprinkle it on and keep working the dough in circles to make sure the board is well powdered. Keep repeating between rolling out each *lefse* when you feel the dough is starting to stick. Again, it is all about controlling the flour addition.

1 pound russet potatoes

4 tablespoons (½ stick) salted butter, melted

1 tablespoon heavy (whipping) cream

1 teaspoon coarse sea or kosher salt

½ teaspoon white granulated sugar

½ teaspoon baking powder

1 cup unbleached all-purpose flour, plus extra for dusting

1. Peel the potatoes and give them a good rinse under running water. Cut them up into smaller pieces, place them in a small saucepan, and cover them with cold water. Bring to a boil over medium-high heat. Partially cover the pan, lower the heat to medium-low, and simmer vigorously until the pieces are fall-apart tender when pierced with a knife or fork, 12 to 15 minutes.

2. Drain the potatoes in a colander and give the colander a good shake or two to rid the potatoes of excess water. Return them to the saucepan. Dry them out over medium-low heat, stirring occasionally, until the surface appears dry, about 1 minute. Some of the pieces will start to break down into smaller morsels.

3. Working in batches if necessary, transfer the potatoes to a ricer and press them directly onto a cookie sheet. (If you don't have a ricer, use a potato masher in the saucepan and fluff them with a fork when completely mashed.) Spread them on the cookie sheet in a thin layer. Allow the potatoes to cool and dry at room temperature. This is an essential step—you want to make sure you don't have to add too much flour because of the moisture in the potatoes. Allow about 4 hours for the potatoes to dry.

4. Once the potatoes are dry, scrape them into a large bowl, partially cover them, and refrigerate them overnight.

5. The next day, add the melted butter, cream, salt, sugar, baking powder, and flour to the chilled potatoes. Stir them in with a wooden spoon and gather the ingredients into a ball. Dust a little flour on your hand and barely knead the dough for a few seconds, just to make sure it is smooth.

6. Lay out a large sheet of wax paper or parchment paper on the counter. Very lightly dampen a clean kitchen towel. Break the dough into 8 equal portions and shape each portion into a ball; set them on the wax paper. Keep the dough rounds covered with the towel to prevent drying as you heat an ungreased griddle to 450°F. (Preferably use a dedicated *lefse* griddle, or a regular round electric one, for even heat; see Tater Tip, page 213, for all the *lefse*-making accoutrements.)

7. Lightly dust a *lefse* rolling board—or a clean, dry countertop—and the rolling pin with flour from a shaker (see Tater Tips, page 131). Lay out a large, clean dry cotton kitchen towel on the counter, next to the griddle. Work with 1 dough ball at a time and keep the others covered. Flatten the ball, then start rolling out the dough on the board or counter, rotating it and dusting it very lightly with flour as required (but you really want to make sure you don't add more than you absolutely need)

to fashion a round with no tears, about 12 inches in diameter. If the dough starts to get too warm, it may not be easy to roll out. Chill the dough balls a bit if needed.

8. Gently transfer the rolled dough to the griddle (see Tater Tip, page 213, about a *lefse*-turning spatula). The *lefse* should start to cook on the underside relatively quickly, with light-brown specks dotting the landscape, 3 to 4 minutes. Flip it over and cook the other side for 2 to 3 minutes. Transfer it to the dry towel. Tear a sheet of parchment paper to lay over this and blanket it with another kitchen towel. Repeat with the remaining dough rounds, stacking each finished *lefse* between sheets of parchment paper and towels.

9. Serve the *lefses* warm or at room temperature, with good-quality butter and some preserves.

TATER TIP

▲ If you're not serving all the *lefses* at one time, once they are slightly cool, fold them into triangles and store them in zip-top bags in the refrigerator for up to a week. They also freeze well in sealed bags for up to 3 months.

SMASHED
SHREDDED
MASHED
BAKED
BOILED
FRIED
ROASTED
RICED

POTATO TORTILLAS

"The man who has nothing to boast of but his ancestors is like a potato— the only good belonging to him is under ground."

—Sir Thomas Overbury, English poet and essayist

The potato, indigenous to South America, did not get to Mexico until the eighteenth century. That the Spaniards took it all the way to Europe before it made its way north is quite unimaginable. Corn tortillas, on the other hand, are distinctly Mexican and Central American, but versions do exist in South America, made with the same masa. The inclusion of other flours is common in Latin America, as is altering the thickness of some of their flatbreads (think Salvadorian *pupusas*). The potato shreds in this recipe offer a purple landscape to a thin, pliable, and flavorful flatbread that puts any store-purchased corn tortilla to shame. And the fact that two out of the four largest crops in the world (corn and potatoes) are in one recipe is so cool in my nerdy estimation. MAKES 16 TORTILLAS

8 ounces purple potatoes

2 cups masa harina (see Tater Tips, page 35)

1 teaspoon coarse sea or kosher salt

¼ cup finely chopped fresh cilantro leaves and tender stems

1 medium-size to large habanero chile, stem discarded, finely chopped (do not remove the seeds)

About 1½ cups hot tap water

1. Fill a medium-size bowl with cold water. Scrub the potatoes well under running water. I like to leave the skin on since it looks pretty. Shred the potatoes through the large holes of a box grater, the fine teeth of a mandoline, or the shredding disk of a food processor. Submerge the shreds in the bowl of water to rinse off the surface starch.

2. Pour the masa harina into a medium-size bowl and add the salt, cilantro, and chile.

3. Drain the potatoes in a colander and rinse them under cold running water to remove any remaining excess surface starch. Give the colander a good shake or two to rid the potatoes of excess water.

4. Add the potato shreds to the masa and give it all a good mix. (I use my hand.) Mix in 1 cup of the hot water. It should start to come together to form a bumpy-textured dough. Add more hot water ¼ cup at a time, making sure it gets incorporated well. The dough should feel bumpy but soft, like a textured Play-Doh, a bit grainy to the touch.

5. Lay out a large sheet of wax paper or parchment paper on the counter. Wet several sheets of paper towels. Break up the dough into 16 equal portions and set them on the wax paper. Roll each portion into a ball. Keep them securely covered under the wet paper towels. The dampness will continue to keep the dough moist.

6. When you're ready to cook the tortillas, preheat a medium-size nonstick skillet or heavy cast-iron pan over medium heat. Cut a 14-inch-square piece of parchment paper or wax paper and fold it in half. Place a dough ball inside its fold and flatten it either with a rolling pin or by pushing down on it with a pie plate. You want a circle roughly 6 inches in diameter. If you have a tortilla press, by all means, use it.

7. Gently pull off the paper and place the tortilla in the hot skillet. It will start to bubble up in places and the underside should have brown patches in 3 to 4 minutes. Flip it over and cook the other side an additional 2 minutes. Transfer it to a plate and cover it with a piece of aluminum foil or a clean kitchen towel. Repeat with the remaining dough. It's important to keep the cooked tortillas covered because the heat from within creates steam that makes them soft and pliable. Serve them warm.

TATER TIPS

▲ If the dough cracks as you flatten it, wet your hand under warm running water and knead the dough with it. You may need to add more moisture as masa has a tendency to dry out quickly.

▲ Cooked tortillas store well in the refrigerator and freezer. I usually stack the tortillas, separated by parchment paper, and seal them in a freezer-safe zip-top bag for up to 2 months.

▲ Because these tortillas are slightly thicker than store-purchased ones, they don't fall apart when you stuff them with a host of ingredients that shape and rock your taco world.

PURPLE POTATO FOCACCIA

A common offering in many regions of Italy, this crusty flatbread is adorned simply with thin-sliced potatoes (purple here for a more dramatic presentation) and drizzled with olive oil, then baked. Fresh herbs are fair game as a topping; I used two headstrong herbs, rosemary and mint, effectively nullifying their individual assertiveness, to create a fine balance of tastes. **SERVES 8**

> "Happy is the man who has a good wife, but I tell you happy is a man who has a south-facing slope where he can grow his own potatoes."
>
> —*Anonymous*

1 package (2¼ teaspoons) instant yeast

About 1¼ cups warm tap water

1 tablespoon unrefined granulated sugar (such as Sugar in the Raw)

2 teaspoons coarse sea or kosher salt, plus extra for sprinkling

3 cups bread flour or unbleached all-purpose flour, plus extra for dusting

Extra-virgin olive oil, for drizzling

½ pound purple potatoes

2 tablespoons finely chopped fresh rosemary leaves

2 tablespoons finely chopped fresh mint leaves

1 teaspoon coarsely cracked black peppercorns

1 teaspoon crushed red pepper flakes

Cornmeal, for dusting

1. Stir the yeast into ¼ cup of the water (I do this in a glass measuring cup). Allow it to sit

TATER TIP

▲ Pizza paddles and stones are an inexpensive investment, and make the pizza process a whole lot easier. Definitely consider buying them, especially if you think you'll be adding homemade pizzas to your dinner repertoire (a very good idea!).

for 10 to 15 minutes as the yeast activates. Stir in the sugar and salt.

2. Pour the flour into a food processor. (Alternatively you can use a stand mixer with a dough hook.) Dribble in the yeasty liquid and the remaining 1 cup warm water through the chute. Pulse the machine to incorporate the liquid into the flour and fashion a soft dough. If it's too sticky, add a little more flour. You don't want it too dry, either. Soft and pliable is what you are going for.

3. Lightly dust a clean countertop with flour from a shaker (see Tater Tips, page 131). Transfer the dough onto the counter and knead to smooth out the dough and create the gluten that gives the crust its chewiness and structure, 3 to 5 minutes. Drizzle a little oil into a bowl large enough to allow the dough to double in volume, and spread the oil around the inside. Gather up the dough and place it in the bowl. Spread a tablespoon of the olive oil over the dough. Cover the bowl with plastic wrap and place it in a warm spot.

4. As the dough rises, prepare the topping. Fill a large bowl with cold water. Peel the potatoes and give them a good rinse under cold

running water. Thinly slice them with a mandoline or chef's knife to ⅛ inch thick. Place the slices in the bowl of water to rinse off excess surface starch. Combine the rosemary, mint, peppercorns, and red pepper flakes in a small bowl.

5. Once the dough has doubled in volume, about 2 hours, position an oven rack in the lower third of the oven. Place a pizza stone or inverted cookie sheet on the rack and preheat the oven to 550°F.

6. Punch down the dough with your fist. Lightly dust the counter with flour and turn out the dough onto it. Roll it out to a circle, 10 to 12 inches in diameter. Liberally sprinkle a pizza paddle or another inverted cookie sheet with cornmeal and place the dough on it.

7. Lay out a clean cotton kitchen towel or several layers of paper towels on the counter, for drying the potatoes. Drain the potato slices in a colander and give them a good rinse under cold running water. Give the colander a gentle shake or two to rid the potatoes of excess water. Transfer the potatoes to the towel and blot them dry.

8. Arrange the slices on the rolled-out dough in a single layer. Top them off with the herbaceous blend. Drizzle another tablespoon or two of oil on top of all that.

9. Slide the focaccia from the paddle onto the heated pizza stone or heated cookie sheet. Bake until the potato slices look slightly crispy around the edges and the crust is reddish brown, 15 to 20 minutes.

10. Remove the focaccia from the oven, sprinkle with a little salt, and cut it into wedges. I love it piping hot out of the oven, but if you plan on eating it at room temperature later, transfer the focaccia to a wire rack to cool so the crust does not get soggy.

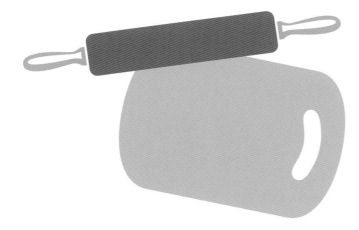

SWEETS
DESSERTS
& GRAND FINALES

Short but sweet—in so many ways. The few desserts that this chapter offers primarily showcase the inherent candied nature of sweet potatoes. Although, admittedly, my die-hard favorite is the simple but luscious salty homemade potato chips dipped in dark chocolate, when it comes to the more traditional desserts, I love a slice of the moist and decadent Chocolate Sweet Potato Pound Cake. The savory spices elevate the honeyed quality of sweet potatoes, a richness that comes through with all that butter! I was bowled over the first time I had a slice of Jim Dodge's apple pithivier: not too sweet, perfect puff pastry layers, finished with a dollop of boozy cream. My adaptation using thin slices of sweet potatoes (like the Jersey variety) yielded a surprise in terms of texture—it was similar to poached pears—but I had the same satiating experience that I did with the original. Oh, and unless your inner child has grown up and become jaded, you will love the Sweet Potato Rolls, akin to cinnamon rolls, warm, slathered with a Creamy Cointreau Glaze—the perfect pick-me-up on Sunday mornings.

North American

THICK-CUT POTATO CRISPS
WITH DARK CHOCOLATE

A cook named George Crum is credited with having created American potato chips at the Moon's Lake House in Saratoga, New York, in the 1870s. He was the first to fry wispy thin potato disks into ultra-crisp chips that were originally called "Saratoga potatoes." I can justify anything dipped in chocolate. But when it's lightly salted homemade potato chips, I would say it's a match made in heaven. Crispy, salty, slightly sweet, and with that depth of richness that can only come from dark chocolate, these are a perfect accompaniment to a bowl of premium ice cream.

These chips are fried twice, just like the Ultimate French Fries on page 175). The first fry, in a lower-temperature oil, removes the moisture from the potatoes, while the second fry, at a higher temperature, makes the chips oh-so-crispy. SERVES 4

TATER TIP

▲ Be sure to use a good-quality chocolate for dipping. You want your chips coated in the best your money can buy for that memorable—make that irresistible—flavor. No . . . you won't be able to eat just one.

1 pound russet potatoes

Canola oil, for deep-frying

Coarse sea or kosher salt, for sprinkling on the chips

8 ounces dark or semisweet chocolate chips (about 1⅓ cups)

Coarse lavender sea salt (or something similar in terms of size, like Maldon sea salt or even just a coarse-grain salt), for sprinkling on the chocolate

1. Fill a medium-size bowl about three-quarters full with cold tap water. Peel the potatoes and slice them lengthwise, into ¼-inch-thick slices, either with a knife or a mandoline. Submerge the slices right away in the water. This prevents them from discoloring and also removes excess surface starch.

2. As the potatoes soak, pour oil to a depth of 2 to 3 inches into a wok, Dutch oven, or large saucepan. Heat the oil over medium heat until a deep-frying thermometer inserted into the oil (without touching the pan bottom) registers 325°F. (I cannot emphasize enough the importance of a thermometer if you wish to make perfect chips.)

3. Lay out a clean cotton kitchen towel or several layers of paper towels on your counter. Line a cookie sheet with several layers of paper towels and set a wire rack on top, for draining the partially cooked potatoes of excess oil.

4. Drain the potatoes in a colander and rinse them a bit under cold running water. Give the colander a good shake or two to rid the potatoes of excess water. Transfer the slices to the kitchen towel and dry them well.

5. Divide the potato slices into 4 equal portions. Gently drop a portion into the oil. You will notice the temperature dip down by 30°F or so. Fry the slices at that temperature, stirring them occasionally to keep the slices from sticking to each other, until they appear a bit soft and pale brown, about 3 minutes. Do not let them sit any longer in the oil. Lift them out with a slotted spoon and spread them out on the rack to drain. Repeat with the remaining potatoes, first returning the oil to 325°F. When you're done, turn off the heat.

6. Once the potato slices have all had a chance to drip excess oil, set aside the rack (with the potatoes still on it). Remove the paper towels from the cookie sheet and give it a wipe to clear off any remaining oil. Transfer the potatoes from the rack to the cookie sheet, spread them out in a single layer, and place them in the freezer for about 10 minutes to chill. (You can let them freeze at this point, if you so wish. Once they have frozen, move them to a zip-top bag and seal the bag. They'll keep, frozen, for up to a month.)

7. When you are ready to refry the chips, again set up a wire rack and towel-covered cookie sheet for draining. Heat the oil (the same oil if you're continuing right away, fresh oil if using frozen chips) until the thermometer registers 375°F. Carefully drop one-quarter of the chilled (or frozen) chips into the oil. The temperature will drop to around 350°F. Make sure the heat under the pan is adjusted to maintain this temperature. As soon as the chips are light brown and crispy, 2 to 4 minutes, fish them out of the oil with a slotted spoon and spread them on the rack to drain. Sprinkle them lightly with the coarse sea

salt. Repeat until all the chips are fried, returning the heat to 375°F for each batch.

8. Lay out a large sheet of parchment paper on the counter next to the stove. Fill a small saucepan halfway with hot tap water. Fit a medium-size heatproof bowl snugly on top. (Make sure the bowl is large enough to fit over the pan without falling in. You don't want any water seeping into the chocolate.) Pour the chocolate chips into the bowl. Bring the water to a simmer over medium heat. Adjust the heat to maintain a simmer. As the chocolate starts melting, whisk to smooth it out. Once it is satin smooth, grab a potato chip and dip it halfway into the chocolate. Place it on the parchment paper. Sprinkle a little of the lavender sea salt on the chocolate-dipped portion. Repeat with the remaining chips and melted chocolate, placing the chips in a single layer. Allow the chocolate-draped chips to cool. Can't imagine you would wait to eat one!

TATER TIP

▲ When possible, I reuse deep-frying oil once or twice more—if I've only used it to fry vegetables (not meat of any kind). After that, the moisture from the vegetables lowers the oil's smoke point, making it no longer good for deep frying. To save oil, let it cool, then strain it through a sieve lined with several layers of cheesecloth. Pour the oil into a clean, dry container with a lid and refrigerate it until the next time. Bring it to room temperature before reusing. If it smells rancid, toss it and start with fresh oil.

SMASHED
BOILED
FRIED
MASHED
SHREDDED
BAKED
ROASTED
RICED

TATER TIP

▲ If you don't have orange liqueur on hand or would rather not add it to the glaze, use 2 tablespoons of orange or lemon juice instead. Be sure to strain the juice before using it in the glaze. For a more intense flavor, use ½ teaspoon orange extract instead of the liqueur.

North American

SWEET POTATO ROLLS
WITH A CREAMY COINTREAU GLAZE

The scintillating aromas of baking cinnamon rolls always elicit enthusiastic anticipation. Sure they're sinful and calorie-heavy, but a mash of antioxidant-rich sweet potatoes makes this version even more appealing. Easy to prepare, they're a downright tasty dessert or great Sunday morning treat, perfuming your kitchen with the warmth of cinnamon, cloves, and cardamom. And that Cointreau glaze? A little morning booze won't hurt you. It's five o'clock somewhere. **MAKES 20 ROLLS**

8 ounces orange or purple sweet potatoes (Jewel or Stoke's, if possible)

1 package (2¼ teaspoons) instant yeast

4 tablespoons (½ stick) unsalted butter, at room temperature, plus 1 tablespoon for greasing the bowl and pans

4 cups unbleached all-purpose flour

¼ cup white granulated sugar

1 teaspoon coarse sea or kosher salt

1 large egg, slightly beaten

FOR THE FILLING

½ cup firmly packed dark brown sugar

¼ teaspoon ground cinnamon

¼ teaspoon ground cloves

¼ teaspoon ground cardamom

¼ teaspoon freshly ground black pepper

4 tablespoons (½ stick) unsalted butter, at room temperature

FOR THE GLAZE

4 ounces cream cheese, at room temperature

2 tablespoons Cointreau or other orange liqueur

1 tablespoon confectioners' sugar

1. To make the dough, peel the sweet potatoes and give them a good rinse under running water. Cut them into large chunks and place them in a small saucepan. Cover them with cold water by a few inches and bring to a boil over medium-high heat. Lower the heat to medium and partially cover the pan. Boil the chunks until they are fall-apart tender when pierced with a fork or knife, 10 to 12 minutes.

2. About 5 minutes into cooking the sweet potatoes, scoop out ¼ cup of the cooking water into a small heatproof bowl. Allow it to cool until tepid. Sprinkle in the yeast and whisk to make sure there are no yeasty lumps. Let it foam and activate, about 5 minutes.

3. When the sweet potatoes are tender, scoop them out and set aside another ¼ cup of the cooking water. Pour the rest out. Drain the sweet potatoes in a colander, giving it a good shake or two to rid them of excess water. Return them to the empty saucepan and add the 4 tablespoons of butter. Mash them well with a potato masher or fork so you have no lumps. No need to rice them—in fact, it doesn't work very well; too much fiber from the potatoes gets left behind in the ricer, and you want that in the dough.

4. Spoon 2 cups of the flour, sugar, and salt into the bowl of a stand mixer and attach the paddle. Run the mixer briefly on low speed to mix the dry ingredients well. Stop the mixer and add the yeast, sweet potatoes, egg, and the saved ¼ cup of water. Mix on medium speed, scraping the insides of the bowl as needed, until a wet dough comes together, about 2 minutes. Sprinkle in another 1½ cups flour and continue to mix until the dough feels soft to the touch.

5. Lightly flour a clean countertop or a large cutting board with some of the remaining ½ cup flour. Transfer the dough to the floured counter and knead it until soft and pliable, making sure you incorporate some of the flour. The dough should not feel sticky.

6. Lightly grease a large bowl (large enough to allow the dough to double in size) with a bit of the 1 tablespoon of butter and use the rest to grease the insides of two 9-inch-round cake pans. Place the dough in the bowl, turning it to coat it with the butter. Cover the bowl with plastic wrap and let it stand in a warm spot until the dough doubles in volume, 1½ to 2 hours.

7. When the dough has doubled in volume, punch it down to release excess carbon dioxide. Lightly flour the countertop again and transfer the dough to it. Roll and pat the dough to a rectangle roughly 20 by 10 inches, sprinkling flour as needed to keep it from sticking.

8. Make the filling by combining the brown sugar, cinnamon, cloves, cardamom, and pepper in a small bowl. Spread the 4 tablespoons of butter on the dough as evenly as you can to cover the entire surface. Sprinkle the spiced sugar evenly over the butter.

9. Roll the dough into a fairly tight 20-inch-long log. Cut the log crosswise in half, then slice each half into 10 equal portions to yield a total of 20 rolls. Place 10 of the rolls in each of the cake pans, pressing against each other. Cover the pans lightly with plastic wrap. Allow them to rest in a warm spot until the rolls have doubled in size and are puffy, about 1 hour.

10. When the rolls are almost ready, position a rack in the center of the oven and preheat the oven to 350°F.

11. Remove the plastic wrap and bake the rolls until they are sunny brown all over, about 30 minutes.

12. Make the glaze as the rolls bake. Whisk together the cream cheese, Cointreau, and confectioners' sugar in a small bowl.

13. Set a wire rack on a cookie sheet, to catch any drips. Remove the rolls from the oven and turn them out of the pans onto the rack. Spread the glaze evenly over the rolls.

14. When the rolls are cool enough to handle, but still warm, pull them apart and dig in. There is nothing like fresh-out-of-the-oven rolls to make the inner kid in you sing with joy. If you have any leftovers (yes, it's possible), store them at room temperature, in a covered container, for up to 2 days. After that, I strongly recommend refrigerating them.

CHOCOLATE SWEET POTATO POUND CAKE

Lovely, moist, and chocolaty, the sweet potato and spices hint of fall and make this a sure crowd-pleaser that's perfect for potlucks or buffets. This is an adaptation of Mary Evans's recipe from her book *Vegetable Creations*. She is a highly skilled teacher, a cooking school operator (she gave me my first chance at teaching 25 years back), a gifted author of multiple books, and a great baker as well. This recipe is a testimonial to her acumen.

The flavors emerge best when the cake is made a day before you plan on serving it. **SERVES 12**

TATER TIP

▲ This pound cake is delicious as is, but no one says you can't dress it up a little. Fresh berries—especially summer raspberries or strawberries—make a beautiful finishing touch. And few folks will say "no, thanks" to a scoop of raspberry sorbet.

TATER TIP

▲ Make sure you use baking spray, not vegetable cooking spray, to grease the pan. Baking spray has flour added and you need that to ensure your cake will release easily from the pan. And make sure your Bundt pan is well coated with spray—especially the center tube—before you add the batter. You definitely want your cake to release in one lovely piece. Once when I missed greasing parts of the flute, I had a gaping tear. And yes, a handful of berries filled that gap really well, serving a double purpose.

8 ounces deep orange sweet potatoes (such as Jewel)

Baking spray, for greasing the pan (see Tater Tip)

2⅓ cups unbleached all-purpose flour

⅔ cup unsweetened cocoa powder

1½ teaspoons baking powder

½ teaspoon baking soda

½ teaspoon freshly grated nutmeg

½ teaspoon coarsely cracked black peppercorns

¼ teaspoon ground cinnamon

¼ teaspoon ground cloves

¼ teaspoon coarse sea or kosher salt

16 tablespoons (2 sticks) unsalted butter, at room temperature

1¾ cups white granulated sugar

1 teaspoon pure vanilla extract

4 large eggs, at room temperature

1. Peel the sweet potatoes and give them a good rinse under cold running water. Cut them into small chunks. Place them in a small saucepan and cover them with cold water. Bring to a boil over medium-high heat. Partially cover the pan, lower the heat to medium-low, and gently boil the potatoes until the pieces fall apart easily when pierced with a fork, 10 to 15 minutes.

2. As the potatoes cook, position a rack in the center of the oven and preheat the oven to 325°F. Spray the inside of a 12-cup Bundt pan or tube pan with baking spray.

3. Sift together the flour, cocoa, baking powder, baking soda, nutmeg, peppercorns, cinnamon, cloves, and salt into a medium-size bowl. Stir with a whisk to blend thoroughly, about 30 seconds.

4. Once the sweet potatoes have finished cooking, drain them in a colander. Give the colander a good shake or two to get rid of excess water. Return the potatoes to the pan and mash them with a potato masher until smooth.

5. Place the butter in the bowl of a stand mixer and attach the whisk. On medium speed, beat the butter until it is very creamy, about 3 minutes. (If you don't have a stand mixer, a handheld mixer will do the trick as well.) Sprinkle in the sugar and continue to beat on medium speed until very fluffy and pale, about 3 minutes. Beat in the vanilla until just blended. Add 1 egg and beat on low speed, just until combined, about 15 seconds. Add the remaining eggs, one at a time, beating on low speed just until combined, about 15 seconds per egg, scraping down the bowl after each addition. Still on low speed, add half of the flour mixture; beat only until just blended, 30 to 45 seconds, scraping the bowl halfway through.

6. Add the sweet potatoes to the batter and beat again on low speed until just combined, about 15 seconds. Scrape the bottom and sides of the bowl. Add the remaining flour mixture and beat on low speed until just combined and smooth, scraping the bowl halfway through, 30 to 45 seconds.

7. Spoon and scrape the batter into the prepared pan; smooth the top with a spatula and tap the pan on the counter to settle the batter.

8. Bake until the top is firm to the touch and a skewer or knife inserted in the cake comes out clean, 55 to 65 minutes. The top of the cake will be rounded and cracked in the center, but that's okay.

9. Transfer the pan to a wire rack and let the cake cool in the pan for about 10 minutes. Invert the pan and turn out the cake onto the rack to cool completely, 2 to 3 hours.

10. Wrap the cake tightly in plastic wrap until you're ready to serve.

TATER TIP

▲ I usually like to serve a slice of this topped with seasonal fruit. For an even more adult offering, place the cake on a rimmed plate and poke multiple holes in the top with a skewer (don't poke all the way through the bottom of the cake). Pour some Cointreau or Kahlúa into the holes, cover with plastic wrap, and allow the cake to absorb the liqueur overnight. Serve slices with a dollop of freshly whipped cream.

French

SWEET POTATO PITHIVIER

A nother great recipe sourced from the incomparable Jim Dodge, renowned pastry chef and friend. I had the opportunity to sample an apple pithivier he had made for a fundraiser hosted at wine producer Margaret Bradley Foley's Petrichor Vineyards in Sonoma County. It was fabulous: homemade puff pastry, the best organic apples dipped in lime juice, and an almond paste filling, brimming with simple flavors and not covered in a truckload of sugar. I was bowled over. My idea of substituting sweet potatoes for the apples works phenomenally well, creating a texture and mouthfeel like poached pears. I cheat and take the ease of frozen puff pastry (a good-quality store-purchased one), which makes the execution very simple. A dollop of boozy crème fraîche pushes it over the top. SERVES 8

TATER TIP

▲ Pithivier may sound a little highfalutin, but really it's just a type of pie, with an upper and lower crust and a thin layer of filling in between. It doesn't have the height of a typical American pie, but it packs a wallop of flavor and makes an impressive statement at the end of a dinner party—even if the rest of the dinner isn't comprised of potato dishes.

SMASHED ROASTED MASHED BAKED BOILED FRIED SHREDDED RICED

TATER TIP

▲ Almond paste has a higher proportion of almonds and is much coarser and less sweet than marzipan (which is more like satin-smooth and pliable candy dough). Almond paste is available in supermarkets and specialty foods stores in tubes or cans. If you would rather make your own almond paste at home, grind together equal portions (by volume) of almonds and confectioners' sugar in a food processor along with 1 egg white for each cup of almonds, and a bit of almond extract if you like. It can keep in the refrigerator for up to a month.

8 ounces sweet potatoes (preferably Jersey)

2 tablespoons salted butter, melted

4 ounces almond paste (store-purchased or homemade; see Tater Tip), softened

8 tablespoons (1 stick) unsalted butter, at room temperature

½ cup white granulated sugar

2 large eggs

1 pound all-butter puff pastry (store-purchased is fine; see Tater Tip, facing page)

Unbleached all-purpose flour, for dusting

1 cup crème fraîche

½ teaspoon pure almond extract

2 tablespoons dark Jamaican rum

1. Position one rack in the center of the oven and another at the lowest level and preheat the oven to 400°F. Line a large cookie sheet with parchment paper.

2. Peel the sweet potatoes, give them a good rinse under cold running water, and dry them with paper towels. Slice them crosswise into ¼-inch-thick rounds, using a chef's knife or mandoline. Place the slices in a single layer on the prepared cookie sheet and brush them with melted butter. Flip the slices and brush the other sides with butter. Roast them on the center rack until they turn light

brown around the edges and are just tender when a wire with a knife or fork, 8 to 10 minutes. Remove the pan from the oven and slide the parchment paper with the potatoes onto a wire rack to cool. Turn off the oven. Let the cookie sheet cool, then line it with a clean sheet of parchment paper.

3. As the potatoes roast, place the almond paste, butter, and sugar in the bowl of a stand mixer and attach the paddle. (If you don't have a stand mixer, you can use a handheld mixer with its whipping blades in place.) Beat on medium speed, until it's smooth and free of lumps, scraping the inside of the bowl as needed to ensure an even creaming, 2 to 4 minutes. Add 1 of the eggs and continue to beat to incorporate the egg and fashion a fluffy whipped batter, scraping the inside of the bowl as needed, 2 to 3 minutes.

4. Lightly dust the clean countertop with flour from a shaker (see Tater Tips, page 131). Unfold the puff pastry on the counter. Cut the pastry so that you have a ⅔ piece and a ⅓ piece. Set the larger piece aside. Roll the smaller piece into a 9-inch circle, lightly dusting the top with flour so the rolling pin doesn't stick. Occasionally stop and rotate the pastry on the counter to ensure that it doesn't stick. Use a dry pastry brush to dust off any extra flour from the top. Flip the circle over and brush any extra flour from the bottom as well. Center the circle on the parchment paper-lined cookie sheet and refrigerate it. Roll the larger piece of pastry into a 12-inch circle, also dusting it with flour, then brushing off any extra.

5. When you're ready to assemble the pithivier, cover the top of the 9-inch pastry circle with the almond batter, leaving an empty 1-inch border at the outside edge. Arrange the sweet potato slices in concentric rings, covering the almond batter. Lightly beat the remaining egg in a small bowl. Brush the border with some of the beaten egg. Refrigerate the remainder for later use. Center the 12-inch pastry circle over the sweet potatoes. Gently press the top and bottom pastry circles together around the edge, sealing them together. If there is an overhang, tuck it under the bottom crust.

6. Using a paring knife, score a decorative pattern through the top layer of dough. Cover the pithivier with plastic wrap and refrigerate to chill the pastry, about 30 minutes.

7. While the pastry chills, again heat the oven to 400°F.

8. Once the pithivier has chilled, brush the top with the remainder of the beaten egg. Bake the pithivier on the lower rack until the top is light brown, 15 to 20 minutes.

9. Rotate the pan from the back to the front. Lower the temperature to 350°F and bake until the top and sides are golden brown, about an additional 20 minutes.

10. Remove the pan from the oven and place it on the rack to cool. Once cooled, transfer the pithivier to a platter. Cover it loosely with plastic wrap and leave at room temperature until you're ready to serve.

11. Pour the crème fraîche and almond extract into the bowl of the stand mixer and attach the whisk. (Again, a handheld mixer works here as well.) Whip the crème fraîche until soft peaks form. Whip in the rum.

12. To serve, slice the pithivier into portions and dollop a tablespoon or two of the boozy crème fraîche over each slice.

TATER TIP

▲ There are some excellent butter-rich puff pastry sheets in the freezer section of your supermarket or specialty foods store. Splurge and buy one of the local or organic brands for an exceptional pithivier.

SPECIAL DIETS

MUNCHIES, MORSELS, TIDBITS & FINGER FOODS

SAVORY SOUPS & STUNNING SALADS

ENTREES, MAINS & FULL PLATES

SMALL PLATES & SIDE DISHES

SWEETS, DESSERTS & GRAND FINALES

SAUCES & DIPS

CONVERSION TABLES

APPROXIMATE EQUIVALENTS

1 STICK BUTTER = 8 tbs = 4 oz = ½ cup = 115 g

1 CUP ALL-PURPOSE PRESIFTED FLOUR = 4.7 oz

1 CUP GRANULATED SUGAR = 8 oz = 220 g

1 CUP (FIRMLY PACKED) BROWN SUGAR =
6 oz = 220 g to 230 g

1 CUP CONFECTIONERS' SUGAR = 4½ oz = 115 g

1 CUP HONEY OR SYRUP = 12 oz

1 CUP GRATED CHEESE = 4 oz

1 CUP DRIED BEANS = 6 oz

1 LARGE EGG = about 2 oz or about 3 tbs

1 EGG YOLK = about 1 tbs

1 EGG WHITE = about 2 tbs

Please note that all conversions are approximate but close enough to be useful when converting from one system to another.

WEIGHT CONVERSIONS

U.S./U.K.	METRIC	U.S./U.K.	METRIC
½ oz	15 g	7 oz	200 g
1 oz	30 g	8 oz	250 g
1½ oz	45 g	9 oz	275 g
2 oz	60 g	10 oz	300 g
2½ oz	75 g	11 oz	325 g
3 oz	90 g	12 oz	350 g
3½ oz	100 g	13 oz	375 g
4 oz	125 g	14 oz	400 g
5 oz	150 g	15 oz	450 g
6 oz	175 g	1 lb	500 g

LIQUID CONVERSIONS

U.S.	IMPERIAL	METRIC
2 tbs	1 fl oz	30 ml
3 tbs	1½ fl oz	45 ml
¼ cup	2 fl oz	60 ml
⅓ cup	2½ fl oz	75 ml
⅓ cup + 1 tbs	3 fl oz	90 ml
⅓ cup + 2 tbs	3½ fl oz	100 ml
½ cup	4 fl oz	125 ml
⅔ cup	5 fl oz	150 ml
¾ cup	6 fl oz	175 ml
¾ cup + 2 tbs	7 fl oz	200 ml
1 cup	8 fl oz	250 ml
1 cup + 2 tbs	9 fl oz	275 ml
1¼ cups	10 fl oz	300 ml
1⅓ cups	11 fl oz	325 ml
1½ cups	12 fl oz	350 ml
1⅔ cups	13 fl oz	375 ml
1¾ cups	14 fl oz	400 ml
1¾ cups + 2 tbs	15 fl oz	450 ml
2 cups (1 pint)	16 fl oz	500 ml
2½ cups	20 fl oz (1 pint)	600 ml
3¾ cups	1½ pints	900 ml
4 cups	1¾ pints	1 liter

OVEN TEMPERATURES

°F	GAS MARK	°C	°F	GAS MARK	°C
250	½	120	400	6	200
275	1	140	425	7	220
300	2	150	450	8	230
325	3	160	475	9	240
350	4	180	500	10	260
375	5	190			

Note: Reduce the temperature by 20°C (68°F) for fan-assisted ovens.

INDEX

NOTE: Page references in *italics* indicate photographs.